THE

BULLY

IN YOUR RELATIONSHIP

THE
BULLY
IN YOUR RELATIONSHIP

**Stop Emotional Abuse and
Get the Love You Deserve**

ANNE-RENÉE TESTA, PH.D.

New York   Chicago   San Francisco   Lisbon   London   Madrid   Mexico City
Milan   New Delhi   San Juan   Seoul   Singapore   Sydney   Toronto

The McGraw-Hill Companies

Library of Congress Cataloging-in-Publication Data

Testa, Anne-Renée.
    The bully in your relationship : stand up to emotional abuse and get the love you
deserve / Anne-Renée Testa.
        p.   cm.
    Includes bibliographical references and index.
    ISBN: 0-07-148136-2 (alk. paper)
    1. Bullying.   2. Psychological abuse.   3. Family violence.   I. Title.

    BF637.B85T47   2007
    158.2—dc22   2007010572

1 2 3 4 5 6 7 8 9 10 11 12 13 14 15 16 17 18 19 20 21 FGR/FGR 0 9 8 7

ISBN-13:978-0-07-148136-6
ISBN-10:   0-07-148136-2

Interior design by RD Studio

McGraw-Hill books are available at special quantity discounts to use as premiums and
sales promotions, or for use in corporate training programs. For more information, please
write to the Director of Special Sales, Professional Publishing, McGraw-Hill, Two Penn
Plaza, New York, NY 10121-2298. Or contact your local bookstore.

This book is printed on acid-free paper.

To the millions of people who
suffer emotional abuse and bullying in silence

contents

acknowledgments

I wish to acknowledge and thank the many people who helped me write this book and bring it to publication. I am indebted to my clients, who have had the courage to discuss their innermost feelings and work with me to change their lives for the better. Obviously, I do not name any of you in the book, because our professional relationship demands strict confidentiality. But I would be remiss not to thank you for your trust and the way you have responded to the method described in the book.

My literary agents at RLR Associates, Ltd.—Gary Rosen, Jennifer Unter, and Tara Mark—assisted me in signing the publishing agreement with the McGraw-Hill Companies. I appreciate their wise counsel and the help they provided in every step along the way. Gary told me that there was no one better or brighter than senior editor John Aherne, who would head up the McGraw-Hill team. I quickly learned how true that is. John was enthusiastic about the project from the outset, and his expert judgment was invaluable. It was a great experience to work with him, and I thank him for that.

John Aherne's team at McGraw-Hill is exceptional. I especially appreciate the meticulous way Sarah Pelz edited the chapters for cohesion, clarity, and detail. Designer Tom Lau came up with that outstanding book jacket. Ann Pryor worked closely with me on publicity and marketing. I am grateful to her and the marketing team—Sarah Love and Eileen Lamadore—for coordinating an impressive program. The publishing process was enhanced by a remarkable staff, including exceptional supervision by project editor Craig Bolt.

I wish to acknowledge and thank Janet Roth and the late Gail North, who worked with me on the initial book proposal, and Marcy Posner, who initiated the contact with McGraw-Hill. During the writing and marketing process, I enjoyed the wise counsel of Karen Zahler and Pierre Lehu, literary professionals whose efforts on my behalf are continuing past the publication date.

I am fortunate to have many friends with whom I have discussed portions of the book and who provided ideas and comment for which I am most grateful. This is probably not a complete list, but I acknowledge and appreciate the contribution of the following persons: Mitchel Agoos, Bea Alda, Ernie Anastos, Emily Anton, Dr. Hugh Barber, Barbara M. Barbera, Heather Bauer, Lois Beekman, Joy Behar, Carol Berman, Howard Berman, Albert Bialek, Sheila Bialek, Linda Calder, Jim Chadlek, Claudia Chan, Tom Dunne, Jackie End, Lewis Frumkes, Steven Gaines, Ed Glavin, Nancy Grace, Tracey Greene, Bernard Grobart, Dr. Laurence J. Guido, Sophia Hall, Alice Harris, Stanley Harris, Tommy Hilfiger, Heather Hurtt, Victor Imbimbo, Linda Heller Kamm, Susan Kiel, Fay Kline, Richard Kline, Sister Margaret Ann Landry, Dr. Sharyn Lawall, Peter Lehu, Kay LeRoy, David Lubell, Tracey Lutz, Patty Marion, Morgan McGivern, Adriana McLaughlin, Ronnie Milo, Karen Parzial, Maury Povich, Jule Ratner, Gary A. Rosen, Katheren Ryden, Randi Schatz, Len Scheer, Allison Winn Scotch, Dr. Thomas Sculco, Jackie Smaga, Gail Steinberg, Dr. Lucy Waletsky, Lisa Wassong, Kevin White, Dr. Donald Williams, Montel Williams, and Barbara and Donald Zucker.

It is not unusual today to communicate on the Internet with persons you have never met. Librarian Karin Suni, one such person on my list, has helped me with her ability to surf the Web and come up with the right answer to any question. Another person, who does not wish to be named, was really a collaborator who worked on the writing with me. While I am responsible for any errors in the book, I wish to acknowledge her major contribution, her talent, and her diligence.

Finally, I thank my wonderful family—my husband, Les Tanner; our children, Joy, Seth, Shari, and Jon; and my sister, Joan Testa—all of whom gave me their love and encouragement. From the day we met and fell in love, Les and I have been each other's partner, best friend, and champion. Having Les at my side while writing this book made the experience special for both of us. My parents, Solomon and Gertrude Testa, are gone now, but I have my memories of the too-few years we were together as a family and sheltered by their love for each other and for my sister and me.

introduction

The Doctor Is In—Help Is on the Way!

Where there is no struggle, there is no strength.

—Oprah Winfrey

You should be proud of yourself, because the fact that you're reading this is a sign that you're brave. You are brave enough to consider the possibility that there's a bully in your relationship. And that takes a lot of guts!

Believe me, I know. I've worked with hundreds of patients who've been bullied. Perhaps just as important, I've been bullied, too. So I really understand what you're dealing with and how you must feel. Most likely, you already know—or at least sense somewhere in the back of your mind—that you aren't being treated right. That you're being pushed around, manipulated, coerced, and subjected to emotional abuse. That you're being bullied by your romantic partner. And maybe, just maybe, you're ready to do something about it.

Maybe that person is your husband or wife, a boyfriend or girlfriend whom you live with, or the man or woman you're dating. Maybe that person's behavior is as obvious as physical threats or as subtle as those seemingly polite but constant quiet criticisms telling you that you should be doing things differently.

The bullying didn't start yesterday; it has been going on for months, even years. And you know it's happening. You can feel that something's wrong, but you're just not sure what to do about it. You might be scared to face it, confused about how to deal with it, or secretly convinced that it's your fault somehow—or even that you deserve it.

Still, the fact that you're reading this book reveals something else—something very important, maybe the most important thing of all. Deep inside, beyond all the fear and the self-doubt, you know in your heart that you deserve better and that you have courage to change.

Damn right you do! And together, we're going to make it happen. Take my hand, borrow my strength, and let me share with you what I've learned. You have absolutely nothing to be ashamed of. You really can do anything you put your mind to; you're capable of so much. And you're not alone. I'm right here with you, and together we'll move mountains and make miracles happen!

MY PERSONAL EXPERIENCE WITH BULLIES

When it comes to bullies, believe me, I've been there. I understand. And I want to share with you the tools and techniques I've learned from my personal experiences and from years of working with clients as a professional psychologist, to help you get up on your own two feet and get on with your life— the fabulous life and loving relationships that you deserve.

I was born and raised in the Bronx in the 1950s, when that area was even tougher than it is today. I grew up in a working-class neighborhood and lived in one room with my mother, father, and sister. I was a small kid, shy, asthmatic, and insecure. I was a walking target—I practically had a

"Kick Me" sign on my back! And every single day, from the time I started school until the time we moved to the Long Island suburbs years later, I was picked on and pushed around and bullied by two neighborhood girls, Mary-Ellen and Roseanne. And I just took it.

Why? Because I didn't have any tools to deal with their behavior. I guess I thought I deserved it. And I didn't have any role models showing me what to do differently, how to stand up for myself. My mother was a quiet woman who did everything she could to avoid confrontations. My father, whom I hardly ever saw because he was always working so hard to provide for us, was often subjected to terrible anti-Semitism, but I never heard him say a bad word about the people who took their ignorance and prejudices out on him—he just accepted it. And though I know my parents loved me and did the best they could to care and provide for us, they just didn't understand how to build a child's self-esteem. That's the way it is with so many parents, and it's not their fault. More often than not, our parents really gave us everything they had to give; they just weren't given the tools by *their* parents to do any better.

Lucky for us, we live at a time when even if we didn't get that nurturing and support from our parents, now we have these wonderful opportunities to fill in the blanks that they left, to learn to find our inner strength, build our self-esteem, and pass those gifts on to our own families. What's past is past. Today it's up to you to take the good from your childhood, heal the wounds, and take the actions that will improve your life—your own and those of the generations to come.

And believe it or not, you have everything you need within you to make those changes right now. Turn the pages of this book, and let me show you the healthy model and help you find the courage to change.

Standing Up to Bullies: I Did It, and So Can *You*

Here's how the changes began for me.

On my last day in that old Bronx neighborhood, I was on my way home from school. Roseanne and Mary-Ellen were waiting for me, right where they always did, to tease and torment me. But this day was different: as I walked toward them, I realized I'd never have to see them again. That meant I had absolutely nothing to lose and nothing to be afraid of anymore. I felt a rush of happiness, and I marched toward them with my head held high, looking straight at them. What did I care what they thought of me? They had no power over me anymore. After all those years of physical and emotional torment, I was free.

As I got closer, I felt the old fear creep back in, but I remembered something I'd heard in stories and songs: that when you're afraid, you should just *make believe* you're brave. And by making believe, you'll face your fears and actually become as brave as you're pretending to be. So that's what I did. I made believe I was brave—and it worked. I kept walking with my chin up. And when those two bullies did what they'd always done, calling me names and threatening to hurt me, I did something I'd never done before in my life. I stood up for myself. I made eye contact with them and talked back to them in a clear, strong voice. Then, when they wouldn't leave me alone, I fought back, and I left that street corner in the Bronx victorious!

I'd won at long last—and not just that confrontation against those two mean girls. This was a much bigger triumph. I'd conquered my own fear, my self-doubt, my deep, secret sense that I didn't deserve any better than to be picked on every day. And I learned some valuable lessons for dealing with bullies, which I use to this day.

The courage that came to me on that long-ago day in the Bronx came because I was about to move. That knowledge gave me a new sense of perspective, which allowed me to experience three very important things that I'd never felt before.

What I Learned from Standing Up for Myself

Over the years, I've come to understand that these three principles are not only essential to dealing with bullies but also the key to healthy relationships and happy lives. These principles have become the basis for the solution I explain in this book: the A.R.T. Method.

The first principle is that what other people think of us has only as much power over us as we let it. We don't have to move out of town to be free from fear of the negative opinions and critical words that some bully is trying to impose on us. We can gain our freedom right this minute, without going anywhere, by reminding ourselves that people are welcome to their opinions about us, but we don't have to share them.

> *What other people think of us has only as much power over us as we let it.*

Ultimately, our opinions of *ourselves* are the only ones that really matter. As Eleanor Roosevelt once said, "Don't let other people tell you who you are!" And as a friend of mine says, what other people think of me is none of my business (even if they try to make it mine). When we truly believe in ourselves, what other people believe about us becomes irrelevant.

Second, we have nothing to lose—nothing, absolutely nothing—that's more valuable than our self-respect, our sense of self-worth. It's true that standing up to bullies might make some waves, but without self-respect, we might sink altogether! Time and again, I've found that it's always better to deal with the consequences of standing up for ourselves than to suffer the consequences of not standing up for ourselves. When we don't, we're treating ourselves as badly as the bullies treat us, basically agreeing with them that we deserve to be treated badly. And we absolutely don't deserve that—no one does. All people, including you, deserve to be treated with kindness, compassion, and respect.

We have nothing to lose— nothing, absolutely nothing—that's more valuable than our self-respect, our sense of self-worth.

Third, and most important, is the lesson that helped me stand up to my bullies: pretend you're brave, even if you're not. Do it scared, but do it. You'll find, as I did, that the more you make believe you're brave, the more you'll discover how brave you really are and all the amazing things you can accomplish once you become willing to face your fears. That's what courage is, after all—not being fearless, but taking action in spite of the fear.

YOU, TOO, WILL STAND UP FOR YOURSELF, USING THE A.R.T. METHOD

Maybe you know what it's like to be bullied every day. Maybe you've been unable to stand up for yourself. Maybe you've tried to ignore the situation, hoping it would just go away, or blamed yourself, or felt hopeless, helpless to do anything about it, and scared that you're not strong enough to live with the consequences of standing up for yourself. If that's the case, take heart! The three basic principles I've just described are all you need to turn things around for good, using my A.R.T. Method's three-step approach (Acknowledge, Reassess, Take action) to take charge of your life and make positive changes in your relationships.

Sound simple? It is. Easy? No way. Everything worthwhile in life takes effort and practice, and my method is no exception. You'll have to remind yourself of these principles every day, maybe every hour in the beginning, maybe even every minute. You'll have to keep reminding yourself of them, like a mantra, until they become part of your life—until they come true. But they will eventually become true for you, and when they do, I'm positive you'll agree that the results are well worth the effort. It may take some time, but I know it works, because I did it. And if I did it, you can do it!

Doing It Scared: How the Trick Took Me Far

When I was eighteen and just out of high school, after my father died, I was grief-stricken. I felt as if I were fighting for my life. And though I didn't have much work experience, it had become my responsibility to support my family, so I found myself fighting for their survival as well. I was terrified, and I didn't know how I was going to do it—so I had to do it scared.

Gathering up every bit of imaginary courage I had and holding my head high, I marched into the headquarters of the biggest company on Long Island. I told the woman at the front desk that I was there to apply for a job and that she should hire me to be the assistant to the president of the company. She gave me such a look ("Who is this kid?") and then told me the president already had an assistant. But, she added, perhaps I'd consider working for the vice president. I guess she liked my nerve—except I didn't really have any. I was scared and sad and desperate, but I pretended to be courageous and confident, and it worked! Once again, I made believe I was brave, and the trick *did* take me far.

The more you make believe you're brave, the more you'll discover how brave you really are.

But then it was showtime. Still young, in what was a big job for me, I had to support my mother and ten-year-old sister and scramble to learn the ropes at work. I was the first one in the office and the last to leave, and I gave my check to my mother on payday. I was determined to succeed but afraid of failing those who depended on me. Those were the days of apprehension over what I had to do and exhilaration when it all came together.

In time, the pretend courage and confidence that got me the job became a reality as my family at home and at work knew they could count on me. More importantly, I knew I could count on me. I saw that my fear had not canceled my courage. In fact, it was a spur to validate what I first thought was bravado. If you want to change your life, you are going to be afraid. The fact is that everyone is scared to make important changes. But if you can make believe you are brave enough to do it, my A.R.T. Method, described in Part 2 of this book, will help you succeed.

That successful outcome with the Long Island company launched my business career. In each subsequent job, I faced new challenges: proving myself once again, afraid that I might not succeed and more confident when I did. I learned how to bring about a change in my own life that worked for me.

Then I started to think about going back to school for professional training I had missed out on after my father died. I was married with two young children. Starting my education anew at that point in my life was daunting, and I was afraid. It was so long since I had been a student.

I was scared when I walked through the doors of Marymount Manhattan College for the first time. But I enrolled, and my major was psychology. When I received my bachelor's degree with honors, the personal satisfaction inspired me to go on for graduate work in psychology. I received my master's degree from Columbia University and a Ph.D. from La Salle University.

What I Want to Do Is Help You

After doing it scared for years, I've become as brave as I made believe I was. Today I'll open any door without worrying what's on the other side, because I'm no longer afraid of what might be waiting there. Whatever life brings, I know I can face it. And you can, too.

For twenty years now, I've practiced psychology in New York City and had the opportunity to meet with hundreds of patients who, in different contexts, have been bullied. This has provided many insights into the ways that being bullied—no matter what the intentions or the face of the bully—can drain the strength and confidence we need to survive and thrive.

The most insidious form of bullying is emotional abuse. The emotional bully could be your spouse, your partner, your boyfriend, or even yourself. What precisely is emotional bullying? It is repeated and often covert behavior that degrades you, makes you feel worthless, and makes you experience a sick feeling of despair. The behavior can range from the most blatant insult to the subtlest criticism. Constant denigration, fault finding, and deprecation all constitute emotional bullying.

Today my passion is for helping other people overcome their fears so they can survive and thrive in their own lives. As you read this book, we'll take the journey of recovery together. Whatever you need to do to deal with the bullies in your life, you can do it. My A.R.T. Method makes it simple. You'll do it scared at first, and then, as you find how brave and strong and deserving you really are, you'll just do it!

So what are we waiting for? Let's get started.

THE

BULLY

IN YOUR RELATIONSHIP

PART 1

Identifying the Bullies in Your Life

That Sick, Sinking Feeling in Your Gut

1

How to Tell if You're Being Bullied

- What is bullying? (You might be surprised by the answers!)
- Are you being bullied?
- How victims are affected—and why they put up with it
- Living out the lie: why the partners of bullies actually seek out abusers
- How victims can stop taking abuse—and start taking care of themselves

The only rights one person has over another are those that are freely given. The only duties they have are those that are freely accepted. Anything else is coercion, and coercion isn't fit to go by the name of love. It isn't a fit transaction for human beings.
—DAPHNE CLAIRE DE JONG

We've all laughed at bullies at one time or another. Think of Simon Cowell, that arrogant, grandstanding judge on "American Idol" who launches vicious attacks on contestants unlucky enough to draw his wrath. We may cringe when he lashes out and shames some particularly naive hopeful, but mostly his arch remarks and witty put-downs make us giggle (and feel glad it's not us!). Same with Al Bundy and his wife, Peg, forever at each other's throats on that old show "Married . . . with Children." In fact, everyone in the Bundy household was a bully and a victim. And while the show played it for laughs, if you ever took that family's dynamic seriously, you probably would have gotten a sick, sinking feeling that made you grab the remote and turn off the television as fast as you could.

Observing a real bully in action isn't any fun at all. Have you ever gone out to dinner and watched the man at the table next to yours demand that his wife order a particular dish, criticize her manners, and comment on her weight, all the while being rude and demanding with the waitstaff? Or stood in line at the movies while trying to tune out the woman behind you nagging her boyfriend about his clothes, his friends, and his job, loud enough for everyone to hear?

Being a bully's target, however, is even worse than watching a bully in action. To the victims of bullies, that sick, sinking feeling is a daily experience. It's the way you feel when someone starts to push you around emotionally, verbally, and maybe even physically. The fear creeps through you like a slow poison. The quiet despair weighs you down, leaving you hopeless, exhausted, and depressed. Anxiety and edginess build, because you never know when the next attack will come. A helpless rage wells up and then stays boiling inside as you find yourself, time after time, incapable of speaking up, talking back, and telling the bully to back off, even though you may imagine doing just that a hundred times a day.

With every day that goes by, these feelings take their toll on you. They eat away at your self-esteem, your sense of self-worth, your health, and your ability to work, love, and experience happiness and peace—in short, your life. Bullying really is that powerful, and it has serious effects that cripple some people for their entire lives.

If you're feeling this way, don't be ashamed. It's not your fault. And you won't have to experience it much longer.

IS THERE A BULLY IN *YOUR* RELATIONSHIP?

When you're involved with a bully, it's all too real. Unlike the cast of "Married . . . with Children" or the contestants and their TV bullies on "American Idol," you can't leave the set at the end of the show. The bully may be your husband or wife, your live-in girlfriend or boyfriend, the man or woman you're dating—someone you can't walk away from, or at least you think you can't.

And unlike Simon and Al, some bullies may not be obvious or recognizable. They aren't always as easy to identify as the kid who tormented you on the playground, the person who cuts in line ahead of you, or the partner who abuses you physically.

Killing You Softly

Let me be absolutely clear: you do not have to be beaten or battered to be bullied. Domestic violence is an extreme form of bullying, a horrible and dangerous form, but emotional abuse is every bit as damaging as physical abuse. Your partner can inflict horrible and lasting pain without ever laying a hand on you or even getting close to you. He or she can wound you with tone of voice, the quality of a glance, body language, or manipulative behavior.

This kind of bullying can kill, too. It kills your spirit, your soul, your ability to love, and your will to live. If you think you're not being bullied because you're not being beaten up, think again. If you think your situation isn't serious or dangerous, just because your partner doesn't hit you, think again.

WHAT IS BULLYING?

Bullying is any repeated behavior that degrades, denigrates, and otherwise makes you feel bad about yourself. Bullying behavior includes the most blatant insults and the subtlest criticism.

Bullying is:

- Bursting into unpredictable rages and issuing threats
- Demeaning or patronizing you, in public or in private
- Nagging, nitpicking, or constantly bringing up past mistakes
- Hijacking control over domestic issues like food, money, parenting, and social life
- Putting down your appearance, domestic skills, career, hobbies, friends, or values
- Withholding affection, sex, or intimacy as punishment
- Demanding sex when you don't want it or sex acts you don't like
- Refusing to communicate for days or weeks at a time

Bullying is also:

- Comparing you unfavorably to others
- Flirting with others in front of you
- Belittling your achievements
- Undermining your value or potential
- Refusing to acknowledge your contributions to the relationship
- Failing to prioritize the relationship
- Threatening to leave the relationship if you don't do what he/she wants
- Making endless "helpful" comments about how you should do things

- Repeatedly urging you to do something you've made clear you don't want to do

These are all forms of bullying. I'm amazed—and saddened—by what people are willing to take from their husbands and wives, domestic partners, boyfriends and girlfriends. I'm amazed by how many people are oblivious to or in denial about the everyday bullying they receive. In fact, every single day in my practice, I hear from clients who are being bullied, and so many of them aren't even aware of it. They feel terrible, they sense that something's not right, but they just can't put their finger on exactly what it is.

You do not have to be beaten or battered to be bullied.

Perhaps something similar is happening to you. Maybe you've heard some of the following types of comments recently:

- **Using sarcasm:** "Those pants are starting to get really tight on you, but I guess you're just too busy to worry about a little thing like how you look."
- **Comparing:** "If you were willing to stay home like John's wife, maybe *our* kids would be in the accelerated classes, too."
- **Guilt-tripping:** "It looks like I just can't expect everyone to give a hundred percent to relationships the way I do."
- **Condescending:** "Well, maybe if you paid attention to the news, you'd understand what I was talking about."
- **Threatening:** "If you don't give me what I want, you can hardly blame me if I go looking for somebody who will."
- **Insulting:** "How can you be so stupid?"

Do any of those remarks sound familiar? If so, you might have a bully in your life.

Are you ready for a closer look? I'm going to share some stories about bullies and their victims. The details of their lives and relationships may not be like yours, but don't be fooled by the specifics. It doesn't matter whether you're a man or a woman, living in shack or a mansion, up in the penthouse or down on the farm. Whatever the superficial differences, the feelings these people have and the problems they experience in their relationships are probably a whole lot like yours.

A Case Study in Bullying: Sandra and Bill

One of my clients, Sandra, is a bright, beautiful woman in her late thirties, with five children, ranging in age from four to fifteen. She married young. Shortly after graduating from college, she met Bill, an ambitious lawyer several years older than she, and they were married less than a year later. Bill asked Sandra to set aside her career plans and start their family. Although Sandra had graduated with honors, a degree in French, and plans to get her teaching certificate, she agreed. She thought that was what she was *supposed* to do and what she *had* to do, to keep her husband happy.

Sixteen years later, Bill is a senior partner at a prestigious corporate law firm, works eighty hours a week, and brings home a seven-figure salary. Sandra's a full-time wife and mother; she never went back to work. The professional ambitions she once had lie dormant, and her personal interests are almost entirely neglected. On the rare occasion that she mentions going back to school or getting a job, her husband is quick to discourage her, pointing out that she doesn't need to work. They live in a luxurious home, drive expensive cars, take vacations twice a year, and send their children to private school. Bill often buys Sandra extravagant presents (though he doesn't ever ask her what she wants) and provides her with a generous monthly allowance for clothes, weekly trips to the spa, lunches with her friends, and membership at an exclusive tennis club.

All Sandra's friends admire their marriage, and they frequently tell Sandra how lucky she is. Unfortunately, so does Bill. He never lets Sandra forget that he's the one who makes her life and lifestyle possible, and that she should be thankful for it. Whenever they fight—which happens more and more often these days—Bill threatens Sandra with divorce. It doesn't seem to matter whether the argument is about something small, like what to have for dinner, or something bigger, like their oldest daughter's report cards. If Sandra disagrees with Bill about anything (and sometimes even when she doesn't), his immediate response is the same.

Emotional abuse is every bit as damaging as physical abuse.

"I want a divorce!" he yells at Sandra, short-circuiting any possibility of dialogue. "Why are you so damn difficult? I do everything for you, and this is how you show your gratitude? I'm out of here! I don't have to deal with this! You think you know better than me? Fine. I'm getting a divorce, and then we'll see how well you do!"

He stomps out of the room or out of the house, slamming the door behind him, and Sandra is left alone with that sick, sinking feeling in her gut, terrified that this time he's really going to do it: he's going to leave her, and she'll end up alone, trying to raise five children on her own with no professional skills, no financial resources, and no love in her life. It's this kind of fear that keeps so many people, rich or poor, trapped in desolate relationships.

What Happens? How Bullying Affects the Victim

Of course, Bill never really leaves; he just keeps threatening to. And Sandra ends up watching her every step, walking on eggshells in order to avoid confrontation. She never dares to disagree with Bill anymore, and she certainly never speaks up about her own needs and concerns. She doesn't want her children to see their father get so angry, and Bill blows his top whether they're around or not, so she feels like it's her responsibility to protect them, by preventing the explosions as much as she can.

Sandra senses that Bill's reactions might be out of proportion, even inappropriate, but she rationalizes that he's under a lot of pressure at work, makes excuses for him, and can't help feeling that it's her fault and that perhaps he's right after all: she's difficult, ungrateful, incapable of taking care of herself. She tiptoes around her own home, terrified that any wrong move will trigger another of Bill's outbursts. She's a prisoner in her gilded cage.

Why on Earth Would Anyone Put Up with It?

What could Sandra be thinking? Why does she put up with it? Why doesn't she stand up for herself or divorce him? To some, Sandra's behavior might not make any sense at all. But as you probably already know, it's not that simple.

None of us *want* to be treated badly, of course—at least, we don't want it on a conscious level. But somewhere inside, deep in our unconscious minds, are ideas about ourselves that were formed a long time ago, when we were children. These ideas were created by the way our parents treated us and treated each other. They became the basis of our identities—the stories in our heads about who we are, which we've been telling ourselves for years.

If we were raised in stable, nurturing homes by protective, supportive adults who taught us with their words and actions that we deserved love and consideration and that our thoughts and feelings were important and should be expressed, listened to, and respected, then we grew up believing these things about ourselves. The story we tell ourselves is that we are valuable and worthy of love and respect. Our self-esteem is high; our confidence is strong. We have no problem standing up for ourselves, and we seek out the warm, loving relationships *that we intuitively understand we deserve.* This is the healthy model.

If, in contrast, we were raised in less-than-perfect homes by less-than-perfect parents (as so many of us were), somewhere along the line, we might have picked up ideas about ourselves that are distorted. If our parents neglected or ignored us as young children, we came to believe, subconsciously, that we are unimportant and unworthy of attention or consideration, that we have been abandoned, and that we deserve it. If our parents were hypercritical, comparing us with other children and denigrating everything we did, day after day, the message we got is that we can't do anything right, that we're never going to be good enough, that we'll never measure up, and that we don't deserve praise, approval, or admiration. And if our parents were abusive to us, we came to believe that we really *are* all the things they told us, through their words and actions: that we are inferior, selfish, stupid, useless, worthless, and that we deserve abuse.

We unconsciously seek out relationships that will provide what we unconsciously believe we deserve: abuse.

Of course, none of those negative beliefs are true. We're not bad, and we don't deserve abuse. No one does. Who would say such things to an innocent child? But unfortunately, too many parents do, without knowing it. The result is that we grow up telling ourselves these awful, untrue stories, usually without even being aware of it. Everything we do, the choices we make, and the situations we get into are informed and motivated by those negative stories.

You have the power to turn things around for yourself.

That means we're likely to undervalue our own feelings and keep our thoughts to ourselves, because we think our opinions and experiences will be criticized or don't really matter. We wind up in jobs far below our real abilities because we think we're good for nothing. And we unconsciously seek out relationships that will provide what we unconsciously believe we deserve: abuse.

Inside the Mind of the Victim

That's exactly what happened to Sandra. She was an only child, raised by an exquisitely lovely woman who didn't want children at all and never should have had them in the first place. Cold and controlling, Sandra's emotionally repressed mother never showed her any affection or approval; in fact, she rarely demonstrated emotions at all. She was even called the Ice Queen! She was obviously a deeply unhappy woman who sublimated her feelings into a chilly drive for control and perfection. From the decor in her den to the curve of her eyebrows, everything always had to be perfect, and that included Sandra. Every aspect of Sandra's life was held to unreachable standards, and nothing—her schoolwork, her friends, her appearance—was ever good enough.

If Sandra brought home a report card that featured mostly A's, her mother would only comment cuttingly on her B-plus in English. When she was selected for her high school tennis team, the first freshman ever to be chosen, her mother pointed out that she had not been picked for first string and that the uniforms would show off her fat thighs. Any minor infraction of the house rules—failing to perform chores exactly as specified or coming home two minutes after curfew—would result in Sandra being grounded for weeks.

It goes without saying that until Bill, none of Sandra's boyfriends were ever up to par! Bill was the first man in Sandra's life her mother ever showed signs of liking. Obviously taken by his clean-cut good looks, impeccable pedigree, and professional accomplishments, Sandra's mother gave the relationship her blessing. However, she also took her daughter aside to tell her how very unlikely it was that a man like Bill would be interested in a girl like Sandra, and that Sandra would have to take great care not to lose him.

The really sad thing about this is that, while her mother's comments infuriated Sandra, she secretly agreed. She was telling herself the story she'd been taught by her mother throughout her childhood: she wasn't good enough, wasn't worthy, didn't deserve love. After all, Bill was a handsome, successful, passionate man who could have any woman he wanted. Why would he want her?

But he did. He aggressively romanced her, showering her with compliments, affection, and attention. And Sandra, starved for this kind of tenderness for so many years, soaked it up like a sponge. She'd seen that Bill had a bit of a temper (shouting at delivery boys, leaning on the horn when he thought someone had cut him off in traffic), but he'd always been gentle and kind with her, and she assumed he always would be.

Sandra could hardly believe her luck when he proposed to her, and even today, after many years of marriage, she still has a subconscious belief that she's not good enough for Bill. "I don't know what I'll do if he leaves me!" Sandra tells me, on the brink of tears. "How would I survive without him? Who else would ever want me?"

Maybe you feel like Sandra. And if you do, boy, do I have news for you: Not only can you survive, you can thrive! You have so many options—and the A.R.T. Method will help you discover them.

It's Time to Stop Living Out the Lie

The reality is that Sandra would do just fine without Bill. Objective outsiders to her situation can see that, in fact, she'd probably be a lot better off than she is now. Maybe she'd have to forgo the Mercedes, the massages, and the manicures, but that's a small price to pay for her self-respect, to say nothing of a safe, sane environment for herself and her children and the future generations.

However, it's always easier to understand someone else's situation than it is to get a handle on our own. These things aren't as clear to Sandra, because her sense of herself has been warped by exposure to the destructive, undermining messages she was subjected to as a child—messages that told her she was worthless and unlovable, which she has continued to listen to, unconsciously, for all these years. *She's living out that lie.* She thinks she doesn't deserve any better than Bill's bullying. Although Sandra is a young, attractive, intelligent woman who has many friends, is actively involved in her community, and has done a terrific job of raising her children, Sandra has absolutely no faith that there might be life after Bill—that she could ever get back into the workforce, be able to support herself, or find a romantic partner who would treat her with love and respect.

Stop listening to the bully in your mind, the one that tells you that you're not worthy of love and respect.

Perhaps you understand how Sandra feels. I know I do. And I know that nobody—not Sandra, not me, and not you—should have to feel that way. The good news is that we don't have to. You have the power to turn things around for yourself. You can stop living out the lies that were forced upon you all those years ago, the lies that have damaged and held you back for so long. You can finally stop listening to the bully in your mind, the one that tells you that you're not worthy of love and respect, that you deserve to be bullied. You can switch gears, let go of the past, and get on with your life. I did it. Sandra did it, using the A.R.T. Method. And you can do it, too. At this point, you might not be able to see how, but stick with me, and I promise you will.

First, though, let's take a different look at the experience of being bullied.

WOMEN CAN BE BULLIES, TOO

The popular conception of the bully is a man throwing his weight around, raising his voice, and threatening people physically. But women can be bullies, too. They can even be that same kind of bully, posturing and yelling. More often, however, female bullies use tactics that are quite different—more subtle, less obvious, but every bit as emotionally damaging to those they bully.

A Case Study: Spencer and Moira

Take Spencer's girlfriend, Moira. She's an actress, an emotive, high-energy woman in her early twenties. For Moira, expression of feelings and demonstrations of affection seem to come as easily as breathing.

When they met nine months ago, Spencer, a shy man in his late twenties, was dazzled by Moira's dynamic personality and the effusive, spontaneous warmth she showed him. She even made the first move. She asked him out, and at the end of their first date, she invited him home to spend the night with her. The next morning, she woke Spencer up with breakfast in bed, showered him with kisses, and told him what a terrific lover he was and how much she liked him. Spencer, who has always longed for a truly intimate relationship but doesn't have much experience with women and tends to develop crushes on women who aren't interested in him romantically, fell head over heels for her. Although his instincts told him to be cautious and proceed slowly, Moira's excitement and enthusiasm were infectious, and in no time, they were seeing each other constantly and spending almost every night together.

It didn't take much longer for Spencer to discover that Moira has what he describes as "sensitive artistic temperament" (and what I call being a big bully). This means that whenever Spencer wants to do something that Moira doesn't want to do, or when Moira wants to do something that Spencer doesn't, her response is to throw a temper tantrum. Suppose he wants to spend a night alone and she wants him to sleep over, or she has been invited to a party and he'd prefer to stay home, or he has planned a trip to the beach and she wants to go camping, or he suggests they go to the foreign film he has been reading about but she wants to see an action movie. No matter what the issue, if Spencer doesn't immediately go along with what Moira wants, she becomes hysterical, weeping, pleading with him (sometimes in public), and accusing him of not loving her enough or respecting her needs.

"You don't care about what I want," she sobs. "If you understood me, you'd get why this is so important to me! You wouldn't be like this if you really loved me!" She pushes Spencer away when he tries to comfort her, so he can't do anything but look on helplessly, at a loss for words, with that sick, sinking feeling in his gut.

What Happens? How Bullying Affects the Victim

In the end, Spencer always ends up doing what Moira wants—spending the night with her, going to the party, vacationing in the mountains instead of at the beach, seeing the movie she wanted to see instead of the one he had picked out. And as soon as he acquiesces, Moira dries her tears and lavishes Spencer with affection, thanking him for his kindness and praising his generous, sensitive nature—until the next time things don't go exactly the way she wants them to.

"Everything always seems to matter to Moira so much more than it matters to me," Spencer tells me. "I mean, of course I'd like it if we could compromise more often, but it's just not worth fighting about. I hate to see her so upset. When she starts to cry, it gets me so panicked I sometimes feel like I'm going to cry myself. I can't deal—it's easier to just give her what she wants."

Inside the Mind of the Victim

Why would a sweet guy like Spencer continue to date a woman like this, who bosses and bullies him and acts like a manipulative child? By now you can probably guess that it has a lot to do with how he was raised. There is no bully gene, and no victim gene either. It's all learned behavior.

Spencer grew up in a dysfunctional family with an alcoholic father who tyrannized Spencer, his mother, and his little sister. A jovial, charismatic man when sober, Spencer's father was likely, after he'd had a few drinks, to fly into rages, threaten Spencer's mother with physical violence, scream at the children, break dishes, overturn furniture, punch holes in walls, and sometimes disappear for days at a time. During these episodes, Spencer would watch his mother weeping and his sister shaking with terror, furious with his father for subjecting them to such treatment, but unable to protect them. This made him feel guilty and ashamed, but he really couldn't do anything. The one time Spencer had tried to intervene on his mother's behalf, at the age of sixteen, his father had hit him in the stomach so hard that Spencer passed out.

For years the entire family's life revolved around this man's drinking. Spencer's mother often vowed to leave him and take the children with her, but she never did. Instead, when he came back or sobered up after one of these jags, she would cover for him, lying to his employers when he was too hungover to go to work and making excuses for him to her increasingly concerned parents and friends. Spencer would listen to her on the phone, explaining to his father's boss that he had the flu again or telling her friends that he was a deeply feeling man with a lot on his mind—and besides, who didn't tie one on now and then? Sometimes she'd even send Spencer up to the bedroom with glasses of juice, cold compresses, and aspirin for his father, who lay in the half dark, nursing his self-inflicted pain. Spencer would deliver the supplies, trembling with fear and rage as he handed them over, sickened by his father's sheepish, apologetic smiles.

Though Spencer's father quit drinking for good shortly after Spencer left for college, the damage had been done. The message Spencer got from his parents' behavior was that he was worthless—not valuable enough to nurture, protect, or take care of—and that his only important role was to stay out of trouble, keep quiet, and accommodate the needs of those around him. He was also traumatized by seeing his mother and sister routinely subjected to such abusive treatment. To this day, he can't stand the sight of a woman in tears; it sets off a deep, irrational anxiety and sense of self-loathing connected to the feelings of helplessness he had as a child.

Still Living Out the Lie

Though Spencer doesn't realize it, he's as drawn to the chaos that Moira creates as he is to her warmth. Life with an intense, dramatic, self-centered person like Moira feels, on a subconscious level, familiar and comfortable to Spencer, because it's what he grew up with.

So he falls into his old role—and the role he saw his mother play with his father—of accommodating and enabling Moira, because of those old, internalized beliefs that his needs are unimportant compared with those of the people around him. Moira's temper tantrums make Spencer feel panicked and deeply anxious because they remind him, on a subconscious or unconscious level, of his father's outbursts and of the pain and fear his mother and sister experienced, which, at the time, he was powerless to prevent. As a result, he'll rush to settle a conflict quickly, to quell Moira's hysteria and the strange terror and grief it stirs up in him. He'll settle for peace at any price—even that of his own needs and self-respect.

You're going to learn how to stand up for yourself. You're going to learn how to say good-bye to the lies.

Now, however, Moira has begun to talk about the two of them moving in together. As much as Spencer cares for Moira, he knows he's not quite ready for such a big move, but she is making it almost impossible for him to say no. Whenever she brings up the idea, Spencer tries to tell her that he's committed to their relationship but wants to wait a while longer before taking such a big step. But no matter how gentle and loving he is, no matter how much he assures her that his desire to wait is not a reflection of his feelings for her, Moira has one of her tantrums. And each tantrum goes on, sometimes for hours, until she and Spencer are completely exhausted and he promises that he'll seriously consider moving in with her in the next month or so.

"I'm really at the end of my rope," Spencer tells me. "I'm not ready to live with her yet. I'm sure I would be, eventually, but she has basically made it seem like it's now or never. I don't want to lose her. She's such an amazing woman, and I'm sure I'll never meet anyone who loves me as much as she does. But I really don't want to move in with her yet. I don't know what to do!"

GET READY TO SAY GOOD-BYE TO THE LIE

We know what Spencer should do. He should tell that bossy, bullying, domineering woman either to stop acting like a spoiled brat and show him some consideration or to take a hike! But it's not that easy for Spencer, because he's living out the lie from his childhood—that quiet, insidious, lying voice in his head, which tells him his role in life is to set aside his own needs and feelings, because they just aren't important or valuable, and take care of whatever trouble-making bully is dominating his life at that moment (just imagine what things are like for him at work!), and that he's so unlovable and unworthy of attention that no woman will ever want him again.

Have you ever felt the way Spencer feels? If so, you'll be very glad to know that Spencer learned to stand up for himself using the A.R.T. Method, and life really changed for him. And you're next. That's right—you. You're going to learn how to stand up for yourself, too. Things can change for you if you decide to make that choice. That change won't be as hard as you think. If need be, you'll do it scared. You're so much stronger and braver than you believe you are. You're going to learn how to say good-bye to the lies—the ones you learned all those years ago, the ones that have been preventing you from getting the love and respect you deserve. You're going to get on with your life.

And I'll be right here with you in these pages to help you, every step of the way.

CHAPTER SUMMARY

GET INTO THE SOLUTION!

➤ Bullying is any repeated behavior that makes you feel bad about yourself. You don't have to take it anymore—and together we're going to make sure you don't.

➤ You don't have to be battered to be bullied. Emotional abuse can be even more damaging than physical abuse, and that sick, sinking feeling in your gut is a sure sign you're being bullied. If it feels bad, it probably is. It's time to start trusting your instincts—and take care of yourself.

➤ You might be stuck in a relationship with a bullying partner because you were raised by bullies and secretly believe you deserve abuse. But you don't! You deserve love and respect, and you're going to learn how to get it.

Why Do They Act like That? 2

Inside the Mind of the Bully

- How bullies get to be the way they are
- The surprising similarity between bullies and their victims
- A guide to the most common types of bullies (Is *your* partner on this list?)
- Can bullies change?

The gods visit the sins of the fathers upon the children.
—EURIPIDES

The oppressor must be liberated just as surely as the oppressed. A man who takes away another man's freedom is a prisoner of hatred . . . I am not truly free if I am taking away someone else's freedom, just as surely as I am not free when my freedom is taken from me. The oppressor and the oppressed alike are robbed of their humanity.
—NELSON MANDELA

In Chapter 1, we looked at what it's like to be bullied and why it's so hard for the victims of bullies to stand up for themselves. You now have a better idea than ever before about just how awful, hurtful, and lonely life is for the victims of bullies. But here's something that might surprise you: it's almost as bad for the bullies themselves.

This may sound crazy at first. After all, the bullies are the ones causing all the pain, creating all these problems! How is that hard on *them*? Why on earth would we think *they* were suffering, too? But the fact of the matter is, they really are. Please don't get me wrong; I'm not saying the way bullies act is OK. Bullying behavior is totally unacceptable, and I would never defend or excuse it. But I can *explain* it, and helping you understand bullies better will help you implement my A.R.T. Method for taking your life back from the person who's bullying you.

Let me take you inside the mind of the bully and show you what this dysfunctional dynamic looks like from the other side.

A CASE STUDY: KELLIE AND MARK

Kellie, a pretty blonde in her early thirties, was cooking dinner for her new boyfriend, Mark. It was the first time Mark had been to her apartment, and Kellie had gone all out. She spent all day (and a good part of the previous day) cleaning, shopping, and cooking. She dusted the entire apartment, washed the floors, cleaned the bathroom and the kitchen, changed the sheets, filled vases with fresh flowers, and stacked all her magazines and newspapers neatly in a corner. She spared no expense on veal shanks, wine, artichoke risotto, and chocolate mousse that she made from scratch.

"I really wanted everything to be perfect!" Kellie told me. "Mark has taken me on such nice dates, so I wanted to make it a special evening for him. I even bought a new dress, this sexy off-the-shoulder thing, and I wore my favorite pair of stilettos. I thought I looked great! And I was so proud of this meal. Mark has told me what a good cook his mother is, and it's obviously something he likes in a woman. I was excited to show off my cooking skills to him."

Kellie went on to say that when Mark arrived, he kissed her on the cheek, looked around the room—and *winced*.

"How can you live in a dump like this?" he asked her. "Don't you ever clean this place?" At first Kellie thought he was joking, because the room was so clean it practically sparkled. But then she saw the cold, cruel look on Mark's face. She was devastated.

"I cleaned it today," she told him. "I thought—"

"You think this is *clean*?" Mark interrupted. "Next time, you better hire a cleaning lady." He glanced at her beautifully set table, where candles were lit and an open bottle of wine waited, and began to shake his head with an expression of disgust. "Did you get this furniture off the street? I can't eat here. Come on, let's get out of this place. I'll take you to a restaurant."

"So," I asked her, "how did that make you feel?"

"Pretty awful," Kellie said. "At first I was really upset and even a little angry. I mean, I'd tried so hard! But then I looked around the place and thought, 'Oh, well, maybe he's right.' I mean, my apartment does get cluttered. And most of my furniture is from my grandparents' farm in Pennsylvania. I inherited it when my grandma died, and I love it because it was hers, but I guess it is pretty shabby. Mark comes from such a nice home; he'd know much better than I about that sort of thing. I guess I'll just have to try harder next time."

Obviously, Kellie's response to Mark isn't much healthier than the horrible way he attacked her. Let's take a look at what was going on for both of them and why they acted, and reacted, in this way.

Inside the Mind of the Bully

What could have made Mark behave the way he did? What triggered his bullying behavior? Let's go inside his mind and make some sense of it.

As Mark drives to Kellie's apartment, he's feeling agitated, experiencing a vague sense of stress and anxiety, feelings that linger from a phone conversation he had with his mother earlier in the day, during which she attacked and criticized him, as usual, dwelling particularly on his lack of consideration for his family. She pressed him repeatedly to join the family for brunch the next day, noting that all of his siblings and their families planned on attending.

It just so happens that Mark would rather be almost anywhere in the world than at a brunch with his family. He doesn't want to see them and have to listen to his mother go on about how unsuccessful he is, how much better his overachieving siblings are doing, and how he should have gone to medical school and become a surgeon like his father. He doesn't want to hear their criticism of his friends, his social life, his personal choices, the many errors of his ways. And he especially doesn't want to deal with the constant undermining and verbal abuse he always gets at family events from his two older brothers, who he feels were his parents' favorites.

And yet Mark knows he won't say no. He'll go to the brunch, as he always does. When it comes to his family, he just doesn't have any voice. Thinking about all of this, he feels impotent—and angry.

Then, out of nowhere, he imagines Kellie at the family brunch. What would they think of her? She's a friendly, outgoing person, and even Mark's best friend, who never likes his girlfriends, told Mark after meeting Kellie for the first time that "she could charm a glacier." But his family? He can just imagine how many things they'd find wrong with her before she even opened her mouth to say hello!

This is Mark's state of mind when he walks into Kellie's apartment. Right away, he's annoyed with her. Her outfit is terrible; she looks like exactly the kind of woman his mother would disdain: trashy, too overtly sexy, obviously trying too hard. Stifling his irritation and judgments, he kisses her cheek and then looks around the room. It's awful, he thinks, cluttered and cheap-looking.

"How can you live in a dump like this?" he asks her. "Don't you ever clean this place?" As the words escape his lips, he feels a sense of power. Yes, he knows he's being cruel (though he doesn't quite realize he's talking to Kellie just the way his mother used to talk to him when he was a child). But he can't help himself. And Kellie's crestfallen expression drives him on; she looks like she's going to cry, which irritates him further.

Why is she so weak, so sensitive? That stack of magazines piled up in the corner annoys him, too; why couldn't she just put them away? She's probably the type to leave clothes lying all over the floor of her bedroom and change her linens just once a month. His irritation builds toward rage. He glances at the dining table. It looks like something from the Salvation Army! The dishes are pure Wal-Mart, and the wine glasses have spots on them.

"This is all wrong," Mark thinks to himself. "She's all wrong. Get me out of here." He turns to Kellie, barely containing his temper. "I can't eat here," he snaps at her. "Come on, let's get out of this place. I'll take you to a restaurant."

What Makes Him Act like That?

You don't need a degree in psychology to see that Mark is just reenacting a scenario from his childhood, carrying forward the anger and abuse his mother showed to his father, his siblings, and himself. He's repeating learned behavior, acting out on Kellie the treatment he has been subjected to by his family.

Mark is demonstrating what I call the "rage of generations." He's unconsciously repeating the bullying he experienced and observed growing up, and in doing so, he's perpetuating the cycle of abuse. Now, you may be thinking, "Wait a minute! In the previous chapter, you told me that people who get bullied as children become the *victims* of bullies when they grow up. Now you're claiming that people who get bullied as children become bullies *themselves*. It can't be both, can it?" Surprisingly, it can. Let me explain.

When children are bullied by a parent or observe one parent bullying the other, they experience all kinds of guilt, shame, fear, anger, and confusion. Different children deal with these awful feelings, these unhealthy role models, in different ways.

Many children think they deserve the abuse they're subjected to. This is because they have no other reality to compare their experiences with. They think the abuse is normal. They turn those stored feelings of rage, hurt, and hate against themselves. These are the children who grow up to become adults like Kellie or like my clients Sandra and Spencer, whom you met in Chapter 1. These people have unconsciously internalized the message they received at the hands of their bullying parents, *that bullying and abuse are what they deserve.* And just as unconsciously, they will put up with (and even seek out) bullying in their relationships—seeking out the sort of treatment they're used to, even if it's miserable, because it's familiar and therefore, in some perverse way, comfortable. This is one manifestation of the rage of generations.

Other children deal with bullying in a very different way. Faced with an enraged, controlling, or otherwise bullying parent who rules the roost, a child might begin to see bullying behavior as normal, as an effective way to gain power in relationships. These children unconsciously identify with the bullying parent. Ultimately, they begin unconsciously mimicking that behavior, becoming bullies themselves. This is another manifestation of the rage of generations.

In this way, both the children who grow up to become bullies and the children who grow up to become the victims of bullies are living out the rage of generations. That means they're behaving in the same way as their own parents, and their grandparents, and their great-grandparents, and so on. Unless bullies and victims learn to acknowledge the patterns they're stuck in, and take action to break out, they pass that rage of generations on to their own children, who will pass it on to *their* children, who will pass it on to *their* children . . . until someone is able to stop this vicious cycle.

Now you can see how bullies get to be bullies. Bullies aren't born; they're made. No one was born a bully, and every single bully started out as a bully's victim.

Unconsciously, bullies feel so weak and frightened that they develop an overwhelming need to command and dominate.

How It Feels to Be a Bully

People like Mark have suffered their whole lives from the pain inflicted on them as innocent children by bullying parents. For years they've carried around a rage bottled up inside, a rage they've been powerless to express. Those toxic, pent-up feelings find an outlet at long last when, as adults, they begin controlling, criticizing, bossing around, and behaving abusively toward their own boyfriends or girl-friends, husbands or wives, sons or daughters.

But while a bully may seem to have power or to be in a position of strength, nothing could be further from the truth. Bullying gives the *illusion* of power—temporarily and almost always at great emotional cost to the bully. In reality, the bully's sense of self-worth and self-image are just as bad, and his or her self-esteem and confidence are just as low, as that of the bullying victim.

In fact, it's the very self-hatred and sense of powerlessness that make bullies behave the way they do. Unconsciously, bullies feel so weak and frightened that they develop an overwhelming need to command and dominate, in order to compensate for how vulnerable they feel. This leads them to choose victims, especially spouses and lovers, over whom they believe they can exert complete control.

As a survival mechanism, children who were bullied take on the anger and fear that fueled their parents' bullying behavior. That very same anger and fear begins eating them alive, leading them to hurt the people they love and to destroy the very relationships that are most important to them.

Inside the Mind of the Victim

This brings us back to our biggest concern: Why do the victims of bullying stick around to serve as punching bags, targets of a bully's displaced anger? What keeps good people trapped in bad relationships?

As we've already discussed, bullies and victims were almost always bullied as children. Both are carrying forward the rage of generations; they just do it in different ways. Bullied children who grow up to become bullies identify with the bullying parent and learn to *externalize* their pain and rage, turning it on the people around them. In contrast, bullied children who grow up to become victims identify with the victimized parent and learn to *internalize* that pain and rage, turning it inward onto themselves; they think they deserve it.

These victim types are usually filled with shame and humiliation. They suffer from feelings of extreme inadequacy and insecurity, and they blame themselves for the bullying treatment to which they're subjected by their partners. They've internalized the negative messages that came from their parents—the lies that they're worthless, useless, not good enough to be loved, not deserving of kindness and respect. The result? The victims' self-esteem is so low that when their partners abuse and demean them, they believe it! This is the behavior we talked about in the previous chapter and identified as "living out the lie."

We saw this pattern manifesting itself in Kellie's behavior. From what Kellie said about her reaction to Mark's behavior, you could probably tell pretty quickly that she, too, had been bullied as a child. Kellie's cold, remote father ignored her, and when he did relate to her, it was clear that he found his role as parent inconvenient and tiresome and Kellie herself clumsy and unappealing. He also criticized Kellie's mother frequently, making disparaging remarks about her appearance and the difference between their class backgrounds.

Bullied children who grow up to become bullies identify with the bullying parent and learn to externalize *their pain and rage. Bullied children who grow up to become victims identify with the victimized parent and learn to* internalize *that pain and rage.*

Through this particular dynamic, Kellie came to believe that she was uninteresting, unattractive, and unworthy of attention. In short, she believes she is totally unlovable. Obviously, this is going to lead her to make bad love choices—until she learns how to break free from the rage of generations.

Bully and Victim: A Perfect (Destructive, Codependent) Match

As you can see, Kellie and Mark are perfect for each other. That is, they're perfectly set up for destruction, for a codependent relationship that perpetuates, for both of them, the rage of generations and the pain, self-hatred, and loneliness that come with it.

When Mark attacked Kellie, his remarks didn't come as a surprise to her; they just echoed the messages she'd received as a child, the lies she's been telling herself all these years. By telling me she thought Mark was right in his criticisms of her, Kellie revealed her own unconscious belief that she's not as good as other women and expected Mark to treat her badly. She thinks that's what she deserves.

When Mark lashed out at Kellie, her unconscious thoughts went something like this: "Gosh, I feel terrible about what he's saying, but who am I to think he'd approve of me? I'll never be good enough for him. He finally found out how flawed I really am. I'm lucky he even bothers with me at all! I should be happy he wants to take me out to dinner instead of breaking up with me right here and now."

You can escape from the rage of generations. You can make sure the cycle of bullying and victimhood ends with you.

Kellie's *introject*—that is, the negative messages about herself that she got from her family—has warped her perceptions of herself and others to such an extent that she can't see the truth that's so obvious to those who know her: that she's a lovely, completely lovable woman, and that her new boyfriend is a big bully!

Fortunately, Kellie didn't have to stay in the dark much longer, and you don't have to, either. You can escape from the rage of generations. Instead of passing that rage and pain on to your children, you can make sure the cycle of bullying and victimhood ends with you. To take your next step toward freedom right now, read the next section and learn how to recognize the different types of bullies and see them for who they really are.

TYPES OF BULLIES

Remember, bullying is any repeated behavior that degrades, denigrates, and otherwise makes you feel bad about yourself, including the most blatant insults and the subtlest criticism. What follows is a list of the most common bullies, with information about how they operate, what makes them tick, and how they carry forward the rage of generations.

Not all bullies will match these behaviors exactly. Many will exhibit characteristics of different types at different times or combine several at the same time. And, of course, you may have experienced bullying behaviors that aren't on this list (unhappy people apparently are endlessly creative about the ways they take out their pain and fear on others). The following descriptions will give you more information about the basic types of bullies and the techniques they employ, but remember that your best guide for identifying

DR. ANNE-RENÉE TESTA'S **GUIDE TO BULLIES**

Here's who you'll be meeting in the following pages:

- The Rage Bully
- The Name-Calling Bully
- The Silent-Treatment Bully
- The Body-Language Bully
- The Temper-Tantrum Bully
- The Control-Freak Bully
- The Money Bully
- The Sex Bully
- The Scorekeeping Bully
- The Passive-Aggressive Bully
- The Guilt-Trip Bully

bullies is *your own intuition*, when that sick, sinking feeling in your gut tells you something's not right.

The Rage Bully

Rage Bullies are among the easiest to identify when they're actually in bully mode. What makes these bullies difficult to deal with is not just their alarming and often violent outbursts (shouting, throwing things, punching walls, threatening physical harm to their partners or children), but also the complete unpredictability of many of the outbursts.

One of my clients who knows this all too well is Muriel, who is married to a man named Frank, a bright, upbeat guy who is a good husband to her and a great father to their three kids about 80 percent of the time. The problem is that the usually easygoing Frank has a hidden temper, and Muriel never knows when he will show it or what will set it off. The sort of thing that Frank won't even notice one day—the kids' toys on the living room floor, a longer than usual wait to be seated at their favorite restaurant, a traffic jam, Muriel having to stay an hour late at work—will send him into a furious rage on another day. He'll shout at their children until he's red in the face, stomp around the house cursing, raise his voice to waiters, lean on his horn and scream at other drivers, and slam doors so hard the house shakes.

Frank's rages never last long; most of the time, they'll go on for just a few minutes—a few hours at most. Then, just as suddenly as his temper flared up, it subsides. He calms down and acts as if nothing has happened. Or he apologizes profusely, begging for forgiveness. Muriel and the children may accept his apologies, but the fear of his rages never goes away. Although days may pass before Frank acts up again, the uncertainty about when it will happen or what will cause it keeps his family constantly anxious and on edge.

Inside the Mind of the Rage Bully. As with most bullying behaviors, the short fuse and violent explosions of the Rage Bully are probably inherited from a parent who modeled that negative behavior—a mother or father whose standard reaction to any anxiety or disappointment, large or small, was to fly into a rage. The children of such parents receive two significant personality-shaping lessons. First, they learn that rage is an appropriate reaction to almost any situation. Second, they sense that they can protect themselves from such rage by deploying it themselves. In adulthood, their understandable fear of the enraged parent becomes an unconscious fear of the world, a deep sense of any environment being inherently dangerous and threatening. The Rage Bully copes with this fear by becoming like that parent. When you see a Rage Bully in action, you're seeing a terrified child who, triggered by a sense that the world is not entirely under his or her control and overcome by a surging sensation of fear and fury, strikes out at whoever is opposing his or her will, making the bully feel out of control. It looks like an attack, but really it's a defense, the bully's way of coping with his or her excruciating sense of vulnerability.

The Name-Calling Bully

Another bully who's hard to miss is the Name-Calling Bully. Resorting to the playground tactics of childhood, Name-Calling Bullies use slanderous put-downs against their partners. Back in school, these bullies taunted their vulnerable classmates by calling them "Four-Eyes," "Brace-Face," and "Teacher's Pet" and by making fun of this one's lunch or calling attention to that one's shabby clothes. As adults, the Name-Calling Bullies may have become more sophisticated, couching painful jabs in backhanded remarks and "constructive criticisms." Sometimes, however, they are just as blunt and cruel as ever, calling their partners names, pointing out their shortcomings, putting down their appearances, abilities, and interests.

Consider the pain this kind of bullying inflicted on Darya, who recently gave birth to twins—an incredible accomplishment and a major challenge for a first-time mother. She'd put on a lot of weight during her pregnancy, especially after her doctor insisted on bed rest for the last two months of the pregnancy. Since then, between feeding, changing, and caring for two newborns (to say nothing of the sleep deprivation), Darya just hasn't had the time or energy to exercise and get back to her old shape and weight.

Although her husband, Gary, was initially supportive, he has grown increasingly abusive about her appearance. The bullying began with subtle snipes: he'd call Darya and the girls his "three roly-poly pudgies" and squeeze the soft flesh on Darya's arms and thighs. But this soon gave way to outright verbal assaults. Only three months after the twins were born, he began to greet her by saying, "Hey, Fatso," and to make remarks like "Nice butt, Porky Pig" and "Wide load, coming through."

Now, though the children are only five months old, he nags her daily about going to the gym, teasing that he'll have to buy her an extra seat on the airplane when they go home to visit her parents for Christmas. And he just won't stop, even when she reminds him that there's no one to take care of the babies while she goes to the gym. For all that Gary pesters her about it, he has never offered to look after the girls for a couple of hours so she could get to the gym—or do anything else on her own, for that matter. Instead, he just retorts that none of the "girls" at his office who have had babies have let themselves "turn into heifers" the way Darya has.

Inside the Mind of the Name-Calling Bully. A Name-Calling Bully is insecure and terrified of being humiliated. Since childhood (which probably included a Name-Calling

Bully for a parent), he or she has felt impotent, afraid, and deeply threatened. These bullies deal with those feelings by lashing out in preemptive strikes. Often the names these bullies hurl at their victims are the dark, awful thoughts they have about themselves.

In some cases, Name-Calling Bullies may just think this sort of verbal abuse is normal communication, an acceptable mode of voicing opinions and desires. After all, it's probably the behavior they grew up with.

The Silent-Treatment Bully

A much more subtle category than the bullies we have discussed up to this point are the Silent-Treatment Bullies. But make no mistake; this kind of bullying is just as aggressive, denigrating, and harmful as the behavior of the Name-Calling Bully or the Rage Bully. It's silent, like a poisonous snake, and just as deadly! Silent-Treatment Bullies attack and manipulate by withdrawing and shutting out their partners completely, leaving them alone, helpless, and feeling abandoned. The Silent-Treatment Bully removes all power from the hands of the victim, forcing him or her to beg and plead for any kind of attention or communication, like a hostage jailed in complete emotional isolation.

Another awful side effect of this behavior is that the bully's silence offers a blank slate onto which the victim will project all sorts of fears and anxieties, without any sense of how to address the problem or even what the problem is: "Is she going to leave me?" "Is he having an affair?" "What's going on in her head?" "What on earth can I do to make this better?" "It's all my fault." This treatment is abandonment of the worst kind; the victims feel as though they have disappeared, that they don't exist.

Barry, for example, went for weeks without receiving so much as a hug from his wife, Carina, who was furious with him for quitting a job that he absolutely hated. Her way of punishing him and trying to bully him into changing his mind was to deny him any attention. She wouldn't talk to him, cast a glance in his direction, or acknowledge his presence in any way. When he came into a room, she would get up and leave. When he tried to speak to her, begging her to talk to him, she would turn coldly from him and refuse to speak. And when he got into bed with her at night and reached to touch her shoulder, she would slap his hand, roll away to face the wall, and literally turn her back on him.

Of course, he didn't change his mind about his job, but he did feel increasingly demoralized and miserable. Was Barry being bullied? You bet he was!

Inside the Mind of the Silent-Treatment Bully. Can you guess how Carina got to be a Silent-Treatment Bully? By now it won't be a surprise to hear that she learned it from her parents. Both of them were Silent-Treatment Bullies who would bully each other, and sometimes their children, parents, and siblings with this cruel treatment. As children, Silent-Treatment Bullies heard this message loud and clear without a word being spoken: the appropriate response to any perceived insult or injury, to something not being done "the right way," is to punish the perpetrator with a chilly wall of silence.

Alternatively, in the case of Silent-Treatment Bullies and other types who employ subtler, stealthier bullying strategies, this bully might have been raised by a Rage Bully or an otherwise verbally or physically abusive parent. In such situations, where any direct expression or confrontation was likely to be met with abuse, the Silent-Treatment Bully learned, as a child, that he or she had to find quiet, covert methods of communicating any feeling of anger or sense of injury. This behavior may have been strategic at the time, but now it creates more pain than it avoids.

The Body-Language Bully

Much more difficult to spot than the Silent-Treatment Bully are the Body-Language Bullies, whose techniques are so subtle that even their victims might not realize they're being bullied. The victims of these bullies might only get "bad vibes" or feel strangely uncomfortable without being able to understand exactly what's disturbing them. Because of this subtlety, the victims might think that they're misinterpreting the bully's behavior or have no right to speak up or take a stand, because it seems like there's not really anything to complain about. But trust me, there is.

Body language is a key component of human communication. I'm sure you've heard the expression "Actions speak louder than words." It's absolutely true, and bullies communicate volumes through imperious bearing, disdainful expressions, or postures that threaten or shut out the victim (crossing arms and legs, leering or rolling eyes, turning away when the other person is speaking, looming menacingly over or looking down upon the victim, to name just a few examples). This body language is every bit as damaging as cruel remarks or raised voices, and it should be taken just as seriously.

Inside the Mind of the Body-Language Bully. The Body-Language Bully might have learned his or her behaviors from a parent. Or, like the Silent-Treatment Bully and other bully types who employ subtle, stealthy bullying strategies, this bully might have been raised by a Rage Bully or an otherwise verbally or physically abusive parent and developed this stealth bullying method in response.

The Temper-Tantrum Bully

You met a Temper-Tantrum Bully in the previous chapter. Remember Spencer's girlfriend, Moira? She was the one who, to get her own way in any circumstance, would cry—sometimes hysterically, often in public—until Spencer agreed to do whatever she wanted and peace was restored (if only temporarily). Moira is a classic example of a Temper-Tantrum Bully, a fully grown adult who resorts to totally childish behavior in order to force his or her victim into doing whatever the bully wants. This bullying behavior may include tears, shouting, sulking, acting out in public, and generally taking the victim hostage with an overwhelming, exhausting, and sometimes embarrassing excess of emotion.

Don't think it's bullying? Think again! This kind of emotional manipulation is every bit as coercive and controlling as physical threats, and it's a lot more insidious, especially as the bullies will often accuse their victims of being cold, insensitive, uncaring, and indifferent to their happiness.

Inside the Mind of the Temper-Tantrum Bully. Even more than with some of the bullies I've already described, it's easy to see that these bullies are badly behaved children who never outgrew their childish behaviors, probably because they grew up with a hyper-emotional role model who used such performances of hysteria to bully their spouses and children into submission. And the family members, like those of the Rage Bully, live in fear and anxiety, never knowing when a tantrum will erupt.

In other cases, Temper-Tantrum Bullies may have grown up with a Silent-Treatment Bully or an otherwise cold or neglectful parent and eventually discovered that the only way they could get attention or provoke a reaction was with the most extreme, exaggerated demonstrations of feeling. Temper-Tantrum Bullies feel powerless, as if they're constantly in danger of becoming invisible or of their needs being misunderstood and unmet. The result? In their unconscious minds, every little disagreement becomes a battle to prove their worth. The real issue isn't which movie you're going to see, or what color the drapes should be, or whatever else it looks like the Temper-Tantrum Bully is making a scene about; it's his or her very existence!

The Control-Freak Bully

Control-Freak Bullies are bossy tyrants. They're sure they know what's good for everyone else, and they persist in trying to make their victims into someone they're not. Whatever goals or pursuits the Control-Freak Bully's partner might have for him- or herself are completely irrelevant; they simply don't factor into the bully's vision of what, who, and how the partner should be. This behavior is very different from that of the husband or wife who lovingly shares a need or asks the spouse to consider making a change for the benefit of the relationship. Control-Freak Bullies are not interested in compromise or in solutions that allow both partners to have their needs met, but only in having their own needs met.

The Control-Freak Bully's approach might be sweet and coaxing or else aggressive and nagging. The victim might get gentle suggestions and "constructive criticism," or angry orders and vicious critiques, or anything in between. Either way, this type of bullying will probably continue nearly nonstop. Whether it's your cooking or your clothing, the work you do or the car you drive, the way you hold your fork or the way you make love, the bully's underlying message is always the same: "You're not good enough the way you are. Your way is wrong, and my way is right. You're broken, and I'm going to fix you." And all too often, the victims of the Control-Freak Bully are inclined to agree with their tormenter, making excuses for the bullying behavior, telling themselves and others, "He just wants to help," or "She only wants what's best for me."

Inside the Mind of the Control-Freak Bully. These bullies are even more fearful than the average bully. Subconsciously, Control-Freak Bullies feel like their lives are always just about to fall apart or go off the rails and can be saved from ruin only if they apply all their energy to make sure everything in their environment happens just so. They're likely to be nitpicky about everything; every person, place, and thing, including themselves, should be immaculately clean, meticulously organized, precisely on time, and performing at 100 percent all the time.

Almost inevitably, Control-Freak Bullies had controlling parents, who also were narcissistic, self-obsessed, rigid, and unreasonably demanding. As children, these future Control-Freak Bullies could see only one way to avoid criticism and feel safe: by doing things "perfectly," that is, in exact accordance with standards of their parents. And all these years later, they're still doing it, while unconsciously imposing unreasonable standards on their partners and children, as their parents did with them.

The Money Bully

In a relationship, the Money Bully is usually the higher-earning person. No matter what socioeconomic level these bullies come from, they use financial status to control and dominate their less-affluent partner. The Money Bully keeps a stranglehold on the purse strings. He or she dictates where the couple will go and when, how much they'll spend and on what. Often these bullies demand detailed accounts of a partner's expenses while being secretive about how much they earn and spend. Money Bullies won't hesitate to play the "I'm leaving" trump card and often threaten abandonment or divorce, fully aware that a split would leave their partner in financial ruin.

The Money Bully also seems to overlook or minimize the value of any other kind of contribution to the relationship or household. It doesn't matter if their partner looks after the children, does the housework, cares for and beautifies the living space, provides emotional support, organizes social and recreational activities, or provides humor and intellectual stimulation, just to name a few ways of enriching one another's lives. It's as if money were the only thing of value that either partner had to offer the relationship.

Take Ginger, a homemaker, and her husband, Phil, a CPA with a six-figure salary. Twelve years ago, when the second of their three children was born just fourteen months after the first, Ginger happily gave up her budding career as an interior designer to stay home with her babies. These days, she juggles the education and activity schedules of three grade-schoolers; serves on the PTA; participates in her daughter's soccer team carpool; does set design for her son's theater productions; does all of the family's shopping, cooking, cleaning, laundry, and gardening; plans family outings and vacations; and hosts occasional dinners for Phil's colleagues and their spouses.

The one thing all these bully types have in common is that they're miserable, frightened people with low self-esteem.

In the past year, Ginger has also started doing the occasional interior-decoration job again, putting in a few hours here and there when the kids are at school. She confessed to me that she's doing it in part so she can have some money of her own to spend without Phil demanding that she account for every last cent. Phil claims the right to do this because, according to him, he is supporting the family on his own. Once Ginger misplaced several receipts for household purchases, which he demands she collect and turn over to him once a week. When she couldn't find the receipts, Phil shouted, "I'm the one providing for all of us! It's my right to know how my money's being spent! When *you* make the money, *you* can call the shots."

Inside the Mind of the Money Bully. Looking at Phil's behavior, it's easy to see he unconsciously believes he isn't valued or appreciated by his family. He abuses his financial position in an attempt to cope with and compensate for these unpleasant feelings. Most Money Bullies, whether rich or poor, were raised by parents who neglected and ignored them, making them feel invisible and beneath notice. Or they were raised by parents who actively abused them, Name-Calling Bullies or Control-Freak Bullies who made them feel that they were stupid, ugly, incompetent, and—worst of all—unwanted or unneeded. The result? As adults, Money Bullies use money like a weapon. They wield the bank balance against their partners in a desperate and destructive attempt to establish their worth in the world.

The Sex Bully

The most primitive of all bullies are the Sex Bullies, who exert power over their victims by either insisting on or withholding sex. A woman may refuse to have sex with her husband until he agrees to apologize for forgetting her mother's birthday. A man may force his girlfriend to perform sexual acts she doesn't like by threatening to go outside the relationship for his satisfaction. For Sex Bullies, sex—which should always and only be an act of love, intimacy, or pleasure—is used as currency, as leverage, as a weapon. This degrades and depersonalizes sexual intimacy within a relationship.

Inside the Mind of the Sex Bully. A Sex Bully may have been raised by parents who used sex as power—mothers who used flirtation, seduction, and sex to get the attention they wanted, to get their needs met, or fathers who treated their wives (and mistresses, female coworkers, and any woman who happened to be passing their way) as sexual objects, conquests to be won, and property to be possessed.

As children, these bullies also may have been sexually abused or given confusing and inappropriate messages about sex.

Alternatively, the Sex Bully may have been raised by *any* kind of bully in an environment that made him or her feel powerless, castrated, and impotent. In adulthood, he or she sexually bullies a partner to overcome an overwhelming sense of insignificance, inferiority, and inadequacy. It's a chest-pounding, I-rule-the-world, Tarzan thing. You'll learn much more about these bullies and what you can do about them in Chapter 4.

The Scorekeeping Bully

Scorekeeping Bullies are constantly bringing the past into the present, using missteps and perceived slights from last week or last year against their partners, penalizing them for past actions for which there is no current solution. The Scorekeeping Bully dredges up offenses, large or small, and throws them back in the victim's face. The time you forgot her birthday. The time you flirted with his friend. The time you stayed out too late without calling him. The time you were short on cash and she gave you a loan that took you a few months to pay back.

Scorekeeping Bullies are grudge holders who collect and hoard ammunition to be used against their partners as leverage in conflicts. The rallying cry of the Scorekeeping Bully is "Remember the time you . . ." This sentence always finishes with some old error that the victim has apologized for (probably more than once) and thought had been dealt with and laid to rest. Or the sentence may be completed by some obscure but long-nursed grievance that the Scorekeeping Bully was just waiting for a chance to use.

Inside the Mind of the Scorekeeping Bully. A friend of mine has a handy trick for getting over resentments and grudges. He just asks himself, "Do you want to be right, or do you want to be happy?" This helps him see that the person he's really hurting by holding a grudge is himself. Scorekeeping Bullies, in contrast, would much rather be right than happy, because being right is what makes them feel safe, even though it also makes them miserable. (Holding a grudge is a lot like trying to wound an enemy by stabbing yourself.) Winning an argument gives the Scorekeeping Bully a sense of power and control, along with the perverse, righteous thrill of proving his or her partner wrong. Unconsciously, the bully feels impotent, in the wrong, and in constant danger of being rejected.

This type of bully may have been raised by an aggressive bully and grown up under constant attack. Or he may have been neglected, ignored, and made to feel worthless. As a result, in adulthood, the Scorekeeping Bully unconsciously lives in fear of disapproval and abandonment. As a "solution," this bully resorts to a kind of Cold War mentality, in which the bully stockpiles weapons of grudge and resentment in an emotional arms race. Then, when frightened or threatened, the bully launches deadly preemptive strikes at his or her unsuspecting partner.

The Passive-Aggressive Bully

Along with the Silent-Treatment and Body-Language Bullies, the Passive-Aggressive Bullies are "stealth" bullies. They're all hard to spot because their bullying techniques are not in your face. In their behavior, Passive-Aggressive Bullies are almost the opposite of the Rage Bully or the Temper-Tantrum Bully. Rather than reacting directly and immediately to a trigger situation (the thing that sets the bully off), Passive-Aggressive Bullies will often take their time and will bully in indirect ways.

I counsel a married couple who are both bullies; the husband, Jamil, is a Guilt-Trip Bully, and the wife, Stella, is a Passive-Aggressive Bully. Instead of addressing Jamil's bullying behaviors in a healthy, mature way that might create opportunities for the relationship to evolve, Stella acts out. For example, let's say Jamil has guilt-tripped her into skipping her family reunion this year. Rather than stand her ground and go to the reunion on her own, Stella stays at work late for a week. Though she knows Jamil hates spending evenings without her (he can barely manage to fix dinner for himself, never mind for their two teenage children), she comes home after ten o'clock every night and then reads in bed for an hour or two, fully aware that the light keeps him awake and that he has to be up at five o'clock the next morning to get ready for work.

And so it goes. Jamil guilt-trips Stella into getting a station wagon instead of the hybrid she wanted; she cuts her hair extremely short, knowing he loves it long. He guilt-trips her into having a dinner party for his

Taking steps to change will have a big effect on the lives of those around you and the lives of those to come.

colleagues; she spends the evening flirting with his supervisor. He guilt-trips her into moving to the suburbs; she has a fling with an old boyfriend. And in the end, who loses? They both do.

Inside the Mind of the Passive-Aggressive Bully. Stella acts the way she does to punish Jamil and get revenge for the pain he inflicts on her. This is standard operating procedure for Passive-Aggressive Bullies, who lack the confidence to stand up for themselves. They're afraid rejection and retaliation will result if they overtly disagree or directly address a conflict with their partners, so they find sneaky, insidious, and corrosive ways of communicating their displeasure—a roundabout response that almost always involves doing something they know their partner won't like.

Many Passive-Aggressive Bullies were raised by a Rage Bully or an otherwise verbally or physically abusive parent. This was the case with Stella. Her mother died when Stella was very young, and she was raised by a resentful, rage-filled father. For years she watched as her older sister, in an attempt to protect Stella, would confront their father and end up receiving beatings as a consequence. Terrified and overwhelmed by her own sense of helplessness, Stella would lie in bed at night screaming into her pillow until she was hoarse, her cries muffled so no one could hear her. The lesson that Stella unconsciously took from her childhood was that it's forbidden, and even dangerous, to state her needs or stand up for herself, and that she must find other ways of expressing her feelings. Unfortunately, the method of expression she chose was as destructive to herself and others as her father's was.

The Guilt-Trip Bully

Guilt-Trip Bullies are so well known and so often made fun of on TV and in movies that descriptions of their behavior might make you laugh. There's the elderly parent who whines, "No, I don't need anything, I'm used to doing everything for myself since you kids moved away and left me alone in my old age." There's the friend who gives you the sweater you asked to borrow for your date, saying sadly, "I never have anywhere to wear it anyway. No one ever asks me out. And now that you're dating, I'll probably never leave the house." And, of course, there's the bullying spouse who sighs, "I'll get my own dinner. Don't worry about me. I'm exhausted from working all day, but never mind," or, "Sure, we can go to the party. You know I don't like going out on the weekends. But if it's more important for you to see your friends than spend time with me, that's fine," or, "Oh, just go ahead and do whatever you want. You always do what you want anyway." (The reality is that the Guilt-Trip Bully's victims *never* do what they want, because they get bullied out of it.)

But however silly these examples may seem, the Guilt-Trip Bully is no laughing matter. Just imagine how this strategy works when the stakes are higher: "When I married you, I never thought you'd be the kind of woman who'd pursue a career instead of staying at home with her children. But I guess not everyone shares my priorities," or, "If you're really so unhappy at that job, you shouldn't worry about how quitting will affect your family. We'll manage somehow." Through steady pressure and coercion, these bullies manage to completely bulldoze their victims and get their own way. They also make those victims feel they're hopelessly self-centered, that their every desire is selfish and unreasonable. This leads the victims to constantly doubt, second-guess, and undermine themselves.

Inside the Mind of the Guilt-Trip Bully. Psychologically, this bully is closely related to the Passive-Aggressive Bully. If the Guilt-Trip Bully wasn't raised by another Guilt-Trip Bully, he or she probably grew up with a Rage or Name-Calling Bully, whose behaviors created such a sense of danger and provoked such anxiety that the child was afraid to speak up and instead developed indirect ways of expressing needs and frustrations. But where the Passive-Aggressive Bully is motivated by a desire to punish and to get even for perceived wrongs, the Guilt-Trip Bully acts on an odd sense of self that combines worthlessness and entitlement. These bullies feel that their needs have never really been understood or met. On the one hand, they're convinced that this is so because they don't *deserve* to have their needs met. On the other hand, after so much perceived deprivation, they feel entitled to have every whim catered to.

Unfortunately, these bullies are playing a lose-lose game. Even when the Guilt-Trip Bully's partner gives in, the bully is unlikely to be satisfied; instead, he or she will be plagued by a sense that the victim didn't really want to comply with his or her demands. Of course this only feeds the bully's feeling of worthlessness and deprivation, because what this person really wants—what all of us want—is unconditional love.

CAN BULLIES CHANGE?

I'm sure you can see now that the one thing all these bully types have in common is that they're miserable, frightened people with low self-esteem. They're trapped by, and living out, the rage of generations. They were bullied as children and now, as adults, are compensating, in the most destructive ways, for how vulnerable, powerless, and terrified they feel. Again, let me be clear that I'm absolutely not excusing bullies for the way they act. But I do think it will help you to know that the bully in your life is suffering, too, that his or her behavior, like yours, was shaped by the negative aspects of his or her upbringing.

And like you, bullying partners are able to change, but *only if they really want to.* You can't make anyone else change. The only person you can change is yourself.

Bear in mind that taking steps to change will have a big effect on the lives of those around you and the lives of those to come. The reason is that you'll be ending the rage of generations. You're setting yourself free from this cycle of abuse. You're ceasing to enable your partner's bullying behavior. And you're also liberating your children, their children, and all the future generations of children to come. That's a pretty profound and amazing change, isn't it? And you're already well on your way!

CHAPTER SUMMARY

GET INTO THE SOLUTION!

➤ When bullies bully, *it's not about you.* They're acting out the rage of generations, the abusive behaviors they learned as children from bullying parents. Their behavior is not your fault. You don't deserve it. You shouldn't take it personally—and you don't have to take it any longer!

➤ What bully and victim have in common is the "introject"—the negative messages received from bullying parents that fuel the rage of generations and keep both bully and victim trapped in a cycle of abuse. But you can break this cycle; upcoming chapters will tell you how.

➤ Being a bully can be almost as painful as being a bully's victim. When you stop taking a bully's abuse, stand up for yourself, and help end the rage of generations, you're doing something loving and caring not only for yourself, but also for your partner—and the generations to come.

Living with the Enemy 3

Are You in Denial About a Bully in Your Relationship?

- What people do to manage the pain inflicted by their bullying partner
- Coping mechanisms (Which ones do you use?)
- Why coping is dangerous for the victim, the bully, the children, and the family's future
- How you can stop *coping* and start *changing*

> *A pirate walks into a bar with a sword sticking out of his chest and calmly orders a tankard of rum. "Blimey!" says the barkeep. "Doesn't that hurt?" To which the pirate responds, "Aye, matey, but only when I laugh."*

Does this joke ring any bells for you? I'll bet it does. People who are in relationships with bullies understand better than most what it's like to be in pain daily—to accept it, ignore it, sublimate it, repress it, cope with it, numb ourselves to it any way we know how, and to live with it until we forget there's any other way to live. Like the man with the sword in his chest, a bullied partner is one of the walking wounded, suffering from the terrible effects of an abusive relationship. But the victim of emotional abuse isn't always aware of just how much pain and danger he or she is really experiencing.

You might be asking yourself, "If the situation is *that* bad, why would victims stay and take it? How could they bear it? If it really hurt *that* much, wouldn't the victims just leave?" These are excellent questions. And it's absolutely true that a person with healthy levels of self-esteem wouldn't stay in a terrible, toxic situation. People who weren't damaged by parental introjects—the negative messages about themselves they learned in childhood—would stand up for themselves. Healthy people set boundaries, state needs, and leave if those needs and boundaries aren't respected. This is the healthy model, the type of response to bullying that we're aiming for.

People who are in relationships with bullies understand better than most what it's like to be in pain daily.

But as I explained in Chapter 1, people who stay with bullies have been programmed from childhood to expect abuse and seek it out in their relationships; they've been conditioned to believe they're worthless, unlovable, and deserve to be abused. It is essential to remember that what happened to you as you were growing up *is not your fault*. You were an innocent child. You should have been loved, supported, nurtured, praised, and protected. If you didn't receive all that good stuff, the reason is not that you didn't deserve it. You deserved love and respect back then—and you deserve it today!

WHY AND HOW THE VICTIM STAYS WITH A BULLYING PARTNER

I can say with confidence that victims who stay with their bullying partners do *not* do so because it's "not that bad." They're not staying because the pain is minor or the situation is merely inconvenient. Just the opposite! They stay because they think they deserve the abuse they're getting. They're living the lie. And the suffering that results, far from being easy to endure, is so extreme that it requires all kinds of coping mechanisms. Here are some of the most common ways people cope:

- Denial
- Excuse making
- Rationalization
- Avoidance
- Isolation
- Destructive distractions

We'll discuss each one of these at length and look at examples later in the chapter.

Such psychological contortions and adaptive behaviors are survival strategies. They allow bullied partners to navigate the war zone of the bullying household. Unfortunately, these strategies are not *solutions*. They're only temporary bandages. They cover up the symptoms of the problem but don't heal the cause. Instead, these "Band-Aids" make it possible for the victim, who is anesthetized and in denial, to remain in a destructive relationship, suffering more and more damage. By and large, victims use these coping mechanisms unconsciously. They do it without knowing how much pain they're in or how hard they're working to cope with it.

As you read on through the descriptions of various coping mechanisms, you may recognize your own behavior in one or more of them. If you do, you'll be making a terrific advance in the improvement of your psychological health and well-being. Why? Because the first step of the A.R.T. Method is to acknowledge. As you know, to acknowledge something is to become aware of and accept it. This is the foundation of any recovery process. When you open your eyes to what's really happening in your relationship, you're making a big, brave start toward your own recovery. So please, take a long, hard look at the coping mechanisms described in this chapter. But be kind to yourself as you do so; don't beat yourself up. Instead of feeling guilty, just take a look and see what's going on.

DENIAL

To be in denial is to refuse or to be unable to recognize and deal with a serious personal problem. This is one of the main ways that bullied partners cope with their daily abuse. Occasionally the denial is conscious. The victimized partners will lie to others and *attempt* to lie to themselves and deny how badly they're being bullied, how much it's hurting. Often, though, the denial is entirely unconscious, a trick the victim's mind plays to manage the pain.

Three of the most common manifestations of denial for the victim of a bullying spouse or partner are to think, "This is normal," "It's my fault," or, "I can fix it."

"This Is Normal"

When the victims of bullying partners tell themselves their situation is "normal," they believe all relationships are like theirs. They think bullying and victimhood are the way relationships are *supposed* to be. They don't see anything wrong with the way their partners treat them.

The victim of emotional abuse isn't always aware of just how much pain and danger he or she is really experiencing.

It's easy to understand how someone who was raised by a bullying parent, especially one who was physically violent or verbally abusive, might indeed believe that an abusive relationship is "normal," since that's what the person experienced in childhood. If one of your parents constantly bullied the other (along with you and your siblings), the same treatment from your own partner or spouse might actually seem perfectly normal. In other cases, such beliefs may be the result of true psychological denial, as the word is used by psychologists: the truth hurts so much that the victim completely numbs it out, because it's easier than facing reality.

How This Type of Denial Looks in Action. Kamalah is a nurse in her fifties. When I first started working with her, she was in deep denial about what was really going on in her relationship with her second husband. Leo, a car dealer whom she'd met through a dating service and married a few years earlier, had initially been a warm, gentle, sexually appreciative partner. This thrilled Kamalah, who'd been widowed young and stayed single for many years following her first husband's death.

What happened to you as you were growing up is not your fault.

Unfortunately, Leo's sweet ways didn't last; he turned out to be a Sex Bully. Six months into their marriage, Leo began getting rough with Kamalah in bed, pushing her to have sex whether she wanted it or not. He took to smacking her derriere, pulling her hair, even slapping her in the face while they were having intercourse—and not in a playful, consensual way. If she resisted, he'd either ignore her and continue what he was doing or else shove her away, call her uptight and a prude, and threaten to visit prostitutes if she didn't "loosen up."

This is pretty obvious and serious bullying behavior on Leo's part, but because of her inner shame, Kamalah couldn't bring it up with me until after two months of weekly sessions. And when she did, she mentioned it casually, as if she were telling me about a trip to the grocery store. In her gut and deepest self, she obviously knew how wrong it was for Leo to treat her that way, or she wouldn't have come to see me. In fact, in her deepest self, his behavior felt *deeply* wrong, but so did the horrible thought of giving up the first relationship she'd had in many years. She was afraid of being alone again. Faced with this seemingly irresolvable conflict, Kamalah went into denial without even knowing it. Her mind blocked from her consciousness how wrong Leo's behavior felt to her, how painful it was to be treated the way he was treating her. But—and this is the important thing—the denial didn't end her pain. It only numbed and shut out her *awareness* of how much she was being hurt by Leo's bullying.

You deserved love and respect back then—and you deserve it today!

Just imagine someone ice-skating or doing hurdles with a broken leg: this athlete might take painkillers to cover up the pain, but the longer the person ignores the damage being done, the worse that damage gets. That's a pretty good metaphor for Kamalah's situation and for any bullying victim who's in denial about the reality of his or her situation. It's easier to numb yourself and pretend everything's OK, because the truth is too painful to face and the fear of change is too overwhelming.

"It's My Fault"

Having read in previous chapters about the psychology and self-esteem issues of people who get into relationships with bullies, you can see how the "It's my fault" form of denial works. Like the victims you've met so far in these pages, such people have been deeply affected by the negative, destructive, undermining messages they got as children—that they were worthless and unlovable—lies they've unconsciously continued to listen to and live out for years. As children, they took to heart—internalized—their bullying parents' insults and abuse, and they blamed themselves for the treatment they were subjected to. They thought they deserved it!

Today, as adults, they take to heart their bullying partners' insults and abuse, continuing to blame themselves for the treatment they're subjected to. They think they deserve it. They think they're responsible for it. But the only thing they're responsible for is that they stay and take it.

How This Type of Denial Looks in Action. Max exhibits this form of denial about his relationship with his wife, Keiko, a Control-Freak Bully. As far as Keiko is concerned, Max can't do anything right. If Max takes Keiko out to dinner, she complains that the restaurant isn't nice enough and tells him he's cheap. If he changes the sheets on their bed, she criticizes him for not knowing how to make hospital corners and putting the bedspread on the wrong way. If he arrives home early from work, she accuses him of driving too fast, not taking his job seriously, or even spying on her.

Sadly, Max believes he deserves Keiko's low opinion and bullying treatment. Raised by a Rage Bully father and a preoccupied, neglectful mother, Max has incredibly low self-esteem, and he's convinced that Keiko is right about him. When I try to point out how unreasonable and unkind her actions are, Max leaps to defend her. "She's not trying to be mean," he tells me. "She's trying to help me. She's got high standards, but she's so good at everything, and things don't come as easily to me as they do to her. I just have to try harder, and then I won't upset her. Sometimes I wish she'd be more patient with me, but I know if I just try harder, we won't fight as much, and I'll make her happy."

> *Victims use these coping mechanisms unconsciously. They do it without knowing how much pain they're in or how hard they're working to cope with it.*

Poor Max! We know he'll *never* be able to make Keiko happy, not unless she's able to make some changes of her own and grow out of her bullying ways. He'll never be able to make her happy—not because *he's* doing anything wrong, but because *she's* a miserable person whose only relief comes from taking her misery out on her innocent partner . . . who blames himself.

"I Can Fix It"

One of my favorite cartoons depicts two women talking over lunch. One exclaims, "You're marrying Attila the Hun?!?" and the other answers, "I can fix him!" Talk about denial!

When I call it denial to claim you can "fix" a bully, I don't mean it's a case of leopards not being able to change their spots. Bullies certainly *can* change, if they really want to. They can change if they're willing to do the work. But one fact is unavoidable: you can't fix anyone but yourself, no matter how well-meaning, well-informed, intelligent, diligent, devoted, or determined you are. That's because no one can *ever* change another person. We can only change ourselves.

How This Type of Denial Looks in Action. Amy isn't in any kind of denial about how rough things are with her longtime boyfriend, Brandon. This guy is a first-class Scorekeeping Bully who finds daily opportunities to get angry about things Amy "did wrong" weeks, months, and even years ago. Amy wants a commitment from Brandon, but whenever she brings up the subject of marriage, he'll dredge up some ancient error or misstep as proof that he can't trust Amy enough to marry her. Then he'll talk about it for hours, until Amy is in tears and falling all over herself to apologize.

Amy sees perfectly well that Brandon's behavior isn't healthy. But she is in denial about what she can do to change the situation. And she's desperate, because she has somehow convinced herself that this guy is the only man on earth who will ever want her.

"He's in so much pain," Amy tells me. "He had such a terrible childhood! Of course he has trust issues and intimacy issues. I don't like the way he's treating me right now, but it's only because he was so hurt in the past. I know I can make it better. If I can just be patient and loving and not complain, he'll work through all that stuff, and things will change."

Will they? Not this way, they won't. By taking Brandon's abuse without standing up for herself, Amy won't accomplish anything except hurting herself and enabling Brandon to continue behaving in a way that's as destructive to him as it is to her. She won't "fix" him, because Brandon is the only one who can do that. What Amy needs to focus on instead is healing *herself.* That's something she really can do—and you can do for yourself.

> *When you open your eyes to what's really happening in your relationship, you're making a big, brave start toward your own recovery.*

EXCUSE MAKING

Sometimes a bully's partner is able to stop denying there's something very wrong in the relationship but is still too scared to take action. In this kind of situation, one coping mechanism that gets used is excuse making. This is exactly what it sounds like: the victim makes excuses for the bully's behavior, the situation, and why the victim isn't doing anything about it. The most common excuses are "He/she is only acting like this because . . . ," "Talking about it won't do any good," and "It's not like there's anything better out there."

"He/She Is Only Acting like This Because . . ."

Victimized partners come up with all kinds of excuses, from the mundane to the ridiculous, for their partners' bullying behaviors. Here are just a few of the excuses I've heard lately:

- "He's only acting like this because he's been working so hard lately."
- "She treats me this way because it's that time of the month."
- "He only yells at me because he hasn't been sleeping well."
- "She's touchy because her birthday's coming up."
- "He's in a bad mood because his team lost again."
- "She gives me the silent treatment because she has a hard time communicating her feelings."

All of these explanations for a partner's bad behavior may hold some truth or validity, but an explanation is not an excuse. Plain and simple, *there is no excuse for being an abusive bully*. It doesn't matter how hard we're working, or what time of the month it is, or how little sleep we had, or even how hard our childhoods were. We all have to take responsibility for our actions—and that goes for the bullies *and* for the victims who've been making excuses for their partners' bullying behaviors.

How This Type of Excuse Making Looks in Action. My shy, meek client Chayanne, a tiny woman with a doll's face, has known for months that her hulking husband, Manny, a Name-Calling Bully, is treating her very badly.

An explanation is not an excuse. Plain and simple, there is no excuse for being an abusive bully.

She understands, at least on an intellectual level, that the way he acts toward her is not OK. But she hasn't yet been able to really acknowledge, deep in her heart and gut, that Manny's behavior is truly unacceptable and that she deserves better —because then she'd have to do something about it, which terrifies her. So instead of holding Manny responsible for his actions, Chayanne makes excuses for him. When we first started working together, she told me that Manny called her "pushy" only because he was so stressed out about his job as a foreman on a tough construction job. The following month, he got fired—and *that* was how Chayanne excused him for calling her a "damn nag" and a few other choice names we can't print here. Now, several months and many inappropriate four-letter words later, Manny has a new job. And according to Chayanne, when he calls her a "lazy cow" and "ingrate," it's only because he's under so much pressure to learn the ropes there.

What do you suppose the excuse will be next week? How long will Chayanne have to suffer these horrible insults and cruel attacks before she sees that there is never an excuse for anyone to treat her that way and stops making excuses for Manny?

"Talking About It Won't Do Any Good"

When the victims of bullies stop making excuses for their partners and start making excuses for the relationship or themselves, that's when I start to hear them say, "Talking about it won't do any good." At this point, the victim has finally been able to face the fact that his or her spouse is behaving badly, and may have even acknowledged that the bullying is not appropriate. But rather than acting on this new knowledge, the victim decides that addressing the situation won't do any good. It's the perfect excuse for not saying anything: "Talking won't help. It won't change things. It won't make things better, and it might even make them worse, so why bother?"

As we can easily see, this excuse isn't true. It's a rare situation that isn't improved by honest, open communication. Even the victim knows that "Talking won't help" is a ridiculous ruse!

What's really happening here? The fear of conflict, confrontation, or consequences is still greater than the pain caused by the spouse's bullying. Therefore, the suffering but fearful victim makes excuses for not speaking up and speaking out, trying to convince him- or herself (and anyone else who might be asking) that there's no point in trying.

How This Type of Excuse Making Looks in Action. Stewart, a tightly wound but very nice journalist in his forties, is married to Robin, a gorgeous, athletic woman—and a serious Passive-Aggressive Bully. She works as a physical trainer at the local gym, and when she's mad at Stewart, she'll make a point of scheduling late-night appointments with her more attractive male clients. If Stewart drops by the gym to visit Robin, she makes a big show of flirting with and lavishly praising her attractive male coworkers. And when she visits Stewart's workplace, she behaves seductively with his coworkers, especially the ones she knows he doesn't like, the ones he feels competitive with.

After many years of suffering from Robin's underhanded bullying, Stewart finally got tired of living with the pain and decided to get into therapy. It didn't take him long to admit to me that he is hurting or to acknowledge that Robin really is a bully, and that the way she treats him is just not OK. But that's where Stewart has been stuck—for months.

"I hear what you're saying," Stewart tells me when I encourage him to discuss the situation with Robin, "but you just don't understand. You don't know Robin the way I do. There's no point in bringing it up with her. Talking to her won't help! She'll just tell me I'm imagining things. If I point out that she's being passive-aggressive, she'll just deny it. And then she'll act out even more! I'm telling you, trying to talk about it with her will only make things worse."

Stewart is terrified of his bullying wife, of confrontation, of change. His fear of facing off with Robin is bigger than the pain that Robin has been inflicting on him. So he has convinced himself he knows exactly how Robin would react if he stood up for himself. He doesn't have any idea how she'd *really* react, but he's too scared to find out.

"It's Not like There's Anything Better out There"

The victim's next line of excuse-making defense is the claim that *no one* is perfect, that *any* commitment requires compromise, that *all* marriages have problems. Any relationship is likely to be more or less like this one, my excuse-making patients tell me. So, their argument goes, there's no point in taking action. And there's certainly no reason to consider walking out. Any other partner would be just as bad as this one—and the devil you know is better than the devil you don't know, right?

The problem with this argument is that it relies on faulty logic. It doesn't make any sense! Of course it's true that no partner is perfect. No relationship is problem-free. That's obvious to anybody who has ever been in one. But there's a big difference between the disagreements that every couple has and the abuse that these victims deal with every day. And there's a huge difference between a bully and an imperfect but self-aware partner who makes occasional mistakes but takes responsibility for his or her actions.

What's really going on here? This excuse is not based on reality, but on what the victim unconsciously believes: that no one in this world will ever offer kindness, respect, and unconditional love, because he or she doesn't deserve it. And that's not true.

How This Type of Excuse Making Looks in Action. Toni used this excuse for ages. She knew her relationship with her boyfriend, Neelish, was bad for her. A Guilt-Trip Bully who kept her on a very short leash, Neelish used his guilt trips to control where Toni went, when, and with whom, until she never went out at all and became completely isolated. She never saw her old friends, never did anything on her own, and practically never left the house without Neelish, except to go to and from work. He didn't even like her to run errands or shop for groceries without him.

Toni often talked about feeling as if she were under house arrest. "You know those dog collars that give the dog an electric shock if it tries to leave the yard?" she said once. "That's what it's like living with Neelish. Except instead of an electric shock, I get that damn broken-up look on his face, and then I know the big poor-me routine is on the way. And before it even gets started, I know I'll give in, because I always do."

But whenever I tried to suggest that Toni deserved better, she shut down. If the discussion turned from acknowledging the problem to looking at a solution, she froze up. And out came her favorite excuse: "Nobody's perfect. So he's clingy. At least he doesn't scream and punch walls like that jerk I dated for years before I met him. He doesn't sleep around the way my father ran around on my mother. He doesn't spend all his time at the bar, like my friend Laura's husband. He's overprotective, but that's because he loves me! So what? I leave him, and then what? I end up with some bum who drinks and slaps me around? No, thanks."

Toni and I kept working together, and by using the A.R.T. Method for dealing with bullies, Toni eventually stood up to Neelish. She really tried to work it out with him. He wasn't able to change, but *she* did. She came to know in her heart that she deserved better than to be manipulated and boxed in by a bully like Neelish. So she gathered together her courage and her newfound self-respect, and she walked out of that abusive relationship. She was terrified, but she did it scared. Today, Toni is married and has two kids with Saul, a great guy who's totally crazy about her and treats her like a queen. Know where they met? A French-cooking seminar—just one of the many things that Toni had wanted to do for herself while she was involved with Neelish and that he wouldn't permit.

RATIONALIZATION

Rationalization is the attempt to justify behavior that would otherwise be considered irrational, by offering apparently reasonable explanations for it. Say, for example, that I'm addicted to jaywalking. I know how dangerous it can be. I've even been in accidents and had to go to the hospital as the result of my strange fixation. But I'm not ready to give it up, so I rationalize. I tell myself and others that the dangers of jaywalking have been exaggerated by the media. I declare I'm not going to be oppressed by the petty tyranny of a bureaucracy that tries to curtail the freedom of Americans by dictating when they can and can't cross the street. I insist that it's my body, my health, my life, and that I should be able to risk it if I want to.

This is rationalization at its finest. Whether or not these arguments are logical, they're also obviously and perfectly ridiculous when linked with the total insanity of a desire to play in traffic or do anything else dangerous and self-destructive. Like excuse making, rationalization is one of the coping mechanisms that a bully's partner tends to use after courageously acknowledging that there are problems with the relationship but while still afraid to do anything about it.

Some of the most common rationalizations for staying in a bullying relationship are "I can't give up my lifestyle," "I don't want to be alone," and "I stay for the kids." Let's see how they keep people stuck in a bad situation—and why they don't really make sense.

"I Can't Give Up My Lifestyle"

Whether you're a man or a woman, in the highest tax bracket or the lowest, it's very easy—and totally human—to get accustomed and even attached to the way you live. Maybe it's your double-wide or your double income, your second home or staying home with the kids, your Neiman's shopping sprees or the neighbors you've lived next door to for a decade, getting weekly beauty treatments or getting your spouse's health benefits, the mutual funds or the mutual friends. Whatever the case, most of us are used to the way we live. We've worked hard for what we have. We've put time and effort into making things just so. And many of us simply can't stand the idea of anything changing.

For bullied partners who feel this way, it's incredibly difficult to think about doing anything that would rock that boat or shake the security and stability of their lives. That's completely understandable. But take a closer look. Does that desire to avoid change really make sense? Is this rationalization rational? Is maintaining the status quo really worth all the abuse you put up with? Is your lifestyle really so great that it's worth sacrificing your happiness, self-respect, physical health, and emotional well-being? I don't think so!

Nothing is worth that much—certainly not the two-car garage or the two-carat diamond or the twice-a-year vacations. Sure, those things are nice. But we're talking about protecting and preserving the most precious things of all: your heart, your spirit, your *life*. Nothing is more valuable than that.

How This Type of Rationalization Looks in Action. Theresa was a prisoner of the lifestyle trap. She came from a truly poor family, and like me, she was the first in her family to attend college. When, at a relatively young age, she met and married Conrad, a wealthy financier, Theresa felt incredible relief. Not only had she found love, but she'd also been rescued from ever again needing to feel the deprivation, fear, and shame she'd felt throughout her childhood.

Unfortunately, this wasn't quite what happened. Oh, Theresa's wishes for *things* were more than satisfied. Conrad bought them a lavish house in an upscale neighborhood and a summer home on the beach. He provided her with all the money she could spend on household and personal expenses. He paid for trips to the Caribbean in the winter and Europe in the summer. But Conrad is an ice-cold Silent-Treatment Bully who gets embarrassed by what he refers to as Theresa's "lack of breeding." He makes note of her every perceived social blunder and faux pas—eating with the wrong fork, using slang he considers vulgar—and he punishes her with days or weeks of chilly silence. During these periods, he won't touch her, cast a glance her way, or acknowledge that she exists. In her suburban palace decorated with beautiful furniture—with her fridge full of fancy food and her closets jammed with expensive clothes—Theresa once again suffers from deprivation, fear, and shame!

But however unhappy she is with the way Conrad treats her, Theresa just can't bring herself to think about doing anything that might jeopardize her marriage and the material riches it provides. "I can't," Theresa wept one day when I suggested that she might be better off without Conrad. "I can't go back to the way I lived before we got married. I couldn't even fit my shoe collection into the apartment I was living in when I met him! I used to eat nothing but beans and rice, and today I eat at five-star restaurants. You can't ask me to give that up! I just can't!"

We're talking about protecting and preserving the most precious things of all: your heart, your spirit, your life. Nothing is more valuable than that.

It would be a million times better for Theresa to live on her own in one room as a woman who respects and loves herself. Instead, she lives in that fancy home with her fancy things, a prisoner to the lie in her head. She subconsciously believes she'll never deserve real love, so she might as well settle for luxury. What Theresa can't see through these rationalizations is that she's paying dearly for what she has. Sure, she may be surrounded by wealth. But it doesn't matter, because she's on her way to being emotionally and spiritually bankrupt.

"I Don't Want to Be Alone"

It's so sad to hear clients say they stay with bullying partners because they don't want to be alone. They remain in abusive relationships because they're afraid of being alone, but they don't realize that they already are!

It's healthy to want companionship, attention, and affection. And it's completely understandable that anyone would feel some reluctance to walk away from the familiar company of a long-term mate. But take a close look at the feelings and dynamics that exist between bully and victim. You probably won't see a lot of the intimacy that most of us with associate with romance. You won't see much of the warmth, tenderness, and comfort that we look for in our relationships.

It's much better to be on your own than to be with someone else and feel so lonely.

In short, you won't see antidotes to feelings of isolation and loneliness. Instead, you'll usually see fear, hostility, sadness, suspicion, confusion, and resentment—the very conditions that make us feel *most* alone. And it's much better to be on your own than to be with someone else and feel so lonely.

How This Type of Rationalization Looks in Action. For several years, Gus has been living with Louise, a funny, attractive literature professor with whom Gus, a writer, has many interests in common. He fell deeply in love with her, and the first couple of years of their relationship were among the happiest of his life.

Unfortunately, Louise is a Rage Bully. At the beginning of their relationship, Gus was so smitten that he overlooked her occasional outbursts, but as the months pass, her abusive behavior is becoming more flagrant and frequent. These days Louise seems ready to scream at anybody about anything, and the people who bear the brunt of her bullying are Gus and Parker, Louise's teenage son from her first marriage. Gus, who never married or had children of his own, adores Parker; in fact, Parker was one of the things that drew him to Louise in the first place. Gus is devoted to both of them, and he even proposed to Louise a few months ago.

He thought the demonstration of his willingness to commit might ease some of the anxiety he blames for her raging outbursts. It didn't; in fact, it seemed to make things worse. Almost every night, Louise lets loose on Gus, shouting at him, insulting him, accusing him of trying to steal Parker's affection from her or of not supporting her career. The argument usually ends with Louise shutting herself up in her study for hours on end, not coming out until late at night when Gus is asleep, and leaving in the morning before he wakes up.

Even so, Gus hasn't left Louise—and he says he won't, because he doesn't want to be alone. I try to point out that the hour or two they're together each day is spent with Louise yelling at him; practically and emotionally, he's alone *right now*. But Gus was raised by a neglectful single mother who worked two jobs, was rarely home, and never attended a single one of Gus's spelling bees or school plays. Now, after avoiding intimacy for years, he has had a taste of what it feels like to be part of a family, and he'd rather suffer any abuse than give it up. He's terrified to let go of his relationship with Louise and Parker, because unconsciously he's convinced that if he does, he'll be alone forever. He's willing to accept the way Louise treats him because of his introject—the lie he's living out—that not only does he not deserve better, he doesn't deserve *anything at all.*

"I Stay for the Kids"

Many of my clients use concern for their children's well-being as their rationalization for staying with a bullying partner. And usually, they really mean it. They honestly believe they're doing their children a favor by holding the family together at whatever cost to themselves. But in fact, the opposite is true. Of course, a two-parent home is the ideal situation for children, but only if it's a happy, healthy home. It's true that separation or divorce can be difficult for children, but the effects are nothing compared with the damage that can be done to children by a bullying parent. And that's the case even when a bully's attacks are directed only at the spouse and not at the children.

Children exposed to a bullying parent are in terrible emotional danger. Innocent and impressionable, they're constantly taking in all sorts of lessons based directly on how they're treated by their parents and how their parents treat each other. These messages will affect them deeply, both in the short term and for the rest of their lives. Just think back to what we've discussed in the examples of victims and their bullying partners—particularly what they experienced as the children of bullies and how these experiences affected them. Those lessons should be more than enough to convince you that "staying for the children," however well intended, might actually be one of the *worst* things you could do for your children.

How This Type of Rationalization Looks in Action. Years ago, I worked with Daisy, whose husband, Tom, was a terrible Temper-Tantrum Bully. Daisy came from a very traditional, conservative family, and it was a point of pride that none of them had ever been divorced. But if you heard about how unhappy those families were, how unkind Daisy's parents were to each other and to their children, you'd agree there wasn't much to be proud of. Daisy's family didn't reject divorce because they valued marriage; they just didn't like to admit mistakes or take responsibility for their actions. People like this would rather stay in horrible relationships that make a mockery of marriage than do the work to have a true partnership or move on and make one with somebody else.

When we first started working together, Daisy was overcome with shame at the prospect of being the first person in her family to get a divorce, and she had succumbed to pressure from family and friends to keep the marriage together for the sake of their children, a six-year-old girl and an eight-year-old boy. "I can't leave him," Daisy wept to me one day. "I don't want our children to be from a broken home! I hate the idea of what that could do to them. What if they're never able to have successful relationships and it's my fault because I didn't try hard enough to make this marriage work?"

"Staying for the children," however well intended, might actually be one of the worst *things you could do for your children.*

But after suffering through another year of Tom's bullying and seeing how edgy, unhappy, and afraid her children seemed, Daisy decided the situation had to change. She met with me once a week, practiced the A.R.T. Method, and tried every option available to make her marriage work. Finally, Daisy did it scared—she filed for divorce, got full custody of her children, and moved on. A few years later, she met and married Steven, a gentle, loving man who adored her and her children.

Our work together finished, and I didn't hear from Daisy for years. But recently I received a call from her. She got in touch to let me know her daughter had just gotten married to a young man the whole family loved. At the wedding reception, Daisy told me, her daughter had pulled her aside with tears in her eyes to thank Daisy for having had so much courage and self-respect that all those years ago she had braved the disapproval of her family and her fear of the unknown to take care of herself—and her children. Just imagine how differently things might have turned out if Daisy had "stayed for the children."

AVOIDANCE

We're all familiar with avoidance, in one way or another. It's a common response to being faced with something we just don't want to do or someone we'd rather not deal with. If you're not ready to address a conflict with a friend, you dodge her calls. When you don't want to face the boss about a recent error, you phone in sick. Hate the idea of spending a holiday with your in-laws? You put off buying plane tickets or gifts until the last minute. This coping mechanism works the same way with bullied partners who've acknowledged that their relationship has problems but aren't ready to take the next step. They've taken the first step of the A.R.T. Method to break the cycle of abuse (acknowledging that a problem exists) but are avoiding the next (reassessing their options).

This victim tries to avoid the bully—or conflict with the bully—by any means necessary. When you avoid the person, you avoid the abuse, at least temporarily. Unfortunately, as we all know, you can avoid a person or problem for just so long. And as with many coping mechanisms, the side effects of avoidance can be nearly as bad for the victim as the bullying itself.

Some of the most common avoidance strategies are overworking or workaholism, engaging in excessive social activity, and always agreeing with, capitulating to, or accommodating the bully. Let's see what these strategies look like and why they don't actually help.

Overworking/Workaholism

Spending long hours at the office. Volunteering to work overtime. Procrastinating until work must be completed over weekends. Picking up extra shifts because "we need the money" or "we're understaffed." Taking as many out-of-town assignments as possible or finding reasons to extend business trips. Making up excuses to "just drop by" the workplace and "see how things are going, just for a minute," which inevitably turns into an hour or many hours. All of these behaviors are tip-offs that a bullied partner may be practicing avoidance. Most avoidance tactics dovetail with denial, and overworking does so more neatly than most. It's all too easy for a bully's victim to convince him- or herself that all this extra time at work is just commitment to the job, rather than fear of facing the bully who waits at home.

How This Type of Avoidance Looks in Action. Aamira went back to work part-time when her children went to high school, but she was quite casual about her job as a salesperson at the local outlet of an upscale clothing chain, until the kids left for college. Then she leaped at the first

The side effects of avoidance can be nearly as bad for the victim as the bullying itself.

opportunity to take a full-time position, signed on for swing shifts and evening shifts whenever possible, and accepted a promotion to manager that involved a lot more work for not much more pay.

Ordinarily, I would applaud a client who showed this kind of enthusiasm for her job. It's so healthy to have work we're passionate about, and it builds self-esteem to put in the time and see the results of our labor. But the fact is, Aamira doesn't really care for her work. Her real interest is music, and she gave up a budding career as a nightclub singer to get married and raise a family with her husband, Roy. Now she's putting in overtime to *avoid* Roy, a Name-Calling Bully whose abuse has gotten much worse since their kids moved out, leaving no witnesses to keep him in check.

Aamira has already acknowledged that the way Roy treats her is not right, but she hasn't yet been able to confront him. Instead, she tells herself that it's really not so bad, because she has this fabulous job, which keeps her busy and takes her mind off things at home. What Aamira really means is that she has an airtight excuse for staying away from the house as much as possible, allowing her to avoid Roy's taunting and insults. But as we know, this is just a temporary reprieve, especially since Roy isn't happy about his wife's increasing absence and makes his displeasure known in totally inappropriate ways. At some point, Aamira will have to face the music.

Excessive Social Activity

The flip side of the overworking coin is engaging in excessive social activity. We could call it "overplaying." Lunch and dinner dates with friends. Long nights out with the boys or the girls. After-work drinks with colleagues until after midnight. Weekends away to visit family, old college pals, or anyone with a spare room or foldout couch. Long vacations in remote locations without one's partner. Book clubs, bridge clubs, bowling teams, neighborhood softball leagues, PTA, community boards, charity work. Doing any of these activities occasionally or in moderation is great. But when activities, outings, and social obligations pile up and keep a bullied partner away from home and spouse for many hours or days at a time, it's a sure sign that the victim is in avoidance.

How This Type of Avoidance Looks in Action. If you took a look at Shawn's social schedule, you'd think he was the most popular guy around. Every day he has multiple plans with multiple friends, drinks with his business partners after work, dinner with a cousin who's in town for work, a colleague's birthday party, a weekend camping trip with his brothers. Then there are basketball practice for his gym's league, the football game on TV at a buddy's house, and his role as assistant coach for his son's track team and his daughter's soccer team. Round it all out with volunteer work with the kids at the Shriners' hospital, the nearby old-folks' home, and the homeless outreach program run by his church. Many people would consider Shawn a happy guy with a very full life. But what I see is a man who married a vicious Silent-Treatment Bully and does anything and everything he can to avoid being at home with her.

As you might expect, Shawn's avoidance only makes the relationship worse. The more Shawn stays away, spending time with everyone in town but his wife, the angrier she gets. And the angrier she gets, the colder her cold shoulders become, and the longer her punishments last. The more those silences stretch out, the more Shawn feels compelled to stay away from home and avoid its frigid, frightening atmosphere. So the destructive, self-perpetuating cycle continues.

Agreeing, Capitulating, Accommodating

The third type of avoidance—agreeing, capitulating, and accommodating—is more commonly known as walking on eggshells. You may have practiced it with anyone, from a waitress with a bad attitude to a friend who's having a bad day. Another version is "roll over and play dead," a form of submission intended to defuse conflict and prevent confrontation. Either way, for the partner of a bully, avoidance can look an awful lot like the path of least resistance.

For the victim of any bully, but especially any of the aggressive types—the Rage Bully, the Temper-Tantrum Bully, the Name-Calling Bully, the Control-Freak Bully— this type of avoidance can seem like the only way to get through the day unscathed. In fact, it may really be the only way until the victim is ready to practice the A.R.T. Method and work through what's wrong with the relationship, instead of working *around* it.

How This Type of Avoidance Looks in Action. Remember Spencer from Chapters 1 and 2? Capitulation was the coping mechanism he used to deal with his Temper-Tantrum Bully of a girlfriend, Moira. He learned quickly that if he didn't immediately go along with whatever she wanted, there'd be nothing but tears and sulking until he gave in. Gradually, the time from initial resistance to "roll over and show your belly" got shorter and shorter. Eventually Spencer no longer even bothered to state a preference about anything. His response to whatever Moira might say was "Whatever you want, honey."

Things were like that with Kellie, from Chapter 2, who continued dating Mark, that uptight Control-Freak Bully with a streak of rage. For a while, Kellie did everything she could to placate Mark and keep the peace. She learned his preferences and pet peeves and altered her behavior accordingly. She changed her wardrobe, hair, home decor, hobbies, and eating habits to suit him. She learned to speak in a soft, low voice after he had commented one too many times on how her natural speaking voice was nasal and loud. She even considered getting breast implants because he told her that he didn't usually find flat-chested women like her attractive! Most of all, Kellie learned to read Mark's moods and adjust her behaviors accordingly, doing whatever she could to avoid setting off the flurries of brutal criticism or angry outbursts that Mark would direct at whoever happened to be nearby—usually Kellie herself.

But after a few months of this, Kellie was a nervous wreck. She was haggard from lack of sleep because she'd developed insomnia, and she kept getting colds that she couldn't shake because her immune system was compromised. She'd put on weight as a result of the snacking she did in an effort to calm and comfort herself. And she was on the edge of a clinically diagnosable anxiety disorder. It all happened because this sweet girl was bending over backward to accommodate a bullying boyfriend who would never be satisfied with anything she did, no matter how hard she tried to keep him happy.

After yet another episode when she had knocked herself out to please Mark and he had responded with criticism and anger, Kellie walked into our weekly appointment ready to make some changes. Within a few weeks, she had stopped trying to take care of Mark and started taking care of herself. Slowly but steadily, Kellie went back to doing what made her happy. She pulled her favorite clothes out from the back of her closet. She put her favorite posters back up on the walls. When Mark told her they would being going out for sushi, which she hated, she spoke up and told him she'd prefer Italian. And then one night, when he lashed out at her, she gently but firmly stood up for herself. She looked him right in the eye. She told him that she could hear he was upset and she'd be happy to talk about it with him, but that raising his voice to her and attacking her weren't OK anymore. When he treated her that way, Kellie told Mark, she felt hurt and disrespected. And she didn't deserve to be treated that way.

And you know what? After reacting and resisting for a few minutes, Mark took in what Kellie was saying, agreed with her, and apologized. She faced her fears, stood her ground, stared the bully down, and got what she deserved: respect!

ISOLATION

Many victims use avoidance to cope with their abusive relationship and put distance between themselves and their bullying partners. But just as often, the victim avoids friends and family, isolating him- or herself. Why? Because facing others often means we have to face ourselves. We look through their eyes and see the truth about ourselves looking back at us. For the victim of a bully, this prospect can be so awful that the victim will do almost anything to avoid it—even if that means retreating from everything he or she cares about or enjoys.

Victims most commonly isolate themselves by staying at home, sleeping excessively, and engaging in solitary or "tuned out" activities. Let's consider each form of isolation and see how it just perpetuates the problem.

Staying at Home

There's nothing wrong with being a homebody. But being shut in is a different story. All too often, that's what happens to the victims of bullies: they begin to withdraw from the world because they're terrified of what the world will see if they go out into it. Bullied partners who isolate by staying at home aren't doing so because they enjoy a lazy afternoon around the house or a cozy night in with the family. They do so because venturing outside could mean being seen in public with a cold, hostile, angry, aggressive, or otherwise abusive spouse. The shame of friend, foe, or total stranger actually seeing the abuse take place is a horrible, humiliating, and sometimes paralyzing prospect. Going out alone poses its own problems; it might involve running into acquaintances or colleagues who ask difficult personal questions for which the victim has no satisfactory answers.

It would be much better, the bullied partner thinks, just to stay at home. Of course, that might mean being with the bully all the time, even being bullied more than usual. But at least there won't be any witnesses. And if no one sees what's happening, the victim's convoluted logic goes, it's somehow not quite as real, so we can go on pretending everything is all right.

How This Type of Isolation Looks in Action. Brooke began staying at home after a particularly embarrassing incident at a local restaurant. Her husband, Cal, a Money Bully, took one look at the menu and began announcing loudly to Brooke and their three children which items they were allowed to order and which were off-limits. When the waiter came by, Cal berated him about the prices for certain entrees. After dinner, when their youngest daughter asked if she could have dessert, Cal flew off the handle, scolding the little girl so loudly that everyone in the restaurant turned to watch. When Brooke tried to step in and calm Cal down, he raised his voice even more and accused her of raising their children to be as greedy and ungrateful as she was.

Everyone in the restaurant turned to watch the scene. Brooke was mortified, especially when she realized that a neighbor of theirs was having dinner just a few tables away. She felt even worse when a friend called her the next day to see how she was doing and told Brooke she'd heard "through the grapevine" about the scene Cal had made at the restaurant.

At first Brooke just avoided public outings with Cal and the kids, which was fine with her cheapskate husband, who made plenty of money but preferred takeout meals to expensive restaurants and the economy of renting DVDs to the price of a family night at the movies. But soon she began limiting her own time outside the house as much as she could. She went straight to work without stopping at her favorite coffee shop. She started skipping her after-work aerobics classes and her weekly bridge night with her girl-friends. She resigned from her commitments at her children's schools. She canceled a long-standing plan to spend a week in Vegas with her sister, who had planned the trip as Brooke's fortieth-birthday present. Eventually she even stopped going grocery shopping; she began to order all the family's food and supplies online and have them delivered to the house. Finally, after calling in sick to work twenty-six days out of sixty, Brooke was let go from her job. A couple of months later, when Brooke came to my office for our initial consultation, it was the first time she'd set foot outside her apartment building in over three weeks.

For bullied partners, usually even the worst dreams aren't as bad as the reality of their waking life with their abusive spouse.

Of course, the stay-at-home syndrome doesn't have to get as bad as it did for Brooke to serve as a wake-up call that something's not right. Perhaps you or someone you care about has started to give up activities that involve leaving the house, getting out, and being seen. If that's the case, it's probably a case of isolation.

Excessive Sleeping

As with staying at home and any comfort or indulgence, there's absolutely nothing wrong with sleeping in now and then. But when bullied partners engage in this type of avoidance, it's usually not just the occasional nap, morning sleep-in, or early bedtime. It may start that way. But the habit will probably progress fairly rapidly. It can escalate to hitting the snooze alarm until the last possible minute (and beyond) on workdays; sleeping ten, twelve, fourteen, or sixteen hours at a stretch on weekends; and catching naps that extend from "just a few minutes of shut-eye" to hours on end.

Before long, the victim is spending any and all free time in the Land of Nod. What more perfect place to isolate oneself from everyone? When you're sleeping, you're on your own, safe, and feeling no pain. No one can get to you. Sure, there may be nightmares. But for bullied partners, usually even the worst dreams aren't as bad as the reality of their waking life with their abusive spouse.

How This Type of Isolation Looks in Action. Victor, a high school teacher, got into the habit of "resting" for an hour or two when he came home from work. He told himself and his wife, Kate, that he was worn out by a heavy class load and after-school responsibilities. The real story? Victor was exhausted by Kate, a champion Guilt-Trip Bully who always seemed to have a long list of ridiculous errands and complicated odd jobs that she wanted Victor to take on, and which she would coax, cajole, sigh, whine, and manipulate him into doing. Of course, the items on Kate's list—recaulking the shower for the second time in six months, fixing the trick latch on her car's glove box, picking up a particular kind of soda sold only at a specialty store on the other side of town—were completely beside the point, though neither she nor Victor was aware of it. All Kate really wanted was the experience of exerting power over her husband, forcing him to meet her demands. And all Victor wanted was to be left alone. But instead of taking action, he took naps. That was the only way he could escape from Kate.

His after-school "rest" sessions began to last through dinner and right up to bedtime. After sleeping for three hours or more, he'd stumble off the couch at ten o'clock and eat cold leftovers by himself in the kitchen. Then he'd stumble into bed and fall asleep again. He and Kate used to have coffee in the mornings before work, but then Victor began sleeping through his alarm, so he had to rush straight out of the house in order to get to work on time. When summer vacation came around—and with it a mile-long list of demands from Kate—Victor found it increasingly difficult to wake up in the mornings and almost impossible to stay awake. He'd sleep until eleven, get up for a couple of hours, fall asleep on the couch in the afternoon, and then wander through the house like a zombie for a few hours in the evening before falling back into bed at around eight o'clock.

Victor himself didn't know why this was happening. He went to his family doctor for a checkup, concerned that something might be physically wrong with him. Fortunately, he had a great doctor, who recognized that his "sleeping sickness" had a psychological cause, and Victor was able to get the help he needed.

Solitary or "Checked Out" Activities

One easy way to isolate oneself is to get involved—as often as possible—in any activity that requires solitude, discourages company, or inhibits interaction. I've seen clients with bullying partners develop spontaneous passions for photography (and lots of solo time in the darkroom), animal grooming (his wife was allergic), opera appreciation (and headphones—her boyfriend hated classical music). I've seen people who'd never read anything longer than the back of the cereal box become bookworms ("I just want to finish this chapter") and sedentary people go on high-energy exercise kicks ("Still can't run on those bad knees? Too bad; otherwise, you could train for this marathon with me"). I've seen men who'd never changed a tire turn grease monkey and log whole days under their cars, and women who didn't know a tulip from a turnip get green thumbs, spending weekends in their flower beds and evenings poring obsessively over plant catalogs.

And, of course, I've seen hundreds of couples who declare that they spend every evening together, which they do—in front of the television. From the time they arrive home in the evening until the time their heads hit the pillows, these couples are looking not at each other but at the television. Instead of talking to one another, they watch show after show, occasionally conversing in the three-minute gaps between segments—usually about nothing more than which detective is going to solve this cold case or who will get voted off the island. Would you call that quality time? I certainly wouldn't! I like television as much as the next person, and I think it can provide great entertainment and great educational opportunities. But in cases like these, all TV provides is a way to escape without leaving your couch, a way to completely isolate yourself while sitting right next to your partner.

How This Type of Isolation Looks in Action. Several years ago, I worked with a young couple, Will and Sarah, who were engaged to be married. Will, though he didn't know it, was a Body-Language Bully. And although he hadn't become physically abusive, he came from a battering background; he and his mother had been beaten by his father. I could see that unless Will got serious about growing emotionally, it was only a matter of time before he continued that cycle of violence in his own relationship. But this had nothing to do with the reason Will and Sarah came to see me, or so they thought. The problem, as they saw it, was that Will couldn't deal with Sarah's new hobby: skydiving.

Although Sarah had never been much of an outdoor person or a thrill seeker, she'd tried skydiving recently, developed a taste for it, and now wanted to spend as much of her free time as possible doing jumps. Here's the kicker: Will was absolutely terrified of heights. He had acrophobia, a clinically diagnosable fear of heights. He obviously couldn't take part in Sarah's new hobby, which was no coincidence. In addition, he could hardly stand the idea of her doing it. Although Will was a bully, he truly loved Sarah, and the idea of her being in any danger upset him greatly. Equally upsetting for Will was how out of character for Sarah the whole thing seemed. He couldn't understand what attracted his usually cautious fiancée to such an activity. And he really didn't understand why Sarah, who was usually so "accommodating," wouldn't quit skydiving. No matter how much he badgered, she wouldn't budge.

Overcoming the rage of generations to build a healthy, loving relationship is a challenge that requires real commitment, but it can be done.

From your perspective, you can probably see that Sarah started skydiving to isolate herself from Will. And when he tried to take that away from her, she finally took a stand against her bullying partner. This may not have been the most important issue in their relationship, but it was a great place for us to start talking about their central issue: the dysfunctional dynamic that was destroying a relationship they both really wanted to work. So together, we spent several months of sessions looking at their codependent relationship. We reviewed their interdependent roles as bully and victim, and they saw that the more they played those roles, the worse the relationship got. Sarah and Will learned the A.R.T. Method and began to practice it in their relationship. Less than a year after they had started therapy, they got married. They recently celebrated their five-year anniversary.

Overcoming the rage of generations to build a healthy, loving relationship is a challenge that requires real commitment, but it can be done. Sarah and Will did it—and so can you!

DESTRUCTIVE DISTRACTIONS

Like other coping mechanisms used by bullied partners, destructive distractions are meant to manage the hurt caused by abusive relationships. But destructive distractions are, by definition, double-edged swords. They might end up causing more harm than bullies could! Ironically, that's often why the victims of bullies unconsciously engage in such behaviors. The feelings that draw victims to abusive partners—low self-esteem, feelings of worthlessness, belief that they deserve pain and punishment—are the very same feelings that lead to diversions almost guaranteed to cause more damage.

> *Destructive distractions are, by definition, double-edged swords.*

The most common destructive distractions are affairs, compulsive behavior, and substance abuse (alcohol, drugs, pills). Let's look at the pitfalls of each one.

Affairs

When things aren't going well at home, it's tempting to look elsewhere for the warmth and attention you aren't getting from your partner. But there are about a million reasons to resist the temptation of an affair, however alluring it might be! Here are just a few:

Getting even is *not* fair play. Your mate may be treating you badly, even cheating on you, but having an affair to get back at that person won't get you anywhere. I guarantee it will ultimately make you feel worse about yourself, not better. It may be exciting at first, to feel like you're taking revenge for the abuse you've suffered. You may feel justified, even righteous. But in the end, you'll have to live with the fact that you've done something dishonest and deceitful. That's disrespectful—to your partner, sure, but more importantly, to yourself. Why let someone else's bad behavior force you to compromise your integrity?

Being bullied impairs your overall judgment. If there's a bully in your relationship, your perspective on relationships is probably a little skewed right now. Given who you're involved with and how you're being treated, your romantic instincts may not be entirely reliable. Think about it this way: if one of your friends were stuck in a relationship with a bully, would that be the friend you'd trust to pick out a good partner for you? Absolutely not! But that's exactly what you're doing when you choose a new partner for yourself before addressing the problems in your primary relationships and the personal issues that led you into those relationships. Otherwise, it's all too likely that the person you get involved with will be nothing more than a new version of the same old thing.

No good relationship begins with bad behavior. Say you're in an abusive relationship that you haven't been able to leave. Then you meet someone you're convinced is the answer to all your problems, the person you're meant to be with. Why wait to get started with the rest of your life? Why bother ending the old relationship before starting the new one?

Here's one very good reason: Imagine what it would be like, years from now, to be asked how you and your current spouse met. How will you feel about telling your friends or your children that the relationship began with lies and betrayal? And how will you feel about acknowledging that truth for yourself? And here's another: If that new love of your life doesn't respect the marriage vow or monogamous commitment you have with your current partner, it's unlikely that any vow he or she makes to you will be respected. There are exceptions to this rule, but in general, I find it to be true:

cheaters cheat. And if they'll cheat with you, they'll probably cheat on you.

Having an affair won't help, and it may hurt. This is the single biggest reason to skip the affair or any other destructive diversion. An affair won't do a thing to fix your relationship. It may provide some temporary relief. But especially if your partner finds out, it will probably also create more problems and complications, whether in the form of more abuse, lost opportunities to make the marriage work, or in the event of divorce, risks to custody of your children.

Compulsive Behavior

A compulsion is an irrational, irresistible desire that forces you to do something. In the victims of bullies, compulsive behavior crops up as a response to the pain of being in a relationship. Unconsciously seeking an outlet for the abnormally high levels of stress and anxiety, the victim will engage repeatedly in behaviors that offer temporary relief. These may include eating, shopping, cleaning, and gambling.

These activities are fine in moderation. Even the occasional indulgence isn't problematic. But it *is* a problem when someone begins to overeat every day, buy things he or she can't afford and doesn't really want, clean obsessively, use pornography excessively, or stay at the blackjack table or poker website for hours at a time.

Compulsive activities may also involve behaviors that are dangerous when carried out to any degree. These include shoplifting and cutting (deliberate and sometimes ritualistic self-wounding).

Substance Abuse

Every day we hear new reports of high-profile celebrities and politicians checking into fancy rehabs. So it's no secret that many of the people who turn to drugs and alcohol for pleasure end up in pain. That's counterproductive, and my goal is for you to feel less pain, not more! So it's important to understand the dangers of using drugs and alcohol to manage your pain, as well as the warning signs that let you know when you may be getting too much of a good thing.

Alcohol. There's nothing wrong with an occasional drink (or even an occasional bender)—unless, of course, you have substance-abuse problems. But be very careful when that cocktail, bottle of beer, or glass of wine stops being just a beverage and starts being something you *need*—to numb the pain of being in an abusive relationship. If you ever catch yourself saying or thinking that you "need" a drink, I encourage you to start keeping a close eye on how much you're drinking and how often.

Pills. The same advice applies to prescription drugs— pills for pain and medications for anxiety, such as Vicodin, Percocet, Xanax, Ativan, Ambien, or Klonopin. Of course, you may have a legitimate medical need for these drugs, but make sure that's the *only* reason you're taking them.

Watch for these trouble signs:

- Taking pills for *any* pain other than the one for which your doctor prescribed them
- Taking more pills than prescribed or taking them more frequently than prescribed
- Borrowing medication from friends, with or without their knowledge
- Trying to convince a doctor you need a prescription refilled or going to a second doctor if the first declines
- Drinking while taking prescription medications

Alcohol is contraindicated for almost all medications used to treat pain, depression, and anxiety, and with good reason.

At best, it can inhibit the medication's effects; at worst, the mixture can be dangerous, even deadly.

Drugs. I hope it goes without saying that street drugs are never safe and never the answer to any problem or pain, no matter how serious or intense. In my years as a psychologist, I've seen too many people try this "remedy," and I can tell you that in *every* instance, it never solved a single problem but caused more trouble and grief than you can imagine. Doing drugs to deal with or distract yourself from the pain of being bullied by your partner is a lot like trying to treat a migraine by cutting your head off! Please—just don't do it.

Believe me, I really do understand what it's like to feel like you're in emotional torment. I truly empathize with the need for relief and release, and the impulse to look for it in a bottle or a pill. But you don't need to try that—because *you can get healing on your own.* You don't need substances.

Emotional abuse can be even more hurtful, damaging, and dangerous than physical abuse.

All you need is belief in yourself, the willingness to change, and my healthy models and strategies. And on these pages, I'll lead you through all the steps to make it happen.

THE DANGERS AND CONSEQUENCES OF STAYING WITH A BULLY

As I say throughout this book, bullying is a very serious matter. Many people suffer consequences even worse than the daily misery and loneliness that inevitably result from being in a relationship with a bully.

Emotional abuse—and that's what bullying is—can be even more hurtful, damaging, and dangerous than physical abuse. The most common dangers of staying in a bullying relationship are risks to physical health, mental illness, and risks to the well-being of one's children.

Risks to Physical Health

It's a well-known fact that stress and sadness can have a big impact on your health. So it's a no-brainer that a relationship with a bully will drain you of energy and vitality and will play havoc with your physical health. Being bullied can literally make you sick!

Many of my bullied patients have one or more of the following health problems:

- Insomnia and/or nightmares
- Exhaustion
- Hypertension
- Clenched jaw and bruxism (teeth grinding)
- Muscle spasms
- Skin problems
- Frequent and persistent flu and colds as the result of a compromised immune system
- Headaches and migraines
- Digestive problems such as stomachache, acid reflux, and irritable bowel syndrome
- Loss of appetite
- Diminished libido and impotence

Mental Illness

Obviously, when you're being emotionally mistreated, what primarily suffers is not your body; it's your heart and mind, your emotional and mental well-being. This suffering can go far beyond mere sadness, frustration, and fear. All too often, my bullied patients begin to suffer from various types of mental illness and mood disorders, including depression, anxiety, panic attacks, eating disorders, stress disorders, hypochondria, cutting and other forms of self-mutilation, and compulsive behaviors.

Risks to Children

If you're a parent in a relationship with a bully, you need to know that your children are at risk for every single one of the physical and mental health problems I've just described, *even if the children aren't being directly bullied by your partner.* A bully-dominated environment is pure poison for kids, even if your partner doesn't bully the children directly. Children in such environments are also likely to develop behavioral problems, do poorly at school, and use drugs.

If you're in a relationship with a bully and have children, your own life is not the only one that's affected. The lives of your children are at risk, too, and their children, and their children.

However, there's an even greater danger to consider. In the previous chapter, you learned about the rage of generations—the legacy of abuse and the way that bullying behavior is passed from parent to child in a sad, sick cycle that continues from generation to generation. So you already know that children who are raised with a bullying parent will almost certainly go on to become bullies themselves or seek out bullying partners and start the cycle all over again. They're going to end up in the same kind of damaging, destructive relationships that you're in right now—and I know you wouldn't want that for your children.

If you're in a relationship with a bully and have children, your own life is not the only one that's affected. The lives of your children are at risk, too, and their children, and their children. It's up to you to protect your future great-great-grandchildren and end the rage of generations.

IT'S TIME TO STOP COPING AND START CHANGING!

Maybe you've recognized that you're using one or more of the coping mechanisms described in this chapter. If so, you shouldn't feel bad! Don't beat yourself up about it. These coping mechanisms are effective strategies for surviving the war zone of a bullying relationship. It's understandable that you would take steps, consciously or unconsciously, to manage your pain. But as we've just seen, the risks of staying in a bullying relationship are much too great for you to keep coping. It's time to start changing!

You've already taken a major step toward making those changes and transforming your relationship with the bully in your life. Just by reading this chapter, you've started to develop an awareness of how you manage your pain in ways that keep you stuck—the mechanisms that numb you to the hurt but don't do anything to end the hurtful situation.

The next step is to *increase* this awareness. And it's not hard to do! You can do it just by paying attention. First, keep an eye on your day-to-day behavior, and try to notice when you're using the coping mechanisms described in this chapter. Then, when you catch yourself coping, don't judge or punish yourself for it. Instead, pause. Stop what you're doing, and ask yourself whether you really want to keep coping with this pain, or if you'd rather be in a relationship where you're treated with love and respect, instead of one in which you're bullied and abused.

The risks of staying in a bullying relationship are much too great for you to keep coping. It's time to start changing!

This exercise may seem silly; after all, who would consciously choose to be in a situation that causes them pain? But that's *exactly* my point. You aren't consciously choosing to accept this situation. Instead, deep unconscious behaviors and thought patterns are keeping you trapped. You're living out the lie! This exercise is designed to help you become conscious of your situation and your choices. Like the rest of this book, it's going to help you learn to make changes and choose something better for yourself—working with me and using the A.R.T. Method.

Ask yourself whether you really want to keep coping with this pain, or if you'd rather be in a relationship where you're treated with love and respect.

CHAPTER SUMMARY

GET INTO THE SOLUTION!

➤ You may be using coping mechanisms to manage the pain of being in a relationship with a bully, either because you're afraid to take action or because you're in denial about the reality of your situation. Now it's time to open your eyes and face your fears. You can do it!

➤ Coping mechanisms may be effective short-term strategies for dealing with a bullying partner, but in the long term, they just keep you in a destructive, damaging relationship. *You deserve so much better.*

➤ Today, working with me, you can stop coping and start changing! Instead of managing the pain, transform that painful situation. Instead of strategizing alone about how to survive a damaging relationship, use this book to strategize with me how you're going make changes that set you free and allow you to thrive.

The Bully in the Bedroom

Let's Talk About Sex—and Sex Bullies

4

- What does your sex life say about your relationship?
- A guide to Sex Bullies
- Do you have a good sex life?
- How to get what you deserve between the sheets
- Five simple steps to great sex—for you *and* your partner

Sex that is not evidence of a strong human tie is just like blowing your nose; it's not a celebration of a splendid relationship.
—ROBERTSON DAVIES

Sex is between the ears, as well as between the legs.
—H. L. NEWBOLD

Talk about sex? For some people, it's a favorite topic of conversation; there's nothing they won't talk about and nobody they won't talk about it with! Others find it excruciatingly difficult to discuss, even with their own sexual partners. But like it or not, we need to address the topic of sex, and now is the best time to start.

Sex is one of the most basic human drives, and our sexual impulses and activities, likes and dislikes are nothing to be shy about or ashamed of. It's really so important for us to get comfortable talking about what we want in bed, because that's the only way we're going to get our sexual needs met. And yes, we do need sex! Sex is natural, fun, and good for us. Whether it's once a day or once a week, mutually satisfying sex is an absolutely essential component of a healthy intimate relationship.

WHAT YOUR SEX LIFE CAN TELL YOU ABOUT YOUR RELATIONSHIP

Your sexual relationship with your partner can be a fairly reliable barometer for your relationship as a whole. Your sex life tends to reflect the overall dynamic and health of your relationship, and vice versa. Simply put, the way things are going horizontally is usually how they're going vertically. In a relationship where partners communicate openly, share responsibilities, express affection, support one another's endeavors, and treat each other with kindness, sensitivity, patience, compassion, and respect, these excellent, healthy, loving behaviors are probably going to extend to their sex life—and make for really great sex.

Your sexual relationship with your partner can be a fairly reliable barometer for your relationship as a whole.

If, in contrast, your partner is a bully who pushes you around, ignores your feelings, and thinks mainly of him- or herself, that's usually how things will go with your sex life, too. If there's a bully in your house, you're probably being bullied in the bedroom. As you can imagine, the reverse is also true. If things aren't going well sexually—if you're not having good sex or not having sex at all—it's probably a sign that you have larger relationship issues to address. If it feels like you're being bullied *in* bed, I'd be willing to bet you aren't being treated the way you deserve when you're *out* of bed.

Are You Getting What You Deserve in the Bedroom?

Sex is such a primal, intuitive, instinctive thing, it goes right to our core. It taps into and draws out what's deepest and most vulnerable in us. For these very reasons, sex can bring us so close to our partners and create such intimacy between us. For the same reasons, being bullied sexually can sometimes feel more frightening, upsetting, and overwhelming than any other kind of bullying. Unfortunately, sexual bullying is something that far too many people live with. Why? Sometimes they can't recognize that they're being bullied; they don't *know* any better. Sometimes they unconsciously believe they don't *deserve* better. And very often, they're just too afraid to stand up and *ask* for better.

If there's a bully in your house, you're probably being bullied in the bedroom.

Let me say it loud and clear: you *do* deserve better! You deserve to be treated with love and respect by your partner, in and out of the bedroom. That means you owe it to yourself to learn how to recognize when, where, and how you're not being treated as you deserve. Once you've done that, you owe it to yourself to learn to say what you want. If you're ready, and if you stick with me and just keep reading, that's what you're going to learn how to do in this chapter. By the time you've finished this chapter, you'll have everything you need to start standing up for what you want in the bedroom. And as I mentioned earlier, the way things go in the bedroom can have a big effect on your relationship—and your life. So let's start in the bedroom and go from there!

SEX: THE GOOD, THE BAD, AND THE BULLY

In my introduction to the Sex Bully in Chapter 2, I explained that Sex Bullies exert power over their victims either by forcing sex or withholding it. For these bullies, sex is not really about sex. Instead, sex—which should always and only be an act of love, intimacy, or pleasure—is about power. Sex Bullies use it as currency, as leverage, as a weapon, which degrades and depersonalizes sexual intimacy within a relationship.

Now, please don't get me wrong. When I say sex should always be an act of love, I'm not saying you should never have rough sex, if that's what you like, as long as it's between consenting adults and no one gets hurt. What I do mean, though, is that sex with your partner should be an expression of your love and respect for each other. It should be about your desire to be closer and to please each other. Above all else, it

Being bullied sexually can sometimes feel more frightening, upsetting, and overwhelming than any other kind of bullying.

should be mutual, meaning that both of you really want to do whatever it is that you're doing together—and that you're really doing it *together*, not just physically but emotionally, too.

Also, sex should *always* be mutual, even if you're just having a one-night stand. Even when it's not about love, you should be treated right.

How do you know if you're having good mutual sex, instead of bad bullied sex? Ask yourself these questions:

- Do you get that sick, sinking feeling when your partner approaches you for sex?
- Do you have sex mainly when your partner's "in the mood," whether you are or not?
- Do you feel pressured or coerced to do sexual things you'd rather not do?
- Do you feel your own sexual needs and desires are often overlooked or neglected?

- In the middle of sex, do you find yourself just wishing it were over already?
- Do you ever fake orgasms?
- After sex, do you feel sad, lonely, angry, hurt, confused, "dirty," or used?

If you answered yes to any of these questions, the sex you're having is *not* mutual. And if it's not mutual, it probably means that you're in bed with a bully.

Inside the Mind of the Sex Bully

How does someone end up being a bully in the bedroom? As I mentioned in Chapter 2, the Sex Bully may have been raised by parents who used sex as power—for example, a mother who used flirtation, seduction, and sex to get the attention she wanted or to have her needs met, or a father who treated his wife (and mistresses, female coworkers, and any woman who happened to be passing by) as sexual objects, conquests to be won, property to be possessed. Alternatively, the Sex Bully may have been raised by any kind of bully in an environment that made him or her feel powerless, castrated, and impotent.

You deserve to be treated with love and respect by your partner, in and out of the bedroom.

In adulthood, this person sexually bullies a partner to overcome an intense and oppressive sense of extreme vulnerability and insignificance. Dominating and controlling a partner gives the Sex Bully a sense of relief and release. But this is only temporary. Soon the feelings of helplessness creep back in, and the cycle of bullying starts all over again. Depending on personal history and predilections, people like this may push their partners around in the bedroom, physically or emotionally, with demands, criticism, coercion, and manipulation. Or they may wage sexual warfare outside of the bedroom, withholding sex, flirting with others, having affairs, or threatening to do so.

The Sexual-Abuse Survivor

The Sex Bully also may have been sexually abused as a child, or may have been given confusing and inappropriate messages about sex by parents or other adult caretakers. In adulthood, people who had these disturbing experiences find sex very confusing. Sex should be fun; it should feel natural, instinctive, and easy; it should bring partners into a deeper intimacy that feels desirable, wonderful, and emotionally satisfying. But for survivors of sexual abuse, sex—or even simple feelings of attraction or arousal—is likely to wake the ghosts of those childhood traumas and make sexual experiences difficult, painful, or terrifying.

For these bullies, sex is not really about sex. Instead, sex—which should always and only be an act of love, intimacy, or pleasure—is about power.

People like this may avoid sex as much as possible. Or they may deal with the confusing mix of emotions that sex brings by getting cold, shutting down, or becoming aggressive or even violent in the bedroom.

Any Bully Can Be a Sex Bully, Too—and Most Are

As I said before, what happens between you and your partner in bed is usually a pretty accurate reflection of what's happening in the relationship as a whole, and vice versa. This means that the average Sex Bully, who focuses most of his or her bullying energies in the bedroom, will probably engage in at least some bullying outside of the bedroom—possibly a lot of bullying. Also, the other types of bullies usually end up bringing their bullying to bed. The Rage Bully and the Silent-Treatment Bully, the Name-Calling Bully and the Passive-Aggressive Bully, and all the other bullies you met in Chapter 2 will turn into Sex Bullies occasionally, or constantly.

Your partner may be a Control-Freak Bully, a Money Bully, or any other kind of bully, but don't be surprised to discover that he or she is also a perfect match for one of the following Sex Bully profiles. Remember, if there's a bully in your house, it's likely that you're being bullied in the bedroom.

TYPES OF SEX BULLIES

Keep in mind my definition of bullying: any repeated behavior that degrades, denigrates, and otherwise makes you feel bad about yourself. That goes for bullies in the bedroom, too.

The following descriptions profile the most common types of Sex Bullies, with a little information about how they operate and what makes them tick. Not all bullies will match these behaviors exactly. Many will exhibit characteristics of different types at different times, or they might even

Dominating and controlling a partner gives the Sex Bully a sense of relief and release.

combine several at the same time. Most will bully in *and* out of the bedroom. And, of course, you may have experienced bullying behaviors that aren't on this list.

The following descriptions will give you more information about the basic types of Sex Bullies and the techniques they employ, but remember this: your best guide for identifying bullies is always your own intuition—that sick, sinking feeling in your gut that tells you something's not right.

DR. ANNE-RENÉE TESTA'S GUIDE TO SEX BULLIES

Here are the bullies you'll be meeting in the following pages:

- The "Put Out or Get Out" Bully
- The "If You Won't, Someone Else Will" Bully
- The "Not Until You . . ." Bully
- The B.J. Bully
- The Grabbing Bully
- The Rough-Sex Bully

- The Tease
- The Critic
- The No-Sex Bully
- The Flirt
- The Cheater
- The Rapist

The "Put Out or Get Out" Bully

The "Put Out or Get Out" Bully is the type of Sex Bully who insists on sex, whether you want it or not. This bully just won't take no for an answer. So what if you're tired, or not feeling well, or just aren't in the mood! That doesn't matter. How *you* feel and what you want is beside the point. In the bully's mind, the only thing that matters is the bully's needs. And those are going to get met, come hell or high water!

The pressure applied by this bully might be aggressive and enraged, as when Clara's husband shouts at her about how it's his right as her spouse to have sex with her whenever he wants to. Or it might be quiet but relentless, the way Alan's girlfriend sulks and pouts and cajoles until Alan reluctantly—and unenthusiastically—tries to give her what she wants. "Put Out or Get Out" Bullies act like spoiled brats who feel entitled to get whatever they want, whenever they want it. But behind the bluster and blind commitment to getting their way are terrified children grabbing at the only power they believe is available to them: the ability to make their partner "put out."

This form of sexual bullying is particularly serious. There's a fine line between being bullied into sex and being raped. Being emotionally manipulated or verbally coerced into sex is, at times, just barely on the legal side of the line. Perhaps you weren't tied up or held down. But if you gave in only because your partner wouldn't take no for an answer—if you were, in essence, forced to have sex—that's dangerously close to what we commonly think of as rape, isn't it?

The "If You Won't, Someone Else Will" Bully

In essence, the "If You Won't, Someone Else Will" Bully is a lot like the "Put Out or Get Out" Bully. These bullies won't take no for an answer, don't take your desires into consideration, and are interested in the sexual needs of just one person—and it's not you! The difference is that the "If You Won't, Someone Else Will" Bully has very specific sexual demands. Using threats of infidelity and abandonment, the bully attempts to force his or her partner into sexual acts that the partner finds distasteful.

For example, after weeks of resisting, Shari agreed to have anal sex with her husband because he told her he'd visit prostitutes if she didn't. Similarly, Byron's girlfriend bullied him into taking her to male strip clubs and watching porn together. He gave in, though he found both repugnant, because she told him that if he didn't, she'd go back to her ex, who would. Christine was talked into a ménage à trois by her boyfriend, who threatened to leave her if she didn't acquiesce. She thought that if she did it once, he'd be satisfied, but the very next day, he started pushing her to plan another one.

Your best guide for identifying bullies is always your own intuition—that sick, sinking feeling in your gut that tells you something's not right.

Now, as I've said before and will say again, there's no sex act that's off-limits if both partners consent and no one gets hurt. If your partner proposes a sexual experiment or adventure, and you're up for it, fantastic! But if there are sex acts, whether tame or wild, that you really don't like, you should just say no. And no means no—which means your partner should respect and accept your decision, no questions asked. If he or she doesn't accept your decision, and uses threats to try to get you to give in, then you can be sure you're dealing with an "If You Won't, Someone Else Will" Bully.

The "Not Until You . . ." Bully

Maybe you've heard of *Lysistrata*, the ancient Greek play by Aristophanes about how the women of Athens stopped a war by refusing to have sex with their husbands until the men agreed to cease fighting. It's funny onstage, and it's certainly a very effective strategy. However, it's not a negotiation technique that anyone would use in a healthy, mutual relationship. Unfortunately, all too many people *do* use it, holding out in the bedroom to get their way outside of the bedroom. And though men have been know to engage in this behavior, these "holdout" bullies are usually women.

> *No means no—which means your partner should respect and accept your decision, no questions asked.*

Sue, Andrew's wife, refused to have sex with him—or even to touch him—until he agreed to let their son go to a private college instead of the more affordable one Andrew favored. She held him hostage for over a month. And who lost out? Both of them! Then there's Roger and his wife, Katie. They didn't have sex for almost three months, until Roger finally cracked and gave in to Katie's demand that they move from their home in Manhattan back to the New Jersey suburb where Katie grew up.

But their tactics were nothing compared with Margot's. In couples counseling with her husband, Geoff, Margot disclosed that she hadn't had sex with Geoff for *seven months* because he wouldn't shave off his beard. On the one hand, it was silly for Geoff to refuse such a minor request. But on the other, this standoff wasn't really about Geoff's facial hair. It was about the balance of power in their relationship and Margot's misguided effort to make herself feel less vulnerable and more in control by exerting influence over her husband, which only deprived both of them of sex for months on end. Ultimately, I have to hand it to Geoff. He stood up for himself and simply refused to let his wife take him hostage—even with a powerful weapon like sex!

> *Don't ever let anyone do* anything *to you that feels hurtful, disrespectful, or dangerous in any way.*

The B.J. Bully

Almost every woman I know has had at least one experience with a B.J. Bully at some point in her life, and usually more than one. (Women can be oral-sex bullies, too, but it's much less common.) That's really too bad, because if you've had the experience, you know how incredibly unpleasant it is. The B.J. Bully's message is "Service me." By gentle or not-so-gentle means, these bullies force their partners to pleasure them with oral sex. This coercion can be as overt as outright force or as subtle as a guiding hand at the back of your head. You don't have to dislike oral sex for the B.J. Bully to be a problem. Even women who enjoy performing oral sex don't like being pushed into it. And that's what the B.J. Bully does—literally.

Does this sound right to you? I don't think so! Remember, your sex life should be characterized by mutuality. And there's just nothing mutual about being forced to pleasure your partner. So the next time you encounter the B.J. Bully, here's what you do. When you feel his hands on your head, *stop what you're doing.* If you don't want to give him oral sex, take his hands off your head, and tell him, gently but firmly, that you don't feel like it. Or if you do want to give him oral sex but don't want to be forced into it, tell that man he can take his hands off your head and put them somewhere else. The appropriate way for either partner to communicate a desire for oral or any other form of sex is to express the desire and ask whether the partner is "up for it." Of course, when that sexual practice becomes a mutually accepted part of your lovemaking, words may be unnecessary.

The Grabbing Bully

The Grabbing Bully is—well, the one who grabs you, rubs against you, or forces you to touch him or her inappropriately in public or in private, morning, noon, and night. This bully is the one with the one-track mind, the one who always seems to be talking about sex, who throws innuendos and double entendres into every sentence. She's the one who undresses you with her eyes while you're trying to have a conversation. He's the one who rarely meets your gaze because he's too busy looking down your blouse or up your skirt. Now, most people like to feel admired sexually. Most people like to hear that they turn their partner on. But up to a point, people! And beyond that point, most of us feel that we're being degraded, objectified, and treated like hunks of meat instead of human beings.

Deedra started dating a Grabbing Bully last year. At first she thought he was just "frisky," a lusty guy with a healthy libido and no inhibitions about expressing it verbally or physically. Also, she was flattered that he was so attracted to her that he just couldn't keep his hands to himself. But Deedra is an emotionally healthy young woman who worked very hard in our sessions to recover from the effects of being raised by bullies. She'd developed good levels of self-esteem. As a result, it didn't take her long to see that the Grabbing Bully's behaviors were disrespectful. Putting his hand up her skirt in a restaurant and putting her hand on his crotch at his office holiday party just weren't appropriate. And his constant references to how horny he was and how hot she looked didn't really have anything to do with her; instead, these behaviors were all about *him*, his insecurities, and his need to debase, degrade, and keep his partners at arm's length by reducing them to sexual objects.

The Rough-Sex Bully

Some people love a little roughhousing between the sheets. And as long as it's *consensual, mutual, and safe*, both physically and emotionally, this can be a perfectly healthy sexual expression for you and your partner. But that's not how things go with the Rough-Sex Bully, whose thrills come from pushing his or her partner around with the intent to dominate and subjugate. Actually making it mutual and consensual would diminish or completely preclude the sense of power and control that is the whole point of the Rough-Sex Bully's violent behaviors.

A Rough-Sex Bully might use physical means to bully his or her partner, or might do so verbally, including with dirty talk, name calling, and insults. Again, if this is what you're into, that's your business. But if you don't like it, don't do it! And please, don't ever let anyone do *anything* to you that feels hurtful, disrespectful, or dangerous in any way. You absolutely, positively don't deserve it, and there's no reason for you to take it.

The Tease

We have to be very clear about teasing, because it can get confusing. Say two people are on a date. Maybe at the end of the date they have a make-out session in the car or on the couch. Now, say Person A expects it will lead to sex, but all Person B wants is to do a little kissing and go home alone. Person A requests sex, gets turned down, and starts accusing Person B of being a tease. Is Person A right? Not a chance! Just because your partner *expects* sex doesn't mean you're under any obligation to have sex. If your partner got the wrong idea somehow, that's not your responsibility.

What makes someone a Tease, in Sex Bully terms, is not failure to conform to a partner's expectations. Instead, it's purposely arousing a partner while planning to leave that person hanging—promising sex with no intention of keeping that promise. The Tease deliberately leads his or her partner on, eliciting desire and then denying it, just for the thrill of power that it gives.

A couple of years ago, Kanisha was dating a man named Whit. She was really smitten with him, and he did seem great on paper, but there was one big problem: Whit was a classic Tease. Early in their relationship, he'd spend the whole evening whispering sweet nothings into Kanisha's ear, telling her how sexy and alluring she was, and how he couldn't wait to get back to her place and make love to her. He'd go on and on about all the things he was going to do to her when they were alone together. He'd lay her out on the couch or carry her to the bed, get her totally worked up, even go so far as undressing her. And then, out of the blue, he'd suddenly remember that he had to be at work early the next morning, kiss her good-bye, and leave. Or he'd get her all hot and bothered and then tell her he wasn't in the mood and just wanted to hold her.

The first few times this happened, Kanisha was baffled but sympathetic. The next few times it happened, she began to suspect that he suffered from some kind of sexual dysfunction. That theory didn't make much sense, because he did have sex with her occasionally. And while the sex wasn't anything to write home about, it seemed clear that there was nothing physically wrong with Whit—he was as capable of intercourse as the next guy. Eventually Kanisha began to notice a pattern to Whit's behavior. She realized that the nights that they *did* end up having sex were the very same nights Kanisha stopped paying attention or responding to Whit's come-ons. If she ignored the sweet nothings, he'd actually follow through on his big talk and make love to her. That would lure her back into listening and hoping. And then the cycle would start all over again.

After several months during which we had a series of conversations about sex bullying, Kanisha called Whit out on his actions. Though she was gentle and kind about it, Whit either wouldn't or couldn't acknowledge and take responsibility for his bullying behaviors. So Kanisha moved on. Today she's engaged to a very sexy man who never misses a chance to make love to her.

The No-Sex Bully

The No-Sex Bully can be easy to confuse with the "Not Until You . . ." Bully or the Tease. All three types bully by withholding sex. But their motives and methods are quite different. The "Not Until You . . ." Bully withholds sex to bully the partner into doing a particular thing. The Tease elicits the partner's desire and then denies it. And the No-Sex Bully is the bedroom equivalent of the Silent-Treatment Bully.

As we discussed in Chapter 2, Silent-Treatment Bullies attack and manipulate by withdrawing and shutting out their partners completely, leaving them alone and helpless, feeling abandoned. The Silent-Treatment Bully removes all power from the hands of the victim, forcing him or her to beg and plead for any kind of attention, like a hostage jailed in complete emotional isolation. The No-Sex Bully works the same way. In fact, Silent-Treatment Bullies are often No-Sex Bullies, and vice versa. Instead of withholding communication and interaction, they withhold sex, but the effect on the victim is similar.

However, you might think you're dealing with a No-Sex Bully when, in reality, your partner is someone who survived a childhood of neglect, sexually inappropriate behavior, or sexual abuse by parents or caretakers. It's entirely possible you wouldn't know about it, even if you've known your partner for years. Sex-abuse survivors have a tremendous fear of intimacy. That fear, not a bullying instinct, is holding them back in the bedroom. Intimacy and trust are aligned and interrelated; someone who wasn't given positive physical contact or who was actually abused will be generally distrustful of people and will resist getting close to anyone. Sex-abuse survivors just don't know how to trust a partner, sexually or otherwise. Such people are likely to make sex cursory, to shut down emotionally during sex, or to avoid it altogether, because the physical and emotional intimacy is just too frightening to deal with. If you suspect your partner is an untreated sex-abuse survivor, help is available—for both of you. Check the resources in Appendix B.

The Critic

Just as the No-Sex Bully is the bedroom equivalent of the Silent-Treatment Bully, so the Critic is the bedroom equivalent of the Control-Freak Bully and the Scorekeeping Bully.

Nothing you do between the sheets will ever be good enough for the Critic. If you're eager to have sex, you'll be accused of having an overactive libido. If you hold back and wait for your partner to make the first move, you'll be charged with passivity. If you do the things you know your partner likes, you're boring and predictable. But if you suggest trying something new or experimental to spice things up, you're a pervert.

According to the Critic, whatever you used to do in bed, or what you refuse to do, will always be more desirable than what you're doing right now. Your body looked better, your kisses were better, and your technique was better. And of course you'll never measure up to your partner's former lovers or your partner's friends' lovers—all of whom say and do all kinds of things that you can't or won't.

The Flirt

There's nothing wrong with flirting, ladies and gentlemen. The day we stop engaging in and enjoying playful flirtation with attractive colleagues, good-looking strangers, sexy exes—that's the day we're officially dead. Flirting is fun, and I wouldn't suggest that anyone give it up. But flirting in front of a partner? That we shouldn't *ever* do (unless, of course, it's done as a mutually agreed-upon form of foreplay).

Flirting when your partner is around is disrespectful, unkind, and even cruel. It plays on any insecurities your partner might have, making him or her feel threatened and unsafe. And it's exactly what the Flirt, as a Sex Bully, does. This type of flirting is a kind of intimidation, a show of sexual force, in which the Flirt lords over the partner how desirable he or she is. Of course, these actions imply a threat: "Look how people respond to me. Look how sexually powerful I am. Look at how easy it would be for me to cheat on you, how quickly I could replace you—so you'd better watch your step!"

The Cheater

Not all sexually straying spouses are bullies. Sometimes a cheater is just a cheater. There's a whole world of psychological explanations for infidelity, including boredom (which often comes from an inability to be intimate), insecurity (and a desire to feed one's ego with conquests), and emotional or sexual dissatisfaction with one's partner, to name just a few. While all these motives are understandable, not a single one of them constitutes an excuse for cheating—because there is no excuse. There's simply no good reason for doing it. It never helps the situation, and it usually makes things worse.

A Sex Bully's cheating is no more acceptable; it's just done a little differently and for different reasons. Instead of cheating to escape, find a diversion, or try getting needs met by someone other than one's partner, the Cheater has a fling or affair for power, punishment, or both. Here's one easy way to distinguish a Sex Bully who's a Cheater from a plain old cheat—a difference that speaks volumes about the difference between them: Plain old cheats will try to keep their infidelities a secret. Sex Bully Cheaters, in contrast, *want* their partners to know about the flings and affairs, because that's where the real gratification comes in. The actual infidelity, the not-so-secret sex, is beside the point for Cheaters. What they're ultimately after is the effect their betrayals have on their victims.

You don't owe sex to anyone. You're not obligated to sexually satisfy anyone. Sex should always be mutual and consensual. That means it's your choice.

Cheaters who act out to punish are the bedroom equivalent of Passive-Aggressive Bullies—taking revenge on or trying to get even with their partners for perceived slights and injuries. Cheaters after power are like Flirts—their motives and goals are the same, but their methods take matters one giant step further.

The Rapist

Rape is the most extreme form of sex bullying. And I'm very sorry to say it, but it's a well-known fact that rape *does* happen in relationships and marriage. Twenty or thirty years ago, date rape was still a dirty little secret, and people didn't give a second thought to blaming a rape victim for the crime committed against him or her. Thankfully, that attitude has begun to change. But despite increasing public awareness and understanding of sex crimes, it's still very difficult for people to accept that if they're forced to have sex with their spouse, lover, or the person they're dating, *that is rape.* If you're physically compelled to have sex against your will, no matter who does it, no matter how well you know the person, that's rape!

Please, make no mistake about it. You don't owe sex to anyone. You're not obligated to sexually satisfy anyone. Sex should always be mutual and consensual. That means *it's your choice.* Being taken out to dinner, away for a weekend, or on a vacation trip does not change that. Making a monogamous commitment, moving in together, or taking marriage vows does not change that one bit!

You know, in your heart and in your gut, that you deserve to be heard, that you deserve to have your needs met and your feelings respected.

If you think you might been forced to have sex, or that it might happen in the future, you need to know this: *It's not your fault.* You do not deserve it. You don't have to take it. And you don't have to deal with it on your own. There are countless support groups, counselors, and survivors of similar experiences. If you want more information about organizations that can help you, check the resources listed in Appendix B.

READY TO IMPROVE YOUR SEX LIFE?

If you've concluded that you've got a bully in the bedroom, just keep reading. It's time to get started on making some positive changes! You're about to learn ways to make your relationship healthier in the bedroom:

- How to talk back to the bully in your bedroom
- How to stand up for what you want
- How to work with your partner to make positive changes in your sex life

Saying No to the Sex Bully

You're not going to believe how simple it is to say no to a Sex Bully. Now, I'm not saying it's going to be *easy*. It probably won't be. You may be really scared—but you can do it scared! And it's not complicated. You say no to a Sex Bully exactly the same way you say no to getting in the car with someone who's intoxicated, eating a food you're allergic to, or doing anything else that's not good for you. You just say no. You don't need to be aggressive, and you shouldn't be hostile. You're not looking for a fight, just looking out for yourself. But don't walk on eggshells either! If you're a mealymouthed mush, the bully won't pay attention.

Always focus on the solution. You have to accentuate the positive in order to eliminate the negative.

You say no politely but firmly. You say no with the courage of your convictions. You say no confidently—because you know, in your heart and in your gut, that you deserve to be heard, that you deserve to have your needs met and your feelings respected. That's all there is to it.

The next time your partner does something that you don't like, stop. Look your bullying partner right in the eye and say, "Don't do that. I don't like it. Don't do it again."

Following Up on "No"

Like many bullies, your bullying partner probably isn't used to hearing the word no very often. So it's likely that he or she will get confused when you suddenly change the rules of the game. It's possible that your partner will feel threatened and afraid when you stand up for yourself. And it's probable that the fear will manifest as anger. He or she might try to take the power back by undermining your strength, using statements like these:

The very best thing you can do for yourself and your partner is to learn how to ask for what you want.

1. "I thought you *did* like it. You never had a problem with it before."
2. "What's wrong with you today?"
3. "Everyone likes this kind of thing."

This kind of defensive reaction on the bully's part might make you uncomfortable. That's totally understandable, but you can handle it. You may want to back down, but *don't*. Trust yourself, and stand your ground.

Take a deep breath, look the bully in the eye, and answer calmly. You might address the three sample comments with the following responses:

1. "You were mistaken, and I'm sorry if I gave you the wrong impression. But I'm letting you know now that I *don't* like it. Want to hear about what I do like?"

2. "There's nothing wrong with me. I'm just letting you know how I feel, so this can be as satisfying as possible for both of us."

3. "Maybe everyone else likes this kind of thing, but *I* don't—and you're with me right now! So let's focus on you and me, and what *we* like."

Speaking Up for What You Want

Notice what the suggested responses do; they turn the focus immediately from the problem to the solution. This is the key to discussing your sex life with your partner and making positive changes together. Always focus on the solution. You have to accentuate the positive in order to eliminate the negative. If you dwell on what *doesn't* work, if you constantly criticize and belabor the bad parts, you and your partner are likely to wind up feeling discouraged, denigrated, and depressed. And that's not a huge turn-on, is it? But if you turn your and your partner's attention to what *does* work, what you *do* like, and what *does* turn you on, you're both going to wind up feeling hopeful, appreciated, and sexually empowered.

Although making changes can be challenging, it can also be a lot of fun. And in the end, your relationship will be stronger and healthier because of it.

So the very best thing you can do for yourself and your partner is to learn how to ask for what you want. Tell your partner, "I don't like it when you do this, but I absolutely *love* it when you do that." Or say, "It hurts me when you do that, but it drives me wild when you do this." Or start a sentence with one of the following statements:

- "My favorite thing that you do is . . ."
- "You're so good at . . ."

- "It turns me on so much when you . . ."
- "There's something I've always wanted to try with you."

Make these statements directly and lovingly. Say them without shame, blame, or fear of rejection. You don't want to be a victim *or* a bully, so avoid any silent sulking or self-pity, and skip the scorekeeping and grudge holding. There's no reason your partner should be able to read your mind, so you have to take responsibility for yourself—and speak up about what you need.

There's no reason you should be able to read your partner's mind, either. So start asking questions about what he or she likes. Make sure that for every sexual favor you request, you try to give one in return. Be as eager to give as to receive. That's mutuality! And I bet you'll find that, in no time flat, your partner's going to be more eager and responsive in bed than you ever would have imagined.

As much as possible, be patient and compassionate with your partner and yourself though this process. Changes like these can take time. Talking about sex takes us to a sensitive, vulnerable place, emotionally speaking. And, of course, so does having sex. Although making changes can be challenging, it can also be a lot of fun. And in the end, your relationship will be stronger and healthier because of it.

Sex is about so much more than just sex. It's not just physical; it's mental, emotional, and spiritual, too. It's an essential part of your relationship, and it's also a reflection of that relationship.

BEYOND THE BEDROOM

The most important thing for you to understand from all of this is that sex is about so much more than just sex. It's not just physical; it's mental, emotional, and spiritual, too. It's an essential part of your relationship, and it's also a reflection of that relationship. The qualities we look for and work toward in bed—open-mindedness, patience, respect, mutuality— are the very qualities we should look for and work toward in our relationships as a whole, and vice versa. That's what you deserve! You shouldn't settle for less, and you don't have to. The tools I've given you are a great way to get started with healing your relationship, in the bedroom and beyond. And we're just getting started; stick with me, and you'll see how good it can get!

CHAPTER SUMMARY

GET INTO THE SOLUTION!

➤ Your sexual relationship with your partner can tell you a lot about your relationship as a whole. The way things are going horizontally is usually how they're going vertically, and vice versa. Improving one will improve the other.

➤ Most bullies are also bullies in the bedroom, and being bullied sexually can be the worst bullying of all. Remember, you don't deserve it, and you don't have to take it!

➤ Your sex life is a great place to start changing your relationship. Saying what you want and need in bed, focusing on the positive, and asserting yourself with your partner are great practice for doing the same out of bed.

You and Your Inner Bully 5

That Voice in Your Head, and How to Shut It Up

- How did that bully get into your mind?
- What the Inner Bully says—and why listening to it will ruin yor life
- How to replace the bully's negative messages with positive boosters that will get you what you want, need, and deserve

> *It is not fair to ask of others what you are unwilling to do yourself. You must do the thing you think you cannot do.*
>
> —ELEANOR ROOSEVELT

You've probably heard people say, "We're our own worst enemies." That's especially true for the victims of bullies. No matter how badly your bullying partner treats you, I bet it's never quite as cruel and cutting as the voice in your own mind. You know the voice I'm talking about. It's the voice telling you that you deserve whatever your partner dishes out, that you're even worse than your partner knows and more deeply flawed than even the most critical companion could see, and that you'll never accomplish anything, amount to anything, or be anything other than a failure and an embarrassment. It's that hateful, vicious voice saying things so incredibly negative and nasty that you'd never even *think* of saying them to anyone else. You know the voice I mean? That's your Inner Bully. And it's telling you lies!

WHERE YOUR INNER BULLY CAME FROM

The psychology term for Inner Bully is *introject*. The introject is the phenomenon I introduced in Chapter 2, when we began to explore the rage of generations. The introject is the sum of all the negative messages that you get from your parents, which you internalize and carry into adulthood.

As I've explained, the way our parents treated us profoundly affects our sense of ourselves and the world we live in—our identity. If our mother and father neglected or ignored us as young children, we come to believe, unconsciously, that we are unimportant, unworthy of attention or consideration. If they were hypercritical, comparing us to other children and denigrating everything we did, day after day, the message we got is that we can't do anything right, that we're never going to be good enough, that we'll never measure up. And if they abused us, we came to believe that we really are all the things they told us through their words and actions—stupid, selfish, ugly, lazy, greedy, useless, ungrateful, unlovable—and that we deserve to be abused.

The introject is the lie you're living out. It's the nonstop, nagging, nitpicking voice in your head, telling you that nothing you do will ever be good enough, that you've missed all your chances and messed up all your opportunities, that you don't deserve love, respect, and happiness. The introject is your Inner Bully.

That's the introject. It's those terrible, negative, untrue ideas you've been carrying around for years, which you received because your parents acted out *their* pain and passed the rage of generations on to you, instead of treating you with the care that you deserved. The introject is the lie you're living out. It's the nonstop, nagging, nitpicking voice in your head, telling you that nothing you do will ever be good enough, that you've missed all your chances and messed up all your opportunities, that you don't deserve love, respect, and happiness. The introject is your Inner Bully.

Your Inner Bully: The Bad News and the Good News

The bad news is that your Inner Bully is a serious, dangerous bully—pushy, powerful, and persistent. In fact, the Inner Bully may be the worst bully you'll ever encounter. And unless you do something about it, that Inner Bully will take charge and run the show, controlling everything you do and sabotaging your entire life. That's because the Inner Bully affects a lot more than your romantic relationships. It also poisons your relationships with friends, family, and colleagues—your daily interactions with every single person you encounter, from the gas station attendant and the grocery store clerk to your boss and your best pals. In fact, whatever actions you take and whatever choices you make about love, work, money, health, recreation, and anything else in your life are all going to be made for you by the Inner Bully—*if you let it*.

The good news is that you *don't* have to let it. You can stop living out the lies that were forced on you all those years ago, the lies that have damaged and held you back for so long. You can reject the introject! You can stand up to your Inner Bully, and that's the first step toward standing up to every other bully in your life.

That's exactly what I'm going to help you do. As you read this chapter, we'll take a closer look at how the Inner Bully works. We'll explore what the vicious voice in your head says and how it affects you. Then you're going to learn to talk back to that voice and take your life back from your Inner Bully.

THE INNER BULLY'S EIGHT BASIC MESSAGES AND HOW TO TALK BACK

You already know the Inner Bully doesn't have anything nice to say. Like all bullies, the Inner Bully says a variety of things in a variety of ways. But most of the destructive, dangerous messages you're likely to hear from your Inner Bully will be a variation on one of the following eight messages:

1. You're unlovable.
2. You're unattractive.
3. You're stupid and incompetent.
4. You're clumsy and weak.
5. Your ideas and opinions are wrong.
6. Your feelings and experiences are irrelevant.
7. You'll never be as good as him/her.
8. Who and what you are is unacceptable.

We're about to explore each one of these messages in depth. After discussing each one, I'll offer you some concrete suggestions for how you can talk back to your inner bully—and refuse to accept the message any longer. To break down and analyze each of the Inner Bully's messages, I'll use my four-point formula:

- **What the Inner Bully says:** How a particular message might sound inside your head.
- **Where the message comes from:** The message's origin in the ways your parents treated you or the things they said to you when you were little. If a particular message sounds familiar, you'll probably recognize some the examples in this section from your own childhood.

- **How the message affects you:** The ways the message leads you to undermine, underestimate, second-guess, and sabotage yourself today.
- **How to reject the introject:** What you should tell the Inner Bully when it tries to give you this message, replacing the negative, bullying message with a positive, empowering message.

As you read the "Reject the Introject" sections, which coach you on how to talk back to your Inner Bully, keep in mind that you'll have to talk back more than once—probably *many* more times—before it stops trying to give you a particular message. The Inner Bully is stubborn and sneaky, so you'll have to be persistent in your efforts to shut it up. It won't happen overnight. But it *can* and *will* happen, when you learn the A.R.T. Method. It'll change your life!

Think of this process of talking back to and silencing your Inner Bully as training an especially tricky and troublesome animal. You *can* tame it.

You can stand up to your Inner Bully, and that's the first step toward standing up to every other bully in your life.

You *must* tame it; your life depends upon it. And you *will* tame it. It's just going to take time and effort. You can do it. So let's get to work.

Your Inner Bully Says You're Unlovable

"You're unlovable" is the kind of thing the Inner Bully says to you after you've had a bad day, or a bad date, or a bad fight with your partner. Inside your head, the message might sound something like this: "No one loves you. No one has ever loved you, and no one ever will love you. No one will ever choose you or cherish you. You don't deserve love or romance, or kindness, warmth, and devotion. You're going to be lonely for the rest of your life, and you'll die alone and unloved."

Where the Message Comes From. Anyone raised by a bullying parent will hear some version of this message from time to time, if not all the time. Our sense of ourselves as people who are worthy and deserving of love begins with our parents. If your mother and father treated you lovingly when you were little—if they held you as an infant, expressed affection verbally and physically as you were growing up, showed warmth and kindness, and took pleasure in spending time with you—the message you got is that they loved you, that you're lovable.

The Inner Bully is stubborn and sneaky, so you'll have to be persistent in your efforts to shut it up. It won't happen overnight. But it can and will happen.

Sadly, all too often, our parents weren't able to provide us with this kind of attention and affection. Of course, this is no reflection on you. It was the result of your parents' own limitations, and it doesn't say anything at all about who you are or what you deserve. But as a child, you can't understand that; you just don't have the critical faculties to sort it out. So, unconsciously, you take responsibility for the way you were treated and blame yourself. Whether you were neglected and ignored or attacked and harassed, you came to believe that the reason you weren't treated lovingly was that you're unlovable.

This terrible, damaging message—that you aren't loved and don't deserve to be—is the main message underlying all of the Inner Bully's other messages.

How the Message Affects You. The unconscious belief that we're unlovable can profoundly damage our lives, as you can imagine. It can, for example, lead you to pursue partners who don't return your affection, accept bullying behavior because you think you don't deserve better, and stay in abusive relationships because you believe that no one else will ever love you again.

Reject the Introject! When your Inner Bully tries to tell you that you're not lovable, take a deep breath . . . and talk back:

> "I know that is not true. And I'm not going to listen to your lies any longer! I am a lovable and loving person. I deserve to give love and to receive love. I've been loved in the past, and I am loved now, and I will be loved in the future. *That* is the truth."

Your Inner Bully Says You're Unattractive

The Inner Bully will spring "You're unattractive" on you at any time of the day or night, but this message is especially likely when you're already feeling self-conscious and insecure. Inside your head, the message might sound something like this: "You're so ugly. Your body's awful! You're really out of shape—how can you even go out in public? You're getting old, your skin is sagging, you're all wrinkled, and look at that cellulite. Your hair's a mess. Your posture's terrible. You're such a slob! What are you wearing? Why don't you learn how to dress decently? No one will ever want you looking like that!"

Where the Message Comes From. For many of us, the origins of this message are all too easy to identify—a parent, grandparent, teacher, or caretaker who all too frequently shared his or her opinion about your physical appearance. You were too fat or too thin. Your clothes were too tight or too baggy. Your hair was too long or too short—and so on. These comments had a subtext; the message you got was that you were unattractive.

Today that message is still with you. The Inner Bully nags and nitpicks about every last detail of your appearance and constantly tells you that no one will ever find you aesthetically appealing or sexually desirable.

How the Message Affects You. The unconscious conviction that you're unattractive can lead to a preoccupation with physical appearance that ranges from the distracting to the downright dangerous. It's bad enough to suffer from low self-esteem and daily concerns about how you look. But when this belief gets out of hand, it can lead to crazy diets, eating disorders, excessive exercise, compulsive shopping (lots of clothes and beauty products you'll never use, putting you thousands of dollars in debt), and even unnecessary plastic surgeries. Besides all these hazards, there's the fact that all of this obsessing with your looks robs you of precious time and energy that you could be spending on much more productive endeavors.

The belief that you're unattractive can also lead to promiscuity. If you lack faith in your own attractiveness, you may end up constantly attempting to prove to yourself (and your Inner Bully) that people *are* sexually drawn to you—and you prove it through conquests. If you have low self-esteem when it comes to sexual desirability, you're likely to treat your sexual self casually and carelessly. You might sleep with anyone who will have you, instead of holding out for worthy, respectful partners who think you're the sexiest, most desirable, and precious creature on earth, because on an unconscious level, you just don't believe that's ever going to happen.

Reject the Introject! The next time your Inner Bully tries to tell you that you're not physically attractive or sexually desirable—that you're too something or not enough something else—take a deep breath and talk back:

> "I know that's not true. And I'm not going to listen to your lies any longer! I'm happy with my appearance. Many people think I'm attractive and desirable—and

I'm absolutely worthy of a partner who finds me irresistibly sexy! I'm grateful to be healthy and whole. And I have better things to spend my energy on than how you see me or how I look. *That* is the truth."

Your Inner Bully Says You're Stupid and Incompetent

When do you hear an inner voice saying, "You're stupid and incompetent"? For most people, this is the kind of attack the Inner Bully launches when we're trying to accomplish something at home or in the workplace and perhaps it's not going as well or as smoothly as we would like it to. Inside your head, the message might sound something like this: "Why are you so stupid? You can't do anything right. What's wrong with you? I don't know why you even bother trying; you're never going to be able to do this. You're never going to be able to do *anything*! You should just give up."

Where the Message Comes From. Negative thoughts about our intelligence and abilities are usually the result of having grown up with overly critical or unsupportive parents who judged, attacked, and demeaned us. When you brought home a bad grade, instead of encouraging and challenging you to do better next time, they told you that you were stupid. When you struggled to build a model airplane, do a science experiment for school, run for student government, or audition for a school play, instead of comforting and rallying you, they pointed out all the mistakes you made. They criticized whatever you did, from your test scores to the way you did your chores, finding fault with everything and merit in nothing.

How the Message Affects You. The unconscious belief that you're less intelligent and capable than you truly are can lead you to quit things you've taken on without seeing them through, leaving friends and colleagues in the lurch. It can lead you to procrastinate and live in fear of making mistakes, constantly anxious about your abilities. It can lead you to accept positions and projects far below your ability level, so you end up with jobs and hobbies that don't demand anything of you, don't engage, excite, or fulfill you, and don't encourage you to grow. Worst of all, this message can lead you to avoid taking on challenges and pursuing your dreams—because you're terrified of failure and don't believe yourself capable of success.

Reject the Introject! When your Inner Bully tries to tell you that you're stupid or incompetent, that you can't do something, and that you should just give up, take a deep breath and talk back:

> "I know that's not true. And I'm not going to listen to your lies any longer! I'm intelligent, competent, and perfectly capable of accomplishing anything I put my mind to. *That* is the truth. And instead of getting frustrated or overwhelmed, I'm going to stay calm and have confidence in myself. I can do this! I'm going to tackle my task one piece at a time until it's done, and do it to the best of my ability today. If it's not perfect, that's fine. I'll learn from whatever mistakes I make and do better next time."

Your Inner Bully Says You're Clumsy and Weak

Your Inner Bully says, "You're clumsy and weak," when you're engaged in some physical activity or one that requires manual dexterity, such as playing a sport, fixing a car, sewing on a button, dancing at a party, or even just walking down the street. If you find the activity at all difficult, even for a moment, your Inner Bully will speak up with a message that sounds something like this: "You're such a klutz! You're all thumbs, aren't you? What's the matter, are you tired already? You can't throw. You're not fixing that; you're just making it worse. You wreck everything you put your hands on! You look like a complete idiot. I've never seen someone so unco-ordinated! What a wimp."

Where the Message Comes From. This message was instilled by overly critical parents who attacked your skills and abilities (usually because they were insecure about their own). They came to your games or meets, and instead of cheering, they yelled corrections and afterward told you everything that was wrong with your performance. They teased you cruelly about your skinny arms, your bad vision, or your two left feet in front of siblings, neighbors, and the person you had a crush on. Your art projects didn't get put on the mantel or the fridge; instead, they were stuffed in a drawer, relegated to the basement, or thrown away.

How the Message Affects You. An unconscious belief that you're clumsy, weak, uncoordinated, or inept can hold you back from engaging in activities that you enjoy, whether it's joining a local sports league, ice-skating with your family, knitting a sweater, or dancing at your friends' weddings. In this way, you deny yourself all sorts of joy and pleasure, not to mention the physical and mental benefits of such activi-ties. And, of course, this sort of low self-esteem and doubt in your physical abilities can have a big negative effect on your sex life.

Reject the Introject! The next time your Inner Bully tries to tell you that you're clumsy, weak, or inept, take a deep breath and talk back:

"That's just not true. And I'm not going to listen to your lies any longer! I may not be the strongest or fastest or most coordinated or artistic person around, but I get by just fine, and nothing's going to keep me from getting out there and doing what appeals to me. Maybe I'll master this activity eventually, or maybe I'll just do it for fun! Either way, I'm going to give it my all and do the best I can today. I'm going to stop judging myself and instead concentrate on enjoying myself!"

Your Inner Bully Says Your Ideas and Opinions Are Wrong

"You're wrong" is a message your Inner Bully sends you at work, at school, over the dinner table, or in any group of people or private conversation. The message sounds something like this: "Don't even bother opening your mouth, because you're going to sound like an idiot. Where do you come up with this stuff? You're totally uninformed. What right do you have to an opinion on this subject? That's the most ridiculous idea I've ever heard. What would you know about it? Why would anyone want to hear what you have to say? Who cares about what you think, anyway?"

Where the Message Comes From. This kind of self-doubt—the fear of sounding stupid—almost always comes from having been raised and schooled by parents, caretakers, and teachers who were unconsciously threatened by a child's enthusiasm and intelligence. Driven by their own fears, they were incapable of encouraging you to speak up, think for yourself, and express your ideas and opinions about the world around you. Instead, they would denigrate your ideas, mock your opinions, rebuff your attempts to participate in conversations, and crush your self-confidence.

How the Message Affects You. As an adult, if you believe that your opinions are wrong or don't count, that belief will lead you to keep things to yourself—at home and at work, with colleagues, friends, or family. You don't offer your ideas on how to improve a presentation for a client, organize a great fund-raiser for your children's school, or rearrange the furniture to make the living room look better.

You don't offer thoughts on your friends' love lives or community politics. You shut down instead of sharing—and everyone suffers as a result.

Reject the Introject! The next time your Inner Bully tries to tell you that your thoughts are not valuable, that your opinions are wrong, take a deep breath and talk back:

> "That's just not true. And I'm not going to listen to your lies any longer! My thoughts and opinions are valuable, and they deserve to be heard. I don't need to be right all the time, and not everyone has to agree with me. If people don't like what I have to say, that's fine. But I'm not going to let fear of being judged or rejected prevent me from sharing my ideas anymore!"

Your Inner Bully Says Your Feelings and Experiences Are Irrelevant

Your Inner Bully may tell you your feelings and experiences are irrelevant anytime, but usually that message comes when you're with someone else or a group of people and your experience of the situation is different from theirs, especially if you're uncomfortable with what's happening and how you're being treated. The message usually sounds something like this: "You're overreacting. Why are you so sensitive? You're too intense. Why do you have to make such a big deal about everything? Nobody cares how you feel. Why are you bothering people with this? No one else has a problem with this situation. It's always all about you, isn't it? Don't make a scene."

Where the Message Comes From. This message starts in childhood with parents, caretakers, and siblings who were too selfish and self-involved to think about your feelings, to hear you out when you got uncomfortable or were happy, or to consider how your experience of an event might be different from their own. Maybe you remember a parent saying to you, "What are you making such a fuss about?" or, "Stop crying, or I'll give you something to cry about!" or, "You're too old to be acting like such a baby." These are classic ways of giving children the message that what they're feeling is unimportant and that their emotional responses are unacceptable.

How the Message Affects You. The unconscious belief that your feelings and experiences are irrelevant, incorrect, or inappropriate can be incredibly damaging. What could be worse than the notion that how you feel doesn't matter to the very people who are supposed to care about you most? And to be told that the way you're feeling, the way the world seems to you, your experience of reality is *wrong*—well, that's just crazy-making! Of course, no one's feelings are wrong. We feel what we feel, and that's that.

When you listen to this message, you go against your own instincts, deny your intuition, and second-guess yourself. Then you end up suffering through toxic relationships, terrible jobs, and injurious experiences of all kinds, even when every fiber of your being is telling you to get out. I'm sure you wouldn't treat anyone else this way; it's the ultimate form of abuse. Yet if you listen to the Inner Bully, you do it to yourself.

Reject the Introject! The next time your Inner Bully tries to tell you that your feelings don't matter, take a deep breath and talk back:

> "That's just not true. And I'm not going to listen to your lies any longer! My experience of this situation, my reactions and perceptions may be different from other people's, but that does *not* make them wrong.

"I'm as sensitive as I am, and my reactions are the size that they are. The fact that they're deeper or bigger than someone else's does not mean I'm too sensitive, or that I'm overreacting, or that my responses are inappropriate. I feel what I feel. I experience things in my own way. Those feelings and experiences deserve the same regard and respect as anyone else's. And today that's what I'm going to insist upon, from myself and everyone else."

Your Inner Bully Says You'll Never Be as Good as Him/Her

The moment you give your Inner Bully an opening by comparing yourself with someone else, the Inner Bully is ready to point out, "You'll never be as good as him/her." Whether that other person is a friend, colleague, sibling, or stranger, whether the comparison is about physical appearance, personal accomplishments, or professional success, the Inner Bully loves nothing better than the opportunity to turn your *comparing* into *despairing*. The message usually sounds something like this: "Look at that car (or career, house, spouse). You'll never have anything that nice. Did you hear about his promotion (her award, their children's report cards)? You'll never accomplish anything like that. What's wrong with you? Why are you such a loser? Why can't you be more like them?"

Where the Message Comes From. It's probably not hard to identify the origins of this message. It comes from bullying parents who constantly compared you unfavorably with siblings, schoolmates, neighbors—anyone at all, since everyone in the world seemed to be better, smarter, more attractive, and more accomplished than you. "John's son just made the varsity football team. Too bad I have such a wimp for a son." "The kids next door always help their parents with everything—not like you selfish brats." "Why don't you have boys calling you all the time, like Linda?" "Your brother and sister manage to get decent grades; what's *your* problem?"

How the Message Affects You. The internalized message that you'll never be as good as other people has the strange effect of leading you to constantly measure your worth or accomplishments against someone else's, to compete with everyone you encounter. Inevitably, when you make such comparisons, you come up feeling like a short, lacking loser—not because you really are, but because that's all the Inner Bully will let you see or feel.

Reject the Introject! The next time your Inner Bully tells you that you're not as good as someone else or tries to make you compare yourself with someone else, take a deep breath and talk back:

> "That's not true. And I'm not going to listen to your lies any longer! My life is not a contest or a race, with winners and losers. I'm not going to compare myself with anyone else, because their triumphs don't take anything away from me, and their disappointments don't enrich me. My success doesn't come from doing or having more than other people. It comes from living according to my own values and measuring myself by my own standards!"

Your Inner Bully Says Who and What You Are Is Unacceptable

The Inner Bully's ultimate message is that who and what you are is unacceptable. This message is the cruel, killing point of everything else the Inner Bully says—a total undermining and rejection of all that you are. The message usually sounds something like this: "You're hopeless, useless, and worthless. You're a disappointment, an embarrassment, a disgrace, a laughingstock to everyone you've ever known. You're disgusting, revolting, vile, and you should be ashamed to even exist. You're just taking up space here. You don't deserve to live."

Where the Message Comes From. This awful message is the direct result of having been mistreated, abused, neglected, and bullied by your parents and other caretakers. They were supposed to support, encourage, and protect you—and most of all to provide the acceptance and unconditional love that you need. But too often they weren't able to do this, as a result of their own pain, damaged emotions, unresolved issues, insecurities, and profound limitations. Instead, they judged and rejected you for reasons that you might never understand— and which they probably don't understand either—and in this way gave you the message that what and who you are is bad, wrong, defective, and unacceptable.

> *Bullying is any repeated behavior that degrades, denigrates, and otherwise makes you feel bad about yourself. That goes for the voice in your head just as much as it does for the person on the other side of the bed.*

How the Message Affects You. I'm sure you can imagine, if you haven't already felt firsthand, the terrible consequences of this message. It leads to you to feel loathing, shame, and revulsion toward yourself and to sabotage and harm yourself by engaging in self-destructive behavior of all kinds, like getting involved in abusive relationships with bullying partners, because you think that's what you deserve.

Reject the Introject! The next time your Inner Bully tells you that you're unacceptable, that there's something essentially wrong with you, take a deep breath and talk back:

> "That's not true. And I'm not going to listen to your lies any longer! There's nothing wrong with me. I'm a human being. I'm a good person, with many strengths and positive qualities, striving to grow and progress, and I have so much to offer. Today I'm right where I'm supposed to be, in the world and in my life. Today I'm exactly *who* and *how* I'm supposed to be."

HOW TO RECOGNIZE THE INNER BULLY: DON'T BE FOOLED!

Remember, the messages we've just analyzed are the Inner Bully's basic, foundational messages, not its *only* messages. Your Inner Bully may have lots of other things to say to you, or it may give you these same messages but in ways that make them sound so different from what I've described that they're difficult to identify. Or you may be so accustomed to hearing such messages that you don't even realize you're hearing them.

Whatever the case may be, don't be tricked into thinking that you don't have an Inner Bully, just because the voice in your head doesn't sound exactly like the one in the previous pages. Instead, listen carefully for any nasty or negative remark that your mind makes about you. When you hear the kind of thoughts you wouldn't say to someone you care about, it's a very good bet that your Inner Bully is talking.

Remember, I've said bullying is any repeated behavior that degrades, denigrates, and otherwise makes you feel bad about yourself. That goes for the voice in your head just as much as it does for the person on the other side of the bed. And as always, remember that your best guide to whether you're being bullied is your own intuition—the sick, sinking feeling in your gut telling you that somebody's not treating you right.

BEYOND THE INNER BULLY TO THE BODY SNATCHERS!

Sometimes, though, that sick, sinking feeling in your gut turns into something even worse: surges of fear, frustration, anger, self-loathing, despair, and helplessness. I call this horrible experience the Invasion of the Body Snatchers, because in such moments, it feels like your body has been completely taken over by your rage and panic. Waves of feeling rush through you like a tsunami, blotting out everything else. And these debilitating sensations make it practically impossible for you to respond calmly or rationally to the situation that triggers them. It's profoundly visceral, overwhelming, even terrifying. And when it happens to you, you know it.

Where the Body Snatchers Come From

What you might not know is that, although you may feel like you're going crazy, this response actually is completely normal. That is, it's a normal response for someone who has experienced chronic trauma as a child—such as the trauma of growing up with a bullying parent.

How Being Bullied Changes Your Brain

Complex trauma can actually interfere with your neurobiological development. Being abused or neglected by your parents or witnessing them mistreat one another can destroy your ability to regulate internal states; that means you can't process your feelings or calm yourself down. It also affects the areas of your developing brain that are responsible for dealing with danger, which impairs your ability to process fear.

What happens? Your reactions to perceived dangers—the fight/flight/freeze responses—are warped. At a physiological level, you respond to even minor fear triggers as if they were life-threatening situations. Your brain and body get confused and behave as if you're in danger of being annihilated. (If you think about it, that's probably exactly how you felt, as a child, when you were being pushed around, threatened, and mistreated by your parents.) And that's what causes the Invasion of the Body Snatchers.

The Body Snatchers' Bullying Message

You can think of the Body Snatchers as the most extreme version of the Inner Bully. They're yet another manifestation of the introject—that expression of the negative messages we got from our parents. The Body Snatchers communicate to us, wordlessly, one of the deepest and most damaging messages we got from the experience of being bullied by our parents: that the world is an unpredictable, dangerous place, and that our very existence is in immediate peril. That message almost always is triggered by something that reminds us, consciously or unconsciously, of the childhood experiences that caused our complex trauma in the first place—such as a confrontation with a bullying partner. Isn't that ironic? At the very moment we most want to be strong, to feel calm and in control, the Body Snatchers turn us into vulnerable, terrified, helpless wrecks.

You can think of the Body Snatchers as the most extreme version of the Inner Bully. They're yet another manifestation of the introject.

But you don't have to take it anymore. It's time to take your mind and body back!

Talking Back to the Body Snatchers

The Body Snatchers get to us at such a gut level that it may feel almost impossible to do anything about them. After all, as I've just explained, they're the result of neurobiological changes. What could we possibly do about that?

Well, you *can* do something about it. You can retrain your brain! It's a mind-over-matter process that's challenging but completely possible. You can deal with the Body Snatchers the same way you deal with your Inner Bully: by talking back. Over time, your brain and body will get the message you're sending, instead of the other way around.

Talking back to these bullies in your head (the Inner Bully and the Body Snatchers) prepares you for talking back to the bully in your relationship.

So the next time you feel the Body Snatchers trying to invade, here's what to do: First, take a deep breath. Then take another one—a long, slow, steady, easy breath. The reason for doing this is that, when our bodies think we're in danger, we get an adrenaline rush, our muscles tense, our hearts race, and every sense goes on alert. We get completely keyed up, ready to freeze, flee, or fight. Deep breathing is a great way to slow your body down and let it know that there isn't, in fact, any need for all that energy and alarm.

Then, as your body gets back to business as usual, talk back to the Body Snatchers. Reject the introject that's trying to take you back to the powerless place you inhabited as a child being bullied by your parents. Open up a space in your mind, and affirm the following, clearly and calmly:

"I'm safe and secure. I'm strong and whole. I'm an adult, and I can take care of myself. I'm not in any danger—the fear that I'm feeling right now is about the past, not the present. And whatever the outcome of the current situation that's triggering these old fears, I'm going to be absolutely fine. Whatever happens, I will survive and thrive!"

You'll be amazed at the effect this has! The Body Snatchers live on irrational fear, and as soon as you take it away from them, they shrivel up and die. They'll be back, of course. But when they return, just take your deep breaths and repeat this affirmation—and they'll disappear again. They'll come back less and less frequently, and when they do, they'll be weaker . . . and you'll be stronger.

Eventually you'll find that the anxiety you experience in triggering situations is the right size for the situation; that it's about the present, not the past; and that you're perfectly capable of facing it and moving forward. You can walk through your fear. You can do it scared!

THE BULLIES IN YOUR HEAD—AND THE BULLY IN YOUR RELATIONSHIP

You're going to find that talking back to these bullies in your head (the Inner Bully and the Body Snatchers) prepares you for talking back to the bully in your relationship: your date, partner, or spouse. The more you talk back to your inner bullies, the more your anxiety diminishes and your self-confidence grows. As this happens, you'll become increasingly less willing to put up with mistreatment—and more inspired to stand up for yourself.

And that's what you'll learn to do in the next chapter, where I introduce you to the A.R.T. Method.

CHAPTER SUMMARY

GET INTO THE SOLUTION!

➤ Your Inner Bully, or introject, says all kinds of terrible things about you—but none of them are true! They're just echoes of the negative messages you got growing up, from adults who were acting out their own pain. And you don't have to listen anymore.

➤ That overwhelming, visceral fear you sometimes feel when you're being bullied doesn't mean you're crazy or a coward. It's the effect of being raised in a bullying family—and you can get over it, and get on with your life!

➤ Talking back to your Inner Bully is an important first step toward talking back to all the other bullies in your life. Responding to the Inner Bully's negative messages with positive, affirming messages will build your confidence and self-esteem, making it easier for you to stand up to your bullying partner.

PART 2

The A.R.T. Method in Motion

The A.R.T. Method

Acknowledge, Reassess, Take Action

6

- Knowledge is power—and you've got it
- The simple three-step solution that will change your life
- *Acknowledging* the problem
- *Reassessing* your options
- *Taking action* to transform your relationship—and yourself

I am not a quitter. I will fight until I drop. That is a strength that is in my sinew. . . . It is just a matter of having some faith in the fact that as long as you are able to draw breath in this universe you have a chance.

—CICELY TYSON

Congratulations! You made it through the difficult first section of this book. In places, it may have been hard to keep reading; facing these harsh realities can sometimes be painful. But by staying with me, sticking it out, and doing it scared, you've opened up your eyes to the truth about bullying in romantic relationships. Knowledge is power, as the saying goes, and in gaining this important knowledge, you've armed yourself with some *very* powerful tools to liberate yourself from the bully in your house (and the bullies in your head), get back up on your own two feet, and get the life—and the love and respect—that you deserve.

DO YOU KNOW HOW MUCH YOU KNOW?

Let's take a quick look at all the knowledge you've gained.

In Chapter 1 you took a closer look at the ins and outs of being bullied—the behaviors involved, the way it affects you, and the psychological twists that keep you in unhealthy, unsatisfying relationships with partners who mistreat you. You also learned that the abuse you've been taking is *not your fault*.

In Chapter 2 you learned what bullies see from their perspective and reviewed the different types of bullies and styles of bullying. You learned about the rage of generations, the legacy of bullying behavior, and what happened to bullies to make them act the way they do. You also learned that, while there may be *explanations* for a bully's behavior, *there are no excuses*.

You've got all the guts, grace, and knowledge required to move forward and put the A.R.T. Method to work for you.

In Chapter 3 you learned about the coping mechanisms that bullied partners use, consciously and unconsciously, to manage the pain of living with a bully in the house. You also saw how dangerous it is for you to stay in denial.

In Chapter 4 you took a look at the bully in the bedroom. You saw what sexual bullying looks like, how it affects you and your relationship, and what you can do to transform your sex life from *bullied* to *blissful*.

In Chapter 5 you learned about your Inner Bully—the introject. You found out how the negative messages you received in your childhood are still playing in your head and controlling your choices. You also learned how talking back to the bullies in your mind is the crucial first step toward standing up to all the other bullies in your life.

This impressive body of knowledge you've gained gives you a solid foundation to stand on as you move forward. You know all about the bullying problem—backward, forward, upside down, and inside out. Now it's time for the solution: my A.R.T. Method.

DR. ANNE-RENÉE TESTA'S A.R.T. METHOD: WHAT IS IT?

The A.R.T. Method is a time-tested approach that I've developed over many years as a psychologist, helping hundreds of clients work through issues, face challenges, and surmount the obstacles that stand between them and the rewarding lives and loving relationships they deserve.

It's a no-nonsense, practical process that allows you to take stock of your situation, take responsibility for your part in the relationship (and let go of everything else), and take steps to change what you can change—your choices and your circumstances.

It's a simple but incredibly effective technique to transform your relationship with the bully in your house. It has just three steps:

1. Acknowledge the problem.
2. Reassess your options.
3. Take action to transform your life.

Sound simple? It is. Easy? Unfortunately, it's not.

But you already know that taking steps to face your fears and change your life requires time, effort, and courage. You know that anything worth having is worth working for. And you're absolutely up to the challenge. You've got all the guts, grace, and knowledge required to move forward and put the A.R.T. Method to work for you.

Before we move forward, let me tell you a little more about each of the A.R.T. Method's three steps, as a quick overview of the journey we'll be taking together.

Step 1: Acknowledge the Problem

It may sound obvious that you have to acknowledge that you have a problem, but really acknowledging the problem goes far beyond a quick admission that your relationship leaves something to be desired. As part of the A.R.T. Method, acknowledging the problem means completely letting go of denial, justification, and excuses; opening your eyes wide to just how serious the problem is; accepting responsibility for your part (and only your part!); and truly acknowledging, in your heart and your gut, that you deserve better and that it's time for things to change.

What other people think of us has only as much power over us as we let it have.

Step 2: Reassess Your Options

To reassess your options means to step back again and evaluate your situation from all sides. You'll take a fresh look at yourself, your partner, and your relationship—what works, what doesn't, what you bring to the party, what you need from a partner, what you want your life to look like, what you can reasonably expect from a relationship, and what you can and should provide for yourself.

As you do this, you're going to "right-size" your perceptions by managing the fear and negative thinking—the introject, the Inner Bully, the Body Snatchers—that have warped your ability to see your situation clearly until now. Today your right-sized vision will enable you to perceive the present and consider your options for the future in a calm, rational, realistic way.

Step 3: Take Action to Transform Your Life

Having acknowledged the problem and reassessed your options, you'll be truly ready and able to take the actions that will transform your life. In Chapter 9 I'll help you develop a strategy, a plan you can implement that will enable you to walk through your fear, stand up for yourself, speak out for what you want, and get the life and love you deserve.

THE THREE GUIDING PRINCIPLES OF THE A.R.T. METHOD

In the Introduction, I described three principles underlying the three steps of the A.R.T. Method. You can use these truths to guide and strengthen you as you follow the A.R.T. Method.

First, what other people think of us has only as much power over us as we let it have. We don't have to go anywhere to get away from our fear of the negative opinions and critical words that some bully is trying to impose on us. We can gain our freedom right this minute, without going anywhere, by reminding ourselves that people are welcome to their opinions about us, but we don't have to share their views. Ultimately, our opinions of *ourselves* are the only ones that really matter. As Eleanor Roosevelt once said, "Don't let other people tell you who you are." And as a friend of mine says, what other people think of me is none of my business, even if they try to make it mine. When we truly believe in ourselves, what other people believe about us becomes irrelevant.

We have nothing to lose—nothing, absolutely nothing—that's more valuable than our self-respect, our sense of self-worth.

Second, we have nothing to lose—nothing, absolutely nothing—that's more valuable than our self-respect, our sense of self-worth. It's true that standing up to bullies might make some waves, but without self-respect, we might sink altogether.

Time and again, I've found that it's always better to deal with the consequences of standing up for ourselves than to suffer the consequences of *not* standing up for ourselves. When we don't, we're treating ourselves as badly as the bullies treat us, basically agreeing with them that we deserve to be treated badly. And we absolutely don't—no one does. All people, including us, deserve to be treated with kindness, compassion, and respect.

Third, and most important, is the lesson that led me to face my bullies: When you're afraid, *make believe* you're brave. Do it scared, but do it! You'll

When you're afraid, make believe *you're brave. Do it scared, but do it!*

find, as I did, that the more you make believe you're brave, the more you'll discover how brave you really are and how many amazing things you can accomplish once you become willing to face your fears. That's what courage is, after all—not being fearless but taking action in spite of the fear.

READY, SET, . . . STEP FORWARD!

Now you know what's coming, and you're ready to get started. The next three chapters will guide you through each of the three steps in the A.R.T. Method with suggestions, exercises, and case studies to help you get started, stay on track, and take the steps toward the life and love that you deserve. As you continue reading, I invite you to think of me as your companion on each step of your journey to a new kind of life.

Acknowledge the Problem

7

No More Denial!

- The challenges of acknowledging the problem
- Applying the first guiding principle of the A.R.T. Method
- Ten questions that reveal the truth about your relationship

All truths are easy to understand once they are discovered; the point is to discover them.

—GALILEO GALILEI

You already know things aren't right in your relationship; that's why you're reading this book. And since you've learned more about bullying, you probably have a good general sense of *why* things aren't right. Now it's time to take the next big step: a really close, fearless, totally honest look at exactly *what* isn't working in your relationship.

With my guidance and encouragement, you'll be examining your partner's behaviors and your own—the destructive habits, failures to communicate, unrealistic expectations, denial, and codependent attitudes—that keep you both trapped in self-perpetuating cycles of hurt and anger. In other words, you're going to acknowledge the problem.

Now, I know this doesn't sound like much fun, but it won't be as tough as you think. And it's an absolute requirement if you want your relationship to improve. Until you really know where you stand—in your relationship and in your life—you won't be able move forward. Until you can see your denial and resistance to change, you'll remain stuck. You have to open your eyes wide to the truth about your relationship—the good, the bad, and the ugly—in order to move forward, because you deserve better.

HOW DO YOU ACKNOWLEDGE THE PROBLEM?

How exactly do you go about acknowledging the problem? How do you assess your relationship? If you're confused, I understand; relationships are so big and complicated, it's almost impossible to know where to start. If you've been in denial, for example, it's hard to know what you might be overlooking or hiding from yourself. If you've been with a bully for a long time, it may be difficult to see just how bad things are. Abusive behaviors and damaging conditions may seem completely normal to you, if you've been living that way for so many years.

You have to open your eyes wide to the truth about your relationship—the good, the bad, and the ugly—in order to move forward, because you deserve better.

It's also possible that you may be feeling so trapped, hurt, and numb that the relationship sometimes seems worse than it actually is. There's a way to improve your situation, a way out, but perhaps you can't see it because you're so overwhelmed. In that case, getting an accurate sense of your relationship can be genuinely challenging. But it can also be incredibly exciting!

If you were in my office, we'd be talking through issues together, face to face. We'd discuss every detail of your relationship, and I wouldn't let you get away with any denial or low self-esteem. But though we can't be in the same room together, I invite you to think of me as being right here with you. So that you can consider the same issues I discuss with my clients face to face, I'm going to ask you a series of questions designed to help you acknowledge the truth about your relationship. To get the most out of this process, you should answer these questions in writing, as thoroughly and honestly as possible. Through your answers, you'll acknowledge the problem. You'll also create the material needed for the work you'll do in the next two steps of the A.R.T. Method: reassessing your options (Chapter 8) and learning how to take action (Chapter 9).

Our opinions of ourselves are the only ones that really matter. When we truly believe in ourselves, what other people believe about us becomes irrelevant.

As you read this chapter, you'll consider each of the following questions. Answering these questions is the first step toward fully acknowledging the truth about your relationship. To help you answer, I'll explain them one at a time.

Questions About Your Relationship

- What does my partner say and do that makes me feel bad about myself?
- Which bully types and bullying behaviors from Chapter 2 remind me of my partner?
- What else does my partner do, or fail to do, that upsets me?
- How have I reacted to my partner's bullying behaviors in the past?
- What do I do, or fail to do, that upsets my partner?
- What do I consider to be my shortcomings in the relationship?
- Which of the coping mechanisms described in Chapter 3 do I use?

- How else do I allow the situation to continue or make it worse?
- Which of the Inner Bully's messages from Chapter 5 do I hear most often?
- What ideas do I have that keep me from speaking up or getting out?

When I say you will acknowledge the problem, I mean *really* acknowledge it, in your brain, your heart, and your gut. I mean you will understand and accept the problem and become completely convinced that it's time for a change.

APPLYING THE A.R.T. METHOD'S FIRST GUIDING PRINCIPLE

As you take the first step in the A.R.T. Method, I'd like you to draw strength and guidance from the first principle of the A.R.T. Method: what other people think of us has only as much power over us as we let it have. And you're not going to let other people's opinions have any power at all. As you answer the questions on the following pages, it's important to be true to yourself and to tell the truth of your experience. Remember, our opinions of ourselves are the only ones that really matter. When we truly believe in ourselves, what other people believe about us becomes irrelevant.

As you work, keep the following guidelines in mind:

- **When thinking about your relationship, trust your gut.** If you feel like you're being bullied, you are. What other people might think of you or how others might see your relationship isn't relevant here. Just stick with how it feels for you.
- **Don't be embarrassed or ashamed about your situation.** Don't judge yourself. You have nothing to be ashamed of! It's not your fault that you're being mis-

treated by your partner. But it *is* your responsibility to acknowledge it—and you're stepping up to take that responsibility. That's something to be proud of.

■ **Know your self-worth.** You can't measure it by how your bullying partner treats you or what other people say. Instead, you need to trust your deepest voice, the one that's even deeper than your introject. You need to trust the intuition that affirms that you are a human being, that you have a human right to be treated with respect and to live with dignity, that you deserve to love and be loved, and that you are lovable. That's the truth!

Are you ready? Then get a pen and a notebook, and start to acknowledge!

> *You need to trust the intuition that affirms that you are a human being, that you have a human right to be treated with respect and to live with dignity, that you deserve to love and be loved, and that you are lovable. That's the truth!*

TEN QUESTIONS TO REVEAL THE TRUTH ABOUT YOUR RELATIONSHIP

As you write out the answers to these questions, remember not to censor or edit yourself. Don't leave anything out because you think it's too small, sounds silly, or feels scary. Don't judge or second-guess yourself. Just write. Get your feelings down on the page. You'll come back and reevaluate your answers in the next two chapters.

Perhaps you feel that you already know the answers to all of these questions and aren't going to discover anything new by doing this exercise. I strongly encourage you to answer every question anyhow, for two reasons. First, you'll need all this material down on paper to complete the exercises in the following chapters. Second, and more important, the act of writing can produce some surprises. Often when we put pen to paper and just let go, all sorts of things come out that we didn't even know we were holding inside. Also, the very things we think we know all too well can end up looking very different on the page in black and white.

So just do it! I encourage you to write down in a personal journal as many answers to each question as you can come up with, and try for at least five items per question.

> **IMPORTANT!** As you answer these first few questions, don't feel bad about focusing on the negative aspects of your partner's personality and behavior. You're going to have a chance to focus on the positive aspects and attributes in the next chapter. And you're definitely going to take a look at your own assets and liabilities as well.
>
> These questions are designed to make sure you look at your relationship from all sides and come up with a thorough, balanced picture. So don't hold back here—or elsewhere.

What Does My Partner Say and Do That Makes Me Feel Bad About Myself?

Does your partner speak sharply or yell at you? Criticize or minimize your contributions to the household, your hobbies or habits? Complain about your appearance or micromanage your spending? Sulk, withhold sex, or give you the silent treatment? Try to think of whatever your partner repeatedly says and does to you that degrades, denigrates, and otherwise makes you feel bad about yourself—that is, bullying behaviors directed at you. Later on, you'll have an opportunity to write about the way your partner treats others and any other of your partner's problem behaviors; for this question, it is important to focus on yourself.

Think carefully, and write down any and all of your partner's behaviors that hurt your feelings, frighten you, insult or humiliate you, belittle or undermine you, or make you feel self-conscious or doubt yourself.

Which Bully Types and Bullying Behaviors Remind Me of My Partner?

Remember the types of bullies I described in Chapter 2. (If you need to refresh your memory, turn to that chapter, especially the box titled "Dr. Anne-Renée Testa's Guide to Bullies.") Perhaps you recognized your partner in one—or more—of those descriptions.

Ask yourself which of those types and behaviors remind you of your partner. Is he or she a Rage Bully or a Money Bully? A Name-Calling Bully or a Scorekeeping Bully? Maybe all of them? Maybe your partner is passive-aggressive on some days and a control freak on others, or combines guilt trips with silent treatments, or is a Rough Sex Bully and also a Cheater (see Chapter 4 to review the types of Sex Bullies).

A bullying behavior doesn't have to be extreme to be a real problem, nor does it have to damage you for it to be called bullying.

Think carefully, be completely honest with yourself, and write down all of the bully types that your partner resembles, all the bullying behaviors he or she engages in. Remember, a bullying behavior doesn't have to be extreme to be a real problem, nor does it have to damage you for it to be called bullying. Maybe your partner acts a certain way only occasionally or doesn't seem as extreme as the types described in Chapters 2 and 4. Maybe she yells "only" once or twice a month, or perhaps he nags you about your spending but doesn't actually control your bank account. Write it down anyway. It's important not to leave anything out in order to create the clearest and most accurate picture of your relationship that you can.

When you've finished, start a second list. Write down all of the bully types and bullying behaviors that remind you of your parents, teachers, guardians, older siblings, and other authority figures from your childhood. Indicate which person reminds you of which bullying type and behavior.

What Else Does My Partner Do, or Fail to Do, That Upsets Me?

Does your partner emotionally abuse or neglect your children? Is your partner rude to your friends or critical of your family members? Is he or she hostile toward colleagues, aggressive with strangers, enraged on the road, condescending or impatient with service workers? Maybe he doesn't call when running late, even though you've asked a thousand times. Or perhaps she makes decisions that affect you without asking for your input. Or doesn't give you holiday gifts, not even for your birthday. Or refuses to help out around the house. Or never bothers to thank you for the meal you made or the errand you ran.

Take an honest look, and then write down all the ways your partner acts toward the people you care about that make you uncomfortable, the things he or she does or fails to do that make you feel unappreciated or taken for granted, and the daily conduct that, though not necessarily bullying, upsets you or contributes to an atmosphere of tension, fear, or anxiety in your relationship and at home.

IMPORTANT! With the remaining questions, it's time to take a first look at your part in the relationship. Once again, please remember not to judge how you've acted in the past. Don't beat yourself up or blow things out of proportion. Instead, just focus your energy on taking this step toward a better future. Get the past down on paper, simply, realistically, and honestly, so you can make peace with it, get over it, and move beyond it.

How Have I Reacted to My Partner's Bullying Behaviors in the Past?

By now you've written enough to have a much clearer idea of how your partner bullies and mistreats you. Now explore how you have reacted to your partner's behaviors. I use the word *react* deliberately, because most victims of bullying *react*, rather than *respond*. That is, they act immediately, automatically, without pausing to think about their motivations or the consequences of their actions. Now, I'm not talking about acting on a good, trustworthy gut reaction or well-founded intuition; I'm talking about letting your fears, your old ideas, your Inner Bully take charge of your life. And we already know that nothing good will come from letting that happen!

What do you do when your partner bullies you? Do you yell or cry? Ignore or attempt to soothe and placate your partner? Do you apologize or retreat and wait for an apology from your partner? Do you quietly submit, thinking your partner knows better? Or do you submit, seething inside and hating your partner for treating you this way? Do you react differently depending on how you're feeling on a particular day, or depending on which bullying technique your partner uses?

Most victims of bullying react, *rather than* respond. *That is, they act immediately, automatically, without pausing to think about their motivations or the consequences of their actions.*

How does your partner react to your reactions?

Also ask yourself if you've ever tried to *respond* to your partner's bullying, instead of reacting to it. Have you ever tried to speak up for yourself, set a boundary, or request that your partner change his or her behavior toward you? Have you ever taken the time to think, in advance, about how to handle a situation with your partner, and then implemented that strategy when the situation arose?

If so, what did you do and say—and what happened?

What Do I Do, or Fail to Do, That Upsets My Partner?

Answering the next question involves a different line of thinking that you might find difficult, but I challenge you to rise to the occasion. Just for the moment, set aside the *way* your partner communicates, and focus on *what* he or she might be trying to say about your behaviors, habits, traits, or values.

It's not easy, but I encourage you to connect with your courage and take this opportunity to ask yourself whether any of your partner's concerns or criticisms of you might be somewhat legitimate, however imperfectly or inappropriately they're communicated. I am absolutely *not* excusing your partner for bullying you; there's no excuse for anyone to bully anyone else, no matter what. So please don't interpret this question to mean that you might deserve to be mistreated. Of course you don't! It is possible, though, that if you look beyond the inexcusable emotional abuse to find out what seems to set it off, you might find real issues, issues that are being obscured by your partner's inability to respond and communicate needs and feelings with you in healthy, adult ways.

If, for example, your partner is obsessive and controlling about the family expenses, constantly taking you to task about fiscal irresponsibility, take a moment to think about whether he or she might have a point. Is it possible that you're not always as financially responsible as you could be? Or if your partner throws temper tantrums, accusing you of being cold, insensitive, or inattentive, try to set aside impulses to deny and defend yourself, and really look at his or her claim. Might it be true that you're not as tender and responsive as you could be?

Of course, you might decide that, in fact, your partner's gripes have no basis in reality and that those shortcomings exist exclusively in his or her mind. But if there's a grain of truth to your partner's gripes—even if you think the things that bother your partner are ridiculous issues to be bothered by, even if they're the very attitudes and attributes on which you most pride yourself—I encourage you to get those issues down on paper. As you do so, remember that although your partner might be right in some cases, it's *always* wrong to react by bullying.

What Do I Consider to Be My Shortcomings in the Relationship?

Now set aside your partner's and anyone else's opinions about you, and take a good look at your *own* sense of what you bring to the relationship, how you come up short, in which areas you could stand to improve a little or a lot. What do you do that erodes trust or blocks intimacy? What behaviors of yours shut down communication or push your partner away? Are you impatient or intolerant of your partner's likes and dislikes, habits and quirks? Are you rigid and unwilling to compromise? Do you put your own wants ahead of the needs of a healthy relationship?

Be honest with yourself, and get it all down on paper.

IMPORTANT! You may be tempted to excuse yourself by pointing out how your partner's bad behavior makes you act the way you do—that you wouldn't be this way if only he or she weren't that way. This response would indicate that you're reacting, rather than responding, to your partner's inappropriate behaviors. You're using someone else's shortcomings as an excuse for your own. But excuses don't do anyone any good; moreover, you don't need to make excuses for yourself. You're perfectly capable of taking responsibility for yourself and your actions—and that's what answering these questions is helping you do.

Which Coping Mechanisms Do I Use?

Remember the coping mechanisms I described in Chapter 3. (If you need to refresh your memory, take some time to review that chapter.) Perhaps you recognized some of your own behaviors in one of those descriptions—or in more than one.

Which of those coping mechanisms might you be using, occasionally or constantly? What do you do to avoid facing the reality of your relationship and to manage the pain of living with a bully? Do you use denial or excuse making, rationalization or destructive distractions—or all of them? Do you tell yourself, "It's not like there's anything better out there," or, "I can't give up my lifestyle," or, "I stay for the kids," or, "I can fix it"?

Of course, it may be hard to tell whether you're doing this sort of thing or not; that's how denial works! But if you get really honest with yourself, you'll most likely be able to see the truth and put it down on the page.

How Else Do I Allow the Situation to Continue or Make It Worse?

The coping mechanisms discussed in Chapter 3 are not the only behaviors that keep us trapped in bullying relationships or compound our conflicts. What else do you do that allows this relationship to continue as it is—or that makes it worse?

When your partner bullies you, do you bully back? Do you act out in other ways, taking the passive-aggressive route? Do you threaten to end the relationship, knowing you won't follow through on your threat? Do you engage in revenge behaviors—anything from doing little things you know your partner won't like to having affairs? Do you talk your partner down to mutual friends, not to seek help and support, but in an attempt to turn them against your partner and get them on your side? Do you set secret deadlines for your partner to change, without asking for those changes or letting your partner know? Do you hold your partner to impossible standards, privately insisting on perfection, rather than improvement?

Write down the ways you sabotage and undermine your relationship or enable and exacerbate your relationship problems. There may be only a few—or there may be *quite* a few. Either way, don't judge yourself.

IMPORTANT! You may be tempted to use these questions as a chance to wallow in negative feelings, think about what a flawed person you are, or take all of the problems of the relationship onto yourself. Don't go there! Blaming everything on yourself is just as counterproductive and bad for you and your relationship as blaming it all on someone else.

Instead, try to keep perspective and balance as you answer these questions. Evaluate yourself, but don't judge. Just take a look and acknowledge your behavior. Acknowledge it, and know that this is just the starting point from which you can change and grow, improving on your shortcomings and expanding your strengths.

Which of the Inner Bully's Messages Do I Hear Most Often?

Remember the discussion about the Inner Bully (the introject) in Chapter 5, including the Inner Bully's eight basic messages. (If you need to refresh your memory, take some time to review that chapter.) I'm sure that some of those messages sounded familiar to you—probably all too familiar.

Which of those messages do you hear most often? Does your Inner Bully tell you that you're unattractive or that you're unlovable? Do you get the message that your opinions are wrong, that your feelings are irrelevant? What variations on those messages does your Inner Bully come up with? Get it all down on paper. Don't hold back, because in the next chapter, you'll learn to talk back and tell your Inner Bully, point by point, how wrong it is!

What Ideas Do I Have That Keep Me from Speaking Up or Getting Out?

It won't be easy to name the ideas that keep you from speaking up or getting out, mostly because the ideas I have in mind are ideas you might not even be aware you have. Like the messages you get from the Inner Bully, these are old notions and assumptions you've had for so long that you don't question or even notice them. These are the lies you're living out without even knowing it—fears, misconceptions, and subconscious beliefs about yourself, your partner, your relationship, and relationships in general. You may have to work hard and dig deep to discover them, but they're down there.

Here are some of the common ideas we have, often without being aware of it, that keep us from taking action to change our relationships with bullying partners:

- I don't deserve anything better than this.
- All relationships are like this.
- All men/women are like this.
- The kind of relationship I want isn't possible/doesn't exist.
- A bad relationship is better than no relationship.
- I know my partner doesn't treat me right, but I really love him/her.
- I'll never have the courage to stand up to my partner.
- Things are never going to change, no matter what I do.
- Anything I say or do will only make the relationship worse.
- It could be so much worse.
- I know it'll get better if I just wait it out.
- It's my fault; I just need to try harder.
- I'm not a desirable partner.
- I'm not attractive enough, intelligent enough, ———— enough.
- If I were a better spouse, he/she wouldn't treat me this way.
- If I leave this relationship, I'll be alone forever.
- No one else will ever love me.
- I couldn't handle being on my own.
- I can't survive without my partner.
- My partner will cut me off financially.
- I'll never be able to support myself.
- I'd feel like a failure if this relationship didn't work out.
- My family and friends won't approve of me rocking the boat.
- Shaking things up will be too hard on the kids.
- My partner will take the kids away from me and prevent me from seeing them.

- I'm too old to move on and start all over again.
- I've put too much work into this relationship to risk losing it.
- I'm afraid of making a mistake, doing the wrong thing, making the wrong decision.

These are just a few of the ideas, conscious or unconscious, that might have kept you from taking action to change your relationship.

Write down as many of these ideas as you can think of. Feel free to include items from this list. And remember, as you write, to include all of *your* ideas, assumptions, fears, and beliefs—even if they seem silly or obvious to you, and especially messages that are embarrassing to admit. If you think or feel it, write it down. It's all important for this process.

A LITTLE PAIN, A LOT OF GAIN!

Whew! You did it. Congratulations—you've just taken a huge step forward. If you've done a thorough job and answered all of these questions to the best of your ability, you've probably written a lot. That's an incredible accomplishment. You've uncovered, discovered, and truly acknowledged the problems in your relationship.

What you wrote may not be pretty to look at, but it's the truth. And as the saying goes, the truth will set you free. Now get ready to put all this effort of yours to use. Take your *next* step toward freedom: reassessing your options.

Reassess Your Options

You Deserve Better!

8

- Reassessing your options: "right-size" your perceptions
- Applying the second guiding principle of the A.R.T. Method
- Seven exercises that will give you a brand-new perspective on old issues

I have not ceased being fearful, but I have ceased to let fear control me. I have accepted fear as a part of life—specifically the fear of change, the fear of the unknown; and I have gone ahead despite the pounding in my heart that says: Turn back, turn back, you'll die if you venture too far.

—ERICA JONG

Now that you've acknowledged the problem, it's time to take your first big step toward addressing that problem; you're going to reassess your options. And because this is the A.R.T. Method, you can bet that reassessing your relationship with your partner isn't about going over the same old stuff in the same old way. Not a chance! Instead, it's about setting aside old, counterproductive ideas from your childhood and straightening out perceptions warped by the way you were treated growing up.

You're going to take a fresh look at your past, your present, and your future. You're going to get a new understanding of yourself, your partner, and your relationship. And you're going to "right-size" your perceptions, by managing the fear and negative thinking—the introject, the Inner Bully, the Body Snatchers—that have impaired your ability to see your situation clearly, up until now.

HOW DO YOU REASSESS YOUR OPTIONS?

So how, exactly, do you go about reassessing your options? It may sound complicated or mysterious, but trust me when I tell you that *you've got all the tools you need*. If you were with me in my office, I'd be able talk this through with you. I could call your attention to the moments when you unconsciously fall back into living out the lies of your childhood. I could let you know personally when you've started to let your Inner Bully run the show. But since we can't be together in person, I've designed a series of seven exercises that will give you a similar experience.

You'll be using all the material you generated by answering the questions in the previous chapter. That will be your starting point for these seven exercises, which will guide you to reassess your past, reevaluate your present situation, reassess your options for the future, and prepare you for the third and final step in the A.R.T. Method: taking action.

The following seven exercises will enable you to reassess your options fully. I'll discuss them one at a time in the coming pages.

Exercises for Reassessing Your Options

- Do I Deserve to Feel the Way My Partner's Bullying Makes Me Feel?
- Are My Partner's Bullying Behaviors Appropriate?
- Am I Ready to Forgive My Partner—and Be Free?

- Are My Reactions to My Partner's Bullying Appropriate?
- What Changes Am I Able and Willing to Make in My Relationship?
- Am I Ready to Stop Coping—and Start Changing?
- Am I Ready to Let Go of Old Ideas and Get a New Life?

All seven exercises are a big project to take on, but you can do it. And I'm 100 percent positive you'll be glad you did, no matter how hard it is. Doing these exercises will straighten out those distorted visions and views that erode your self-esteem, lower your self-worth, and keep you trapped in emotionally abusive relationships and toxic situations.

That's worth the effort, isn't it? You bet it is!

APPLYING THE A.R.T. METHOD'S SECOND GUIDING PRINCIPLE

As you take the second step in the A.R.T. Method, I'd like you to draw strength and guidance from the second principle of the A.R.T. Method: we have nothing to lose—nothing, absolutely nothing—that's more valuable than our self-respect, our self-esteem, and our sense of self-worth. As you do the following exercises, it's very important for you to remember that nothing else in your life is worth sacrificing your self-esteem, because nothing else you have or get can be of much value or good without it.

As you work, keep the following thoughts in mind:

- **You deserve to be treated with kindness, compassion, respect, and love—by yourself first and foremost.**
  Being treated with respect, and believing you're worthy of it, starts with treating yourself that way.

So beginning right now, keep your eyes and heart open, and keep asking yourself these fundamental questions: Am I treating myself the way I would treat someone I love and respect? Am I showing myself the kindness and compassion, the patience and tolerance I would show to my best friend, a valued teacher, a beloved partner? Am I conducting myself with the integrity and dignity of a self-respecting person? Remember, above all else, you deserve your own love and respect.

■ **What you're afraid of losing may not be worth keeping.** When you take steps to protect your self-esteem, to treat yourself with respect and require others to do the same, you might upset those who are accustomed to walking all over you. You might have to face angry or frightened reactions from people who are used to mistreating you and don't like your messing with the status quo. Ultimately, it might even turn out that the bullies in your life just can't handle your newfound self-esteem. They could leave, blaming you for the rupture, although you've done nothing more than ask to be treated decently.

This outcome might seem like a tragedy at first, but think about it this way: if you lose a relationship because the other person doesn't think you deserve even basic kindness, courtesy, and respect, is that really such a loss? I don't think so!

■ **Almost anything that we put ahead of preserving and protecting our sense of self-worth we will lose— whether relationships, friendships, family, or career.** That's because, without self-respect, self-esteem, and a healthy sense of self-worth, we won't be in any shape to show up for the other things in our lives. We must put our own emotional well-being first, so that we can nurture, maintain, and tend to everything else.

Are you ready to take a fresh look at your life, get a new perspective on your relationship, and reassess your options? Then let's do it!

SEVEN EXERCISES TO HELP YOU REASSESS YOUR OPTIONS

In Chapter 7, I advised that as you do the exercises, you shouldn't censor or edit yourself. What I said about answering those questions goes for these exercises as well. Also, do your best not to skip any of the steps, even if some of them seem ridiculous, frightening, or redundant.

You might be tempted to take shortcuts, but doing these exercises as they're described here is a great way to reassess—with your heart as well as your brain—all of the important points from the earlier chapters. The seven exercises give you a way to experience, on an instinctive, gut level, what I've been telling you all along: that you deserve to be treated with love and respect, and that you don't have to accept abusive behavior or stay stuck in a bullying relationship.

> *We have nothing to lose that's more valuable than our self-respect, our self-esteem, and our sense of self-worth.*

Do I Deserve to Feel the Way My Partner's Bullying Makes Me Feel?

In the previous chapter, you asked yourself, "What does my partner say and do that makes me feel bad about myself?" Then you wrote down all the bullying behaviors to which your partner subjects you.

Now go back to your responses to that question, and look at them from another angle. This time, ask yourself, "Do I really deserve to feel the way my partner's bullying makes me feel?" This question may seem silly at first. After all, you've already acknowledged that you don't deserve to feel that way. Of course you don't! Yet assuming you've stayed in an emotionally abusive relationship for some time, even if you *consciously* know you don't deserve ill treatment, your actions indicate that you *unconsciously* think you do deserve it. That's what we're working to change.

As you reflect on these ideas, complete the following steps of this first exercise:

1. Review your list of the bullying behaviors you've been subjected to. For each behavior you listed, ask yourself how it really makes you feel. Next to each behavior on your list, write your feelings—and be specific. Instead of settling for a general phrase like "It hurts my feelings" or "I get angry," dig deeper. Does a particular bullying behavior make you think you're going crazy? Do you feel humiliated? Perhaps you fear for your physical safety or want to scream and cry from frustration. Whatever the case, write it down. Get it all out on paper. It won't be fun to think about this stuff, but there's a very good reason for doing it—which you'll understand in just a minute.

2. Look back over your lists of the bullying behaviors and how they make you feel. Really take it in. Let yourself truly see and feel how deeply you're affected by the way your partner bullies you.

3. Close your eyes, take a deep breath, and imagine someone you really love—a sibling, a best friend—being subjected to these same bullying behaviors. Imagine the person you love being made to feel the way you feel when you're treated that way. It's an awful thought, isn't it? Most likely, you feel terribly sad, terribly angry, or both, just thinking about it. I'll bet you'd do just

about anything to protect your loved one from having to experience that kind of situation, right?

If so, why would you think it's OK for *you* to be treated that way? My point is that it's not! It's not OK for *anyone* to be treated that way, including you.

Reassess the Situation. It's time to get rid of the old idea that you don't deserve compassion, consideration, and respect—the very things you instinctively know are due to those you love. And it's time to start including yourself in the category of people you love. The next part of this exercise will help you get started:

It's time to start including yourself in the category of people you love.

1. Pull out your lists of your partner's bullying behaviors and how they make you feel.
2. As you try to think of yourself as someone you love, someone who deserves to be treated with love, reassess each item on your list of feelings. Consider each of the bullying behaviors one at a time, and recognize that no one, including you, should ever have to feel the way that bullying makes you feel.
3. Beside each description of how you feel, write how you want to feel instead. Describe whatever feelings you want to experience—being loved, respected, adored, admired, protected, cared for, treasured, whatever. If your self-esteem falters, just think of what you know your best friend or sibling or other loved one deserves to feel, and write that down.

When you're done, study your list, and affirm for yourself that you absolutely, positively deserve to feel all those good things. And you absolutely, positively deserve to have people in your life who treat you in ways that let you feel all those things. That's the truth: you don't deserve to feel the way your partner's bullying behaviors make you feel. And doing this exercise should help you to get that, in your gut.

Are My Partner's Bullying Behaviors Appropriate?

In Chapter 7 you asked yourself, "Which bully types and bullying behaviors from Chapter 2 remind me of my partner?" Then you wrote down all the bully types and behaviors that remind you of your partner. You also listed authority figures from your childhood (parents, guardians, teachers, and so on) and indicated which bully types and bullying behaviors reminded you of these people.

Now you're going to go back to those responses and look at them from another angle. Ask yourself, "Are my partner's—and others'—bullying behaviors appropriate? Do I really deserve to be treated that way?" Again, you're probably perfectly aware on a conscious level that bullying behaviors are not appropriate, but this exercise is designed to help change your *unconscious* ideas about such behaviors. Let's get started:

You don't deserve to feel the way your partner's bullying behaviors make you feel.

1. Reread that list of authority figures, bullying types, and behaviors they subject you to. Really take it in. Think about how you were treated by the bullies in your life as you were growing up. Think about the way your partner treats you now. Consider each one of the bully types and bullying behaviors you've written down and what it looks like in action.
2. Close your eyes, take a deep breath, and visualize yourself as a small child being subjected to these bullying

behaviors. Imagine a vulnerable, innocent child being mistreated, pushed around, punished, neglected, and bullied the way you were by your family or are by your partner. Imagine a little boy or girl feeling the way you do when you're bullied; imagine the child feeling degraded and less than human. It's terrible to think about, isn't it? And it's so crystal clear when we look at it this way—how very wrong it was for the people we grew up with to treat our child selves the way they did.

I hope you can also see, and really feel, in your heart and gut, that it's every bit as wrong for your partner—or anyone else—to treat you that way today. Though we're adults now, inside we're still those vulnerable, innocent children that we once were. So why would we decide it's OK for people to treat us badly now, just because we're older? That doesn't make any sense. But unfortunately, one generation does it to the next until one person wakes up and says, "Enough!" You can be that person.

Reassess the Situation. It's time to get rid of the old idea that bullying treatment is anything but completely and totally unacceptable and unjustifiable. It's time to affirm that you don't now, never did, and never will deserve to be bullied. Follow these steps to reassess:

1. Pull out the list of the bully types and bully behaviors that remind you of your partner and the list of feelings these behaviors bring up.
2. Thinking of yourself as a child, reassess each item on these lists. Imagine yourself as a child being subjected to each bullying behavior. Recognize how completely inappropriate that behavior is. Recognize that no one, including you, should ever be treated that way, for any reason. You deserve better. Also recognize that today

you have power to take care of yourself that you didn't have as a child—and the responsibility to do so.

3. Next to each item on your list of feelings, write down how you want *and deserve* to be treated instead. Next to each type of behavior, make a note of what you want instead. For example, if your partner expresses frustration with you by shouting or giving you the silent treatment, write down how you want him or her to express frustration instead, noting the respect with which such feelings should be communicated.

   If you have any doubts about how you deserve to be treated, think about how much kindness you would show to a little child, how much respect and consideration you would show to the people you love most. Remind yourself that you deserve just the same.

4. When you're done, study your lists of what you want, and affirm for yourself that you absolutely, positively *deserve* to be treated with kindness, consideration, and respect. Also, affirm that you absolutely, positively deserve people in your life who will treat you this way.

That's the truth: your partner's bullying behaviors are *not* appropriate, and you do *not* deserve to be treated that way. I've said it before many times, but now that you've done this exercise, you should be able to believe it in a new way.

Am I Ready to Forgive My Partner—and Be Free?

In the previous chapter, you did a lot of writing about the way your partner treats you and others, as you answered the first three questions:

■ What does my partner say and do that makes me feel bad about myself?

- Which bully types and bullying behaviors remind me of my partner?
- What else does my partner do, or fail to do, that upsets me?

Now you'll return to your answers to those first three questions and examine your partner's hurtful behaviors, both bullying and nonbullying, from another angle. Ask yourself a truly challenging question: "Can I forgive my partner—without excusing his or her bullying—in order to be free and move forward?"

Follow these steps:

1. Review the answers you gave, in Chapter 7, to the first three questions. Reread everything you wrote about how your partner bullies you and others, the different ways he or she mistreats you, your friends and family members, colleagues, and strangers.
2. Consider the origin and causes of these behaviors. Begin by thinking about your partner's family and the environment in which he or she was raised. Write down everything you can remember that your partner has told you and everything that you've observed that might have shaped your partner's personality. Then consider your partner's insecurities, vulnerabilities, and fears, including the ones your partner won't admit or isn't aware of. Write those down as well.

> *Your partner's bullying behaviors are* not *appropriate, and you do* not *deserve to be treated that way.*

Reassess the Situation. Become willing, just for the moment, to set aside the anger, hurt, blame, and shame you understandably feel about your partner. Then, with as much compassion and love as you can summon, review the list you just made.

As you do so, try to think of your partner in the same way you thought of yourself in the previous exercise: envision your partner as an innocent child who, like you, has been bullied and abused. See him or her as a fragile, feeling human being whose perceptions and behaviors, like yours, are warped by a destructive force, governed by a relentless Inner Bully. Remember what I explained in Chapter 2: both you and your partner are affected by the rage of generations—you're just manifesting it in very different ways.

1. Allow yourself to see that, like you, your partner is living out the lies of his or her childhood. As you know, this means living with pain and fear, often without even being aware of it. You should be able to see without out much difficulty that your partner's bullying behaviors are the way that he or she unconsciously acts out that pain and fear.

   Of course, acting out is an entirely inappropriate way for your partner to deal with those feelings, but this exercise should help you see those behaviors in a different light. Also, it should make something else perfectly clear: your partner's bad behaviors have absolutely nothing to do with you. Instead, your partner's mistreatment of you and others is only about the hurt that he or she feels, the old lies that he or she is living out. Meditate on this, and really let it sink in: You're not responsible for the bullying. You're not the cause of it. It's not a reflection of you, or even of your partner's real feelings for you.

You're not responsible for the bullying. You're not the cause of it. It's not a reflection of you, or even of your partner's real feelings for you.

This means that it's time for you to stop blaming yourself, in any way, for the way your partner treats you. Let go of all of that blame and guilt. From now on, the only thing you're going to take responsibility for is the way you behave. You accept responsibility for responding rather than reacting and for treating yourself with love and respect.

Optional: If you find this exercise useful, I strongly encourage you to try it on any and all of the other bullies in your life, past and present, starting with the other people on your list of authority figures. Do it the same way, except replace "partner" with "father" or "sister" or "coach." You'll be amazed at how forgiving these people will liberate you.

2. With all this in mind, put the lists of your partner's bullying behaviors next to the list of his or her childhood experiences and present-day issues. Take a deep breath, and look over these pages. See how your partner is suffering from the rage of generations. Then take another deep breath, and to the best of your ability, summon a feeling of forgiveness for your partner.

   This might feel incredibly difficult, even impossible. But remember, you're not excusing your partner's behavior. In fact, it's almost the opposite. In this instance, forgiveness is about accepting that your partner's behavior is completely inexcusable—and letting go of the anger anyway. Why? Because hanging on to anger about it will help neither you nor your partner. But when you let go of it, you're letting go of those feelings of anger, hurt, blame, and shame that have kept you trapped by the rage of generations all this time. When you forgive your partner, you're setting yourself free.

When you forgive your partner, you're setting yourself free.

Of course, though you may achieve a sense of forgiveness today, your feelings of hurt, blame, and anger will probably come back. And that's OK—you're only human. But from now on, when those feelings come up, just remember this exercise. Then, instead of indulging your hurt, blame, and anger, take a deep breath, and summon a sense of forgiveness for your partner again, knowing that it's your ticket to freedom.

3. Finally, make a list of all your partner's good qualities. Which of your partner's personality traits do you love? Which attributes do you admire? Which talents and accomplishments do you respect? Write down everything you like about your partner, big and small, and the best aspects of your relationship and life together.

IMPORTANT: In the remaining exercises, you'll take another look at *your* behaviors. Remember, you won't be judging, just evaluating. So be as honest as you possibly can be—and avoid beating yourself up. Keep in mind that you're looking at how you've reacted *in the past*—and reassessing those behaviors. You'll be taking a new look at anything you've done in the past that didn't work and you don't have to do anymore. This is your chance to make a change.

Are My Reactions to My Partner's Bullying Appropriate?

In the previous chapter, you asked yourself, "How have I reacted to my partner's bullying behaviors in the past?" When you answered that question, you created a list of all the ways you react to your partner's bullying. Now go back to that list, and look at your responses from another angle. Ask yourself, "Were those reactions appropriate? Were they effective?"

To prepare yourself for reassessing your options, take these steps:

1. Look over the list of ways you've reacted, in the past, to your partner's bullying behaviors. Remember, don't judge; just evaluate.
2. Beside each reaction on that list, write down what happened. What did your partner do? Was that response the effect you wanted or expected?

Remember that expectations can be lethal when they're not based in reality. You might also ask whether your expectations for your partner were realistic, given who he or she is.

Reassess the Situation. Before you begin to reassess, try to set aside completely any arguments about how badly your partner might have been acting. It's probably true that he or she was acting inappropriately, and you might be inclined to justify your reactions. But just for the moment, forget about how your partner acted, and focus exclusively on you.

Here's how to reassess the situation:

1. Look over your answers and ask yourself whether your reactions were appropriate. Are you proud of the way you behaved? If you were in that situation again, would you make the same choices? You may well find that sometimes you can answer in the affirmative, and that's wonderful. But it's just as likely that you're not comfortable with or proud of your behavior and would do it differently if given the chance. If so, that's completely understandable. In situations where you're being bullied by your partner, it's very difficult to respond rather than react. But it's *not* impossible, and you're in the process of learning how to do just that—right now.

It's also possible that your partner would have kept up the bullying behavior and reacted badly no matter what you had said or done. But his or her bad behavior doesn't justify your own bad behavior.

You can't control anyone else's actions, but you *can* be responsible for your own. As you take responsibility for your own actions, it gets easier and easier to see that your partner's inappropriate behavior is not your responsibility. So make a decision that from now on, you're going to do your best to respond in a way you can be proud of, showing respect and consideration for yourself and your partner, no matter how your partner acts.

2. Go back to your list, and beside each item, write down how you'd like to act in the future if a similar situation arises. In each situation, imagine that you are standing up for yourself calmly but firmly. Be strong and confident in the knowledge that your partner's bullying has nothing to do with you, that you're not the cause of your partner's bad behavior (no matter what he or she says), and that you deserve to be treated with respect and consideration. Let this knowledge guide what you envision as the appropriate response, and write each one down. Don't worry about how your partner might react—just about how you want to respond.

3. When you're finished, reread the list of what you intend to do. Affirm to yourself that you can and will conduct yourself according to these new ideals, to the very best of your ability, each time such a situation arises again in the future.

What Changes Am I Able and Willing to Make in My Relationship?

In the previous chapter, you asked yourself, "What do I do, or fail to do, that upsets my partner?" You listed your attributes and attitudes—behaviors, habits, traits, values, and so on—that your partner takes issue with. You also asked yourself, "What do I consider to be my shortcomings in the relationship?" Setting aside your partner's opinions, you wrote down the ways in which, as a partner, you fall short of your own ideals.

Now go back to those responses, and look at them from another angle. Ask yourself, "Are these attitudes and attributes that I can change? If so, am I willing to make such changes?" To do that, follow these steps:

1. Begin by taking a close look at your responses to the questions about what upsets your partner and how you feel you fall short as a partner. Don't beat yourself up for what's there. Just take in each item on the list.

2. Give some thought to each one of these attitudes and attributes. Consider how the habits were formed, what motivates the behaviors, how you developed the values, when certain traits became part of your personality, and so on. Think about how each one serves you, whether it helps or harms you, and how it affects your relationship and your life in general. Note your thoughts next to each item on your list of responses. Be as honest and thorough as you possibly can.

Reassess the Situation. Remember, when looking at qualities in yourself that you dislike, don't be too hard on yourself. This is your opportunity to reassess how you've been living, so you can take action to make changes. The person you've been in the past doesn't have to be the person you will be in the future!

Also keep in mind that not every item on these lists will be a negative. Just because your partner doesn't approve of the way you balance the family checkbook, for example, that doesn't mean there's anything wrong with the way you balance the checkbook. And if you wish you were better at, say, expressing affection, that doesn't mean the way you do it now is bad, just that there's room for improvement—and that you want to improve.

Finally, understand that there's a difference between *who we are* and *what we do*—between our character and our behavior. We can change our behaviors, but we can't really change our personalities. For example, if you're naturally introverted, that's part of your character, and there's nothing wrong with it. There's no reason on earth you should become an extrovert—and no way you could. But if your partner is a very social person who wants to go out every weekend, you might consider making compromises, modifying your behavior, and joining your partner occasionally for a night on the town. Or suppose you're a tidy person by nature, and you can't and don't want to "loosen up" about keeping your home clean and orderly. Your partner might be more lackadaisical about tidiness and order. You can find ways to compromise without being made to feel ashamed about your character or pressured to change who you are. You could work together to designate areas of the home where your partner could make messes without intrusion, or you might create a cleaning schedule that you can agree upon and share.

Know the difference between what you can change and what you can't—and make sure that both you and your partner understand and respect those differences.

However you decide to handle problem areas, it's tremendously important for you to know the difference between what you *can* change and what you *can't*—and make sure that both you and your partner understand and respect those differences.

Now let's get started with reassessing your options:

1. Pull out your list of things you do or fail to do that upset your partner. For each item on that list, ask yourself these questions:

   ■ Is that attribute or attitude one that you're *able* to change? If not (if it's part of who you are, rather than a behavior), just make a note of that.

   ■ If it's something you *can* change, is it something you're *willing* to change? The answer may be no, and that's fine. You may feel strongly attached to attitudes and attributes that serve you well; if so, you may be committed to maintaining them, whatever your partner's opinion. When that's the case, write down why the particular behavior, habit, trait, or value is important to you, how it works for you, and why you don't want to change it.

   ■ If it's an attribute or attitude you *are* willing to work on, what might a compromise in this area of your life look like? Write down a couple of ideas for how you might modify this particular behavior, habit, trait, or value so that you and your partner can both be comfortable with it.

2. Next, turn to the list of ways in which you feel you fall short as a partner. For each item on that list, ask these questions:

   ■ What is the *opposite* of the shortcoming? Write down what the opposite, ideal attitude or attribute would look like. If you feel you're too sensitive to criticism, for example, perhaps the *opposite* would be something like "Be completely open to feedback, always willing consider others' opinions and suggestions about me with an open mind." Or if you think you don't spend enough quality time with your family, the opposite might be "Achieve a perfect balance between home and work, devoting undivided attention to partner and children during the times we set aside to be together."

- ■ What would the realistic, attainable version of that ideal be? Write that beside the description of the ideal behavior.
- ■ What can I do to work toward the realistic idea? Write down a couple of steps you can take toward putting the realistic version into action.

3. When you're finished, reread these lists. You have a new awareness regarding which of your attitudes and attributes are problematic for you and/or your partner, and what you want to do about them.

Affirm that each day, with perseverance and patience, you will grow toward the attainable ideals you've determined for yourself as a partner.

Affirm to yourself that you will respect the aspects of your character that you can't change and honor your commitment to the attitudes, attributes, and actions that work for you. Affirm that in your relationship you will work on making compromises and modifying behaviors when appropriate, in the spirit of partnership and for the good of the relationship. Finally, affirm that each day, with perseverance and patience, you will grow toward the attainable ideals you've determined for yourself as a partner.

IMPORTANT: What the following exercises ask you to do might feel especially challenging—even more than the other exercises in this very challenging chapter. These exercises can be emotionally intense and labor-intensive, because you may need to look at a lot of painful issues and write a lot. But you're up to the challenge. And I promise you that you're really going to reap the benefits of the effort you put in.

Am I Ready to Stop Coping—and Start Changing?

In the previous chapter, you asked yourself, "Which of the coping mechanisms described in Chapter 3 do I use?" You listed the coping behaviors you employ in your relationship. You also asked yourself, "How else do I allow the situation to continue or make it worse?" You wrote down the ways that you sabotage and undermine your relationship or enable and exacerbate your relationship problems.

Now you'll go back to your responses to those questions and look at them from another angle. Ask yourself now, "Am I ready to give up those behaviors in order to open myself and my relationship to change?" To answer, take these two steps:

1. Pull out your list of coping mechanisms you use and your list of behaviors that maintain the toxic status quo in your relationship or make things worse.
2. Considering each item separately, write how you use each behavior or mechanism—in which situations you act that way, what feelings or events set you off, and what exactly you do to cope. If one of your coping mechanisms is excuse making, for example, write down the situations that lead you to make excuses—to others or to yourself—for your partner's bullying behaviors, how those situations make you feel, who you make excuses to, and what sort of excuses you make. Or if you tend to be passive-aggressive with your partner, acting out indirectly in response to your partner's bullying, record the kinds of occasions and the ways you get passive-aggressive.

Reassess the Situation. You already know, in a general way, that these behavior patterns aren't benefiting anyone—not you, not your partner, and not your relationship. But

now you'll take a closer look at just how counterproductive
they really are and why you need to set them aside, however
painful it might be, in order to open up yourself and your
relationship to change. Here's how:

1. Turn back to your lists, look at each coping mechanism or problematic behavior, and ask yourself what
   happens when you act that way. How does it make
   you feel? What effect, if any, does it have on your
   partner? What effect does it have on the situation
   in the moment? How does it erode your relationship
   over time? Write down your answers in your personal
   folder.

2. Reread your answers in the previous step. More than
   likely, you'll see that these mechanisms and behaviors
   aren't making things better and, in most cases, are
   making things much worse.

   If you've been honest and thorough, you should
   begin to understand, not just with your head but
   in your heart and gut as well, two points I made in
   Chapter 3: First, people use coping mechanisms to
   deal with the pain of being in bullying relationships,
   instead of just leaving their emotionally abusive partners, because they unconsciously believe they deserve
   to be treated badly and to feel bad. Second, coping,
   acting out, and enabling behaviors don't fix or solve
   any problems. Instead, by numbing, denying, defer-
   ring, shutting out, or acting out on the true pain of
   being bullied, these behaviors make it possible for the
   bullied partner to stay in a destructive relationship,
   suffering more and more damage.

3. With these thoughts in mind, reread your answers
   again. Recognize that by coping or suffering patiently,
   you haven't been sparing yourself from pain at all;
   rather, you've been staying stuck and stunted where

you're most likely to continue being hurt. By coping, you haven't been doing your partner or your relationship any good. Instead, you've been enabling your partner to continue acting in a way that's disrespectful and destructive for *both* of you. And you've been allowing the relationship to continue deeper and deeper into an unhealthy groove.

Don't beat yourself up about any of this. If you've been coping, repressing, and denying up to this point, that's totally understandable. You've been in a lot of pain, and you didn't have any other tools to deal with it. But now you do! Starting today, you don't have to live that way anymore. You're now truly ready to give up these behaviors—and open up yourself and your relationship to change.

As you do the rest of this exercise, draw on what you now know in your heart and gut from doing the previous exercises in this chapter: *You don't deserve to be bullied, you don't deserve to feel bad, and you don't have to live in denial or act out anymore, because now you have the tools to stand up for yourself and address your partner's bullying behaviors directly.*

4. Once more, go back to your responses: which coping behaviors you use; when, why, and how they manifest; and what effect they have on you, your partner, and your relationship. For each item on the list, ask yourself if you really want to continue these behaviors, knowing how counterproductive and even destructive they are. Are you willing to let them go and open yourself up to the possibility of a relationship in which you're treated with love and respect, instead of one in which you're bullied and abused?

5. Take a moment to really experience your willingness to make a change in this behavior. Then, beside each behavior or mechanism, write down what you'd like to

do and how you'd like to act instead—the new, healthy model.

6. Finally, affirm that from now on, you can and will follow this new, healthy model, instead of the old, destructive one. Destructive behaviors die hard, but you *will* move forward toward a new kind of relationship and a new way of living, instead of staying in old patterns that you know don't work.

You've given up coping and started the process of changing—for the better!

Am I Ready to Let Go of Old Ideas and Get a New Life?

In the previous chapter, you asked yourself, "Which of the Inner Bully's messages from Chapter 5 do I hear most often?" You listed all the negative, destructive thoughts and attitudes that are the products of your introject. You also asked yourself,

You're rejecting the introject and saying good-bye to the lies you've lived by in the past.

"What ideas do I have that keep me from speaking up or getting out?" You listed the old ideas and assumptions—about yourself, your partner, and relationships in general—that keep you from taking action to make changes in your relationship.

Now you'll go back to your responses to those questions and look at them from another angle. Ask yourself, "Knowing that these old ideas and messages from my Inner Bully simply aren't true, am I ready to reject them and embrace the truth?" To answer, follow these steps:

1. Pull out the list of messages from your Inner Bully and the list of your old ideas and assumptions.
2. Consider each item, and write down the origins of each idea or message. Who first sent you the message that

you're unattractive, that you aren't as good as other people, or that your feelings aren't important? Where did you first get the idea that a bad relationship is better than no relationship, or that this is just how partners treat each other?

The Inner Bully's messages have been like a warped and dirty window through which you've seen the world. Now you've taken charge of your present, taken responsibility, and washed that window sparkling clean; you can finally begin to see things as they really are.

Also write down how each of these ideas and messages affects you. When does it come up? How does it make you feel? How do you act as a result of having each idea or message?

3. Review your answers. Take a moment to really absorb how much damage and violence you've been doing to yourself by hanging onto these ideas and listening to these messages. *You deserve so much better.* I really hope you can feel that now, in your heart and gut.

You know now that the messages your Inner Bully sends you are just not true. They're the voices of people from your past who were caught up in the cycles of the rage of generations. And you're not going to listen to them anymore. Remember, the ideas you have that hold you back and keep you from taking action to make changes are old ideas that came to you from people who were in pain—and probably were trapped by their own destructive, self-defeating thoughts in unhealthy relationships. These ideas aren't your ideas. They don't work. And you're not going to hold onto them anymore!

Reassess the Situation. To reassess, go back to your list of messages from your Inner Bully.

1. Taking one message at a time, draw a line through it, to signify that you reject it. You know it's not true, you know it doesn't work, and it's not going to be any part of your life from now on.

2. Beside each crossed-out item, write down the new, true, positive, healthy message or idea that you're going to live by from now on.

3. Affirm that, from now on, you can and will listen only to these new, healthy messages and be directed by these new, healthy ideas instead of the old, destructive ones. You're rejecting the introject and saying good-bye to the lies you've lived by in the past. You're moving forward into a new way of living that builds your self-esteem and nurtures your self-worth. You're embracing the healthy model, which enables you to treat yourself with love and respect and insist that others do, too—because that's what you deserve.

REASSESS YOUR THINKING

Bravo! You've just completed a *very* challenging set of exercises. In doing so, you've given yourself an amazing gift: the chance to live in a whole new way.

As you've probably realized by now, what you've been reassessing is your thinking. The work you've done in this chapter is about throwing out the old ideas, distorted perceptions, and negative attitudes forced on you during your childhood. It's about breaking free from the rage of generations and shutting out the destructive messages from your Inner Bully.

The Inner Bully's messages have been like a warped and dirty window through which you've seen the world. Now you've taken charge of your present, taken responsibility, and washed that window sparkling clean; you can finally begin to see things as they really are.

You can see your past for what it was, accept it for what it was, and put it behind you.

You can see yourself as you are: a loving, self-respecting person who's working to follow the healthy model, and who deserves to be treated with love and respect.

And you can see your future for what it is: a bright, wide-open world full of options and opportunities that you can move toward with strength and confidence. And that's just what you're going to do in the next chapter, as you take the third step of the A.R.T. Method: taking action to transform your life.

Take Action 9

Do It Scared!

- Why wait? The time to act is now
- Applying the third guiding principle of the A.R.T. Method
- Six strategies for transformative action you can use today

When we are no longer able to change a situation, we are challenged to change ourselves.

—VIKTOR FRANKL

This is it! You've acknowledged the problem and reassessed your options, so there's nothing left for you to do but take action. The prospect of putting into practice all that you've just learned might be daunting. You might find yourself making all kinds of excuses for why you can't get started until tomorrow, next week, next month, after the holidays, after the family reunion, or after the kids leave for college. But you've already shown what an incredibly brave, strong person you are by making a decision to change and persevering through the challenging exercises in Chapters 7 and 8. You don't need to make excuses, because you can do this.

Why wait? You have everything you need to start taking the actions that will transform your life. By acknowledging the problem, as you did in the first step of the A.R.T. Method, you accepted—in your heart and gut, in black and white—that there really is a problem. By doing the second step of the A.R.T. Method, you learned that the situation doesn't have to stay the way it is; you have options, and you deserve better. And you've come to understand that you have the power to change and the responsibility to yourself, as someone you love and respect, to not spend another day accepting emotionally abusive treatment from a bullying partner. Trust me: you're completely ready, even if you don't feel as if you are.

Don't panic; you don't have to change everything all at once. In fact, you shouldn't even try. But, as Chinese philosopher Lao-tzu says, even the journey of a thousand miles begins with a single step. For you, that journey has already started. It began the moment you first picked up this book. And you've already taken all kinds of transformative action by reading the book and taking the first two steps of the A.R.T. Method, as you did in the previous two chapters.

The third step of the A.R.T. Method is just the next step in your journey. You're already well on your way, so why wait? The time to take action is now.

HOW DO YOU TAKE ACTION TO TRANSFORM YOUR LIFE?

So exactly how do you take action to transform your life? You just do it. Don't believe it's that simple? Trust me; it really is.

Think about how simple it is to make a sandwich. What could be easier? You know where the bread is, where you keep the peanut butter and jelly, which drawer the knives are in, and which shelf the plates are on. You could do it with your eyes closed. And why? Because you have all the ingredients, all the tools, and all the information you need, and you're so confident about your ability that you do it without a second thought.

Well, because you've read this book and worked the first two steps of the A.R.T. Method, today you have all the ingredients, all the tools, and all the information you need to take the third and final step of the A.R.T. Method. Taking action to transform your life is like making that sandwich; all it takes is common sense to apply the knowledge you've gained from doing the work, plus the confidence to just do it.

If you were meeting with me in my office, I'd be able to talk through each action you need to take in your relationship with your partner. I'd be able to strategize with you about how to apply your knowledge to each situation, and I'd cheer *You have the power to change.* you on, every step of the way. But since we can't be together in person, I've created six strategies that you can adapt to your particular situation. And you can bet that even though I'm not right there next to you, I am cheering for you, every step of the way.

Here's a list of the strategies, which I'll describe in detail in this chapter:

The First Three Strategies: Dealing with Your Partner

- Speak out and say, "No more bullying!"
- Stand up for yourself and your feelings.
- Respond instead of reacting.

The Second Three Strategies: Living the Healthy Model . . . for Yourself

- Be a healthy partner.
- Live the healthy model.
- Maintain a healthy attitude.

You can think of these strategies as behavior blueprints to help you apply what you've learned about bullies and about yourself. They're basic guides for taking positive, transformative action in your relationship and your life.

Applying the A.R.T. Method's Third Guiding Principle

As you take the third step in the A.R.T. Method, draw strength and guidance from the third principle of the A.R.T. Method: Do it scared! While you're considering your strategies and preparing to take action, it's very important to remember that if you make believe you're brave, you'll really be brave.

As you work, keep the following thoughts in mind:

- **Courage isn't about being fearless; it's about not letting your fear hold you back.** Courage is the ability to face danger, uncertainty, or pain without being overcome by fear. You know those heroes you hear about—the ones who go running into burning buildings, racing into battle, diving into deep waters, risking their lives to save the lives of others? It's not that they aren't scared; of course they are. Who wouldn't be? But they don't allow themselves to be *overcome* by the fear.

  Heroes feel fear but don't let it stop them. They're scared, but they do the right thing. And you can do it, too.

- **Act as if.** Act as if you're confident. Act as if you're completely sure of yourself. Act as if you're bold, and before you know it, you won't just be acting anymore. You'll find that you actually begin to have all those qualities you were pretending to have.

  A friend of mine says it's easier to act your way into right thinking than to think your way into right action. What he means is that your actions, your experience, will change your attitudes much faster than the other way around.

You can sit around forever waiting to become strong, secure, and self-loving enough to take an action, or you can just take the action. And if you do that, you'll very likely find that, in doing so, you've become strong, secure, and self-loving. Taking action builds those qualities in you. The more you act as if you're brave, the more you'll discover how brave you really are.

Heroes feel fear but don't let it stop them. They're scared, but they do the right thing. And you can do it, too.

■ **If nothing changes, nothing changes.** Or here's another way to say this: If you keep doing what you've always done, you'll keep getting what you've always gotten. Or: If you keep going in the same direction, you'll probably get where you're going. However you express this idea, it means that if you *want* something different, you're going to have to *do* something different. That can be scary. But it's also necessary.

If you want a different kind of relationship, you'll need to start by relating to your partner differently. And you'll start doing things differently by summoning your courage, acting as if, and changing what you can change. Make believe you're brave, and you'll be amazed by how far the trick takes you.

THE FIRST THREE STRATEGIES: DEALING WITH YOUR PARTNER

The first three strategies for taking transformative actions are about your interactions with your partner:

1. Speak out and say, "No more bullying!"
2. Stand up for yourself and your feelings.
3. Respond instead of reacting.

Specifically, these strategies focus on your partner's bullying and other emotionally abusive behaviors. Even more specifically, they're focused on transforming how you deal with your partner's bullying and emotional abuse, because we can't change anyone else's behavior, only our own.

Each strategy uses a short, simple four-part approach to take you through the process of developing and implementing an action plan:

■ **The situation:** Describe how you and your partner are behaving in a particular aspect of your relationship and what needs to be done about it.
■ **The scenario:** Envision a whole new way of addressing or dealing with the situation.
■ **The strategy:** Plan the details of your new approach.
■ **The action:** After practicing by yourself or with a friend, take action and implement your new approach.

Remember, you're responsible only for your own attitudes and actions. How your partner reacts or responds to your new approach is out of your hands. Once you've taken the action, your work is simply to pay attention, see what happens, and use that information to help you decide what further action needs to be taken.

How to Speak Out for What You Deserve: No More Bullying

In the first step of the A.R.T. Method, you acknowledged your partner's bullying and otherwise emotionally abusive behaviors. In the second step of the A.R.T. Method, you gained a new awareness of just how unacceptable and unjustifiable those behaviors truly are. Also, you made decisions about how you want to be treated in the future and about which behaviors you won't accept any longer.

Now it's time to enact these decisions in your relationship with your partner. In this section, I'll help you strategize how to do that most effectively.

The Situation. You know your partner's bullying behavior patterns. You've got them down in black and white! You know what to look out for, whether it's angry outbursts after a bad day at work, passive-aggressive revenge behaviors, or nonstop nit-picking. And the next time it happens, you'll be ready to respond—to speak out for what you deserve and refuse to accept unacceptable behavior any longer.

The Scenario. Begin by imagining a typical scenario in which your partner subjects you to bullying behavior. (If your relationship with your bullying partner is anything like most such relationships, you've probably had the same kind of interactions over and over again, so this shouldn't be too hard.) First, imagine your partner beginning to do whatever he or she usually does, whether it's screaming or the silent treatment, threats or guilt trips. Next, imagine yourself beginning to react to your partner's bullying the way you usually have in the past. Now *stop*.

Push the pause button on this scene. Rewind it back to the beginning, and play it again. But this time, when your partner starts doing what he or she always does, you're going to do something different. You're going to respond, rather than reacting, and change the scene by taking action and speaking up for yourself.

The Strategy. To start developing your strategy, think back on your acknowledgment that you don't deserve to be bullied and the decisions you made about how you deserve to be treated instead. Let your new ideas and attitudes guide you as you imagine responding to your partner in a whole new way.

Play the scene again, and when you get to the part where your partner begins to bully you, pause. Imagine yourself taking a deep, calming breath and summoning your courage. In your mind, hold your head up high, look the bully in the eye, and in a clear, firm, strong voice, say something like this:

The more you act as if you're brave, the more you'll discover how brave you really are.

> "Don't talk to me that way. Don't treat me that way. I don't like it. I understand that you're upset, but that doesn't make it OK for you to act this way. I'd like to discuss this with you, but I need you to speak to me and treat me respectfully. If you're too upset to do that right now, then let's talk later."

The Action. I suggest that you play this scene through for yourself more than once, to get familiar with what you want to say. You might even want to write it down. If you have a close friend who understands your situation and is supportive, ask that friend to discuss your strategy and help you practice.

Your response to your partner doesn't need to be perfect. *How* you say it is much more important than *what* you say. But you'll probably be more comfortable taking action when you feel confident about what to say and your right to say it. However, don't use that as justification for procrastinating. Don't wait any longer than absolutely necessary to implement your new approach.

You're ready. You've got everything you need. And the next time your partner tries to bully you, put your strategy into motion. Take action!

How to Stand Up for Yourself: Requiring Respect and Consideration

In the first step of the A.R.T. Method, you acknowledged that your partner's bullying and otherwise abusive behaviors are unkind, insensitive, and disrespectful. In the second step of the A.R.T. Method, you took a new look at how bad those behaviors make you feel and just how inappropriate they really are. Also, you affirmed that you don't deserve to feel that way and that in the future you should and will be treated with love, kindness, consideration, and respect. Now it's time to put those affirmations into action in your relationship.

The Situation. You know your partner's bullying makes you feel awful—sad, angry, hurt, ashamed, guilty, desperate, useless, worthless. And now that you know you absolutely don't deserve to feel that way, it's time to let your partner know it, too. You're going to stand up for yourself. You'll make it clear to your partner that, from now on, you expect to be treated thoughtfully and with sensitivity, with respect and consideration for your feelings, needs, and boundaries.

You don't have to wait for your partner's next attack to take action. In fact, sometimes it's better to be proactive, take charge, and address the situation in a moment of your choosing, when your partner is most likely to be receptive. That's just what you're going to do. Instead of waiting until you get hurt again, take care of yourself—by making the first move.

The Scenario. Begin by thinking about what sort of situation will be conducive to a calm, quiet, honest conversation with your partner. Perhaps it would be in the evening after dinner, during a morning walk, or on a leisurely weekend afternoon. Whatever the case, envision yourself with your partner in a relaxed setting, quietly enjoying the moment and one another's company. Next, envision preparing for your big talk. Imagine getting ready to tell your partner about how you're affected by his or her bullying.

Pay attention to how you feel in this imagined moment as you prepare to raise the subject. Do you feel resentful and angry at your partner, or sad and vulnerable? Are you second-guessing your right or ability to stand up for yourself? Are you getting anxious that your partner will react badly and mistreat you?

Now . . . *stop*. Push the pause button on the scene. Rewind it back to the beginning, and play it again. Except this time, when you begin to feel uncomfortable, you'll respond, rather than reacting to your own feelings.

These feelings are the product of old messages and ideas you have about yourself, your partner, and your relationship. They won't help you, so set them aside. Change your attitude, and act as if you're calm, confident, and courageous. Draw strength from your new convictions, and start a conversation with your partner about the way you want, need, and *deserve* to be treated.

The Strategy. To start developing your strategy, think back on your acknowledgment that bullying behaviors affect you deeply and your affirmation that you absolutely don't deserve to feel that way. Also remember the process of forgiveness you went through, recognizing that, like you, your partner has been trapped by the rage of generations. Your partner has inappropriately acted out the pain he or she feels by bullying you. You're not responsible for the bullying. You didn't cause it. It's not about you, and you've done nothing to deserve it. Keep all this in mind as you play the scene again in your head.

When you get to the part where you get ready to start the conversation and feel anger or anxiety begin to creep in, take a moment. Imagine yourself pausing and affirming your love and respect for yourself, and your right to be treated with love and respect. Then envision yourself taking a deep, calming breath, looking your partner in the eye, and in a firm, clear voice saying something like this:

> "I have something I'd like to share with you. I'd like you to just listen until I'm finished, and then we can discuss it together. I want to let you know that when you raise your voice to me, I feel frightened and uncomfortable, and I really don't like it. I don't deserve to feel that way, and I'm sure you don't want me to feel that way.
>
> "I'd like us to make an agreement that you won't raise your voice to me anymore."

The Action. As in the previous strategy, I encourage you to play this scene through more than once, think about what you want to say, and even write it down. If you have a close friend who understands your situation and is supportive, ask that friend to discuss your strategy and help you practice. You certainly don't have to stick with the language I suggested; you can say it in any way that seems right for you and your partner. But I encourage you to keep the following guidelines in mind as you consider what you're going to say and how to say it:

- **Pick just one or two bullying behaviors to address, and stick with those.** Don't overwhelm your partner, and don't give yourself too much to deal with at once. This is already challenging enough. You can address other behaviors at other times. Whether you choose the bullying tactics that hurt you the most, the ones that are easiest to talk about, or something in between, keep it simple.
- **Keep the focus on yourself and your feelings.** Concentrate not on your partner's bullying behaviors, but on how those behaviors affect you. Try not to get into blaming or finger pointing.

If possible, avoid talking about how your partner "makes" you feel. Remember, you're not going to be a victim anymore. No one *makes* you do or feel anything. Recognize that something happens (your partner yells at you), and you have a feeling about it (frightened, uncomfortable). Your partner's actions have an effect on you, but that's not the same as making you do or feel anything.

Instead, own your experience. Take responsibility for it. You may be surprised by how this simple shift in how you talk about cause and effect will change your attitude. You may also find your partner is more receptive to what you're saying, since you're not blaming him or her for "making" you feel a particular way.

■ **Be strong and firm but also warm and positive.** After all, at this point, you're taking action to find a solution, with the hope that you can learn how to work together to establish a true partnership. Bring that love, hope, and affirmation to the conversation.

Now all that's left to do is pick a date for your conversation. Choose a time that you know will work for your partner—one when he or she is usually relaxed, receptive, and in a good mood. Also consider planning an activity that will set both of you at ease. Then, whether it's tomorrow or a week from now, write this date on your calendar, make a commitment to follow through, and take action!

How to Respond Instead of Reacting: Be Strong When the Bully Strikes

In the first step of the A.R.T. Method, you acknowledged how you've reacted to your partner's bullying behaviors in the past and what the result has been. In the second step of the A.R.T. Method, you gained a new awareness about which of your reactions to your partner were inappropriate or ineffective. And you envisioned how you'd prefer to respond to your partner's bullying behaviors in the future.

Now it's time to make those visions a reality!

The Situation. As I mentioned earlier, if your relationship with your bullying partner is like most such relationships, you probably have the same sort of interactions over and over and over. It's as if you're stuck playing out the exact same scene, repeating the same lines of dialogue in the same old way, day after day and week after week, with the same awful results: Your partner bullies you, and you react. Your reaction plays into your partner's rage, and more bullying ensues. You react again, and your partner bullies more. And on it goes, until one of you ends the interaction (probably by leaving the room and slamming the door).

As I've said, if nothing changes, then nothing changes! But now you're ready to break the cycle and transform this old scene. You can do that by writing yourself a new part.

We've just looked at two different approaches to changing the way you deal with your partner's bullying—responding instead of reacting by planning in advance what you want to say and do. Unfortunately, you won't always have the chance to practice exactly what to say when your partner starts bullying. In fact, it's possible that when you take the actions outlined in the previous two strategies, your partner's initial reaction could be one of fear, confusion, or anger. If so, you should be ready to respond, rather than react.

To prepare, create a flexible strategy that helps you stay calm, treat yourself and your partner with respect and dignity (even if your partner can't return the favor), and respond sanely and strongly to whatever your partner throws at you.

The Scenario. To begin, think about how your partner might react to an approach like the ones I described in the two previous strategies. Of course, you can't know for certain how your partner will react. It's entirely possible that he or she will accept your affirmations, agree to your requests, engage in a dialogue with you, or be shocked into retreat. But it's just as likely that your partner will push back and try to place all the blame on you, instead of hearing what you have to say, accepting responsibility, and owning up to his or her part. That's what you need to prepare for.

So first, imagine that you've taken action, implemented your new approach, and responded to your partner's bullying by firmly, calmly telling your partner that you won't accept bullying behavior anymore. Next, envision your partner's reaction. You know him or her well enough to make a pretty good guess about what this might be. Here are some common reactions:

- "Why are you so sensitive? Nobody else has a problem with the way I act."
- "What's the matter with you today? You've never had a problem with this before."
- "You're always nagging me. You're never satisfied with anything I do."
- "What makes you think you can tell me what to do?"
- "If you don't like it, you can leave."
- "What about you? Who are you to talk when you do X, Y, and Z?"
- "I don't know what you're talking about. I don't act that way. You're crazy."

You aren't crazy, of course. But reactions like these are pretty crazy-making! And when your partner provokes you with statements like these, it's so hard not to get drawn back into the bully's no-win wrestling match and blame game. But it's absolutely crucial that you don't.

So *stop* right here. Push the pause button on the scene. Rewind it back to the beginning. Play it again, and take a closer look at the bully's statements. Can you see what they all have in common? They're defensive reactions, motivated by fear. That's because the bully feels startled, cornered, caught behaving badly, and threatened with judgment, punishment, and rejection. Obviously, such reactions have little or nothing to do with you. Instead, they're a manifestation of your bully's Inner Bully, the introject, the rage of generations. They're a sign that your partner is experiencing pain and fear.

Now, as you know without a doubt, that doesn't excuse your partner's bullying. But it does explain why your partner reacts that way. You can use that information in the moment to change your role in this scene.

The Strategy. To start developing your strategy, think back on your acknowledgment that your old way of reacting to your partner's bullying didn't work, as well as your commitment to doing something different, responding in a way that accords both of you respect, consideration, and dignity, even if your partner isn't capable of doing the same. With these thoughts in mind, play the scene again. When you get to the part where your partner reacts defensively, tries to put things back on you, and utters provocative, crazy-making statements and you feel as if you want to react and counterattack in the same old way, take a pause.

Envision yourself taking a moment to breathe deeply and calm down. Silently remind yourself that your partner is acting out pain that has nothing to do with you. Reaffirm your commitment to respond in a way that is respectful to both of you. Then look the bully right in the eye, and in a firm, strong voice, respond with confidence and dignity to your partner's bullying reaction.

Here are suggested responses to the common reactive statements listed previously:

THE BULLY: "Why are you so sensitive? Nobody else has a problem with the way I act."

YOU: "I don't know whether I'm sensitive or not, but I do have feelings about this, and I'm just letting you know what they are. Other people may not have a problem with this behavior, but I do. And right now we're talking about you and me, not those other people."

THE BULLY: "What's the matter with you today? You've never had a problem with this before."

YOU: "Nothing's the matter. I'm just communicating with you about how I feel. And whether it has been a problem in the past isn't the point. It's uncomfortable for me *now*, which is why I'm letting you know."

THE BULLY: "You're always nagging me. You're never satisfied with anything I do."

YOU: "I'm sorry that I've given you that idea, because that's not at all what I'm saying. I don't feel that way, and I definitely don't want you to feel that way. I want each of us to feel loved and respected by the other. Let me try to be clearer. What I'm trying to say is that I feel anxious and frightened when you raise your voice, and I'd like us to agree that you won't do that anymore."

THE BULLY: "What makes you think you can tell me what to do?"

YOU: "I'm not telling you what to do. I'm sharing with you how I feel and what I need as your partner. What you do with the information is up to you. But I do hope you'll think about my request and consider honoring it, because this is important to me."

THE BULLY: "If you don't like it, you can leave."

YOU: "I sincerely hope you don't mean that. I care about you, and I want our relationship to work, but this aspect of the relationship really isn't working for me, which is why

I brought it up with you. Are you saying that you're not willing to compromise or modify your behavior at all for the sake of our relationship?"

THE BULLY: "What about you? Who are you to talk when you do X, Y, and Z?"

YOU: "I would never want to do anything that made you feel bad, and I'd be glad to discuss any issues you have with my behavior. But right now I'd like to stay focused on the issue at hand."

THE BULLY: "I don't know what you're talking about. I don't act that way. You're crazy."

YOU: "I can understand that it may not feel that way to you. What I'm saying is that it *does* feel that way to me, and I hope you can hear and respect that."

The Action. You can put this strategy into action on any occasion when the bully strikes. The very best way to prepare for implementing this strategy is to move on to the next three strategies. Why? Because they're all about taking action that will help you feel good about yourself and take care of yourself, build up your self-esteem and self-respect, and reinforce the sense that you deserve to be treated with consideration and respect. The more you develop that sense, the more you'll be able to respond rather than reacting to your partner. The more you value yourself, the easier it will be to say no to mistreatment by others.

Remember that what you're asking for—to be treated with consideration and respect—is not merely reasonable. It's a basic, fundamental component of any relationship, of any kind, between any two people. A partner who loves you will be glad that you're taking care of yourself, grateful that you're taking action to make change possible for both of you, and happy to modify his or her behavior or discuss compromises to make sure you're happy.

If your partner doesn't immediately respond this way to your new approach, don't give up! You two have been doing things the same way for a long time, and it may take a little while for your partner to catch up with your changes. Try the approach a second time, and a third. What if you do that, but things still don't change, and your partner continues to respond in the same way? It doesn't mean you're doing anything wrong. All it means is that your partner isn't ready, willing, or able to hear what you're trying to share.

That may not be what you were hoping for, but it's valuable information that will help you make decisions about how and when to take action next.

> **IMPORTANT:** Remember that, no matter what happens with any of these strategies, no matter how your partner reacts or responds, the important thing is that, by taking action, you're affirming that *you deserve better.* You deserve to be treated with consideration and respect. You're telling your partner—and yourself most of all—that you won't be bullied any longer. You're taking responsibility for yourself and your part in the relationship. You're acting as if you have tremendous self-confidence, self-esteem, and self-respect. And we know what happens to people who act like that: they end up actually having those very qualities!

THE SECOND THREE STRATEGIES: LIVING THE HEALTHY MODEL

The second three strategies for taking transformative action are all about you. They're about taking what you've learned from the A.R.T. Method's steps and principles and applying that knowledge to your life every day. Almost all of us need help making a big change in the way we live. So I've designed three strategies that help you take your big change one day at a time:

1. Be a healthy partner.
2. Live the healthy model.
3. Maintain a healthy attitude.

Each strategy uses a simple four-part exercise that you can practice daily, weekly, or as necessary to make sure you keep changing, growing, and moving toward the new goals and ideals you've established for yourself. Here are the parts of the exercise:

- **Challenges and changes:** You'll make a list of the particular challenges you face and changes you've committed to making.
- **Morning affirmations:** At the beginning of each day, you'll review your challenges and changes, and recommit yourself to them for the day.
- **Daily practice:** Throughout each day, you'll do your best to honor the commitment you've made to yourself. Whenever a challenge arises, you'll use it as an opportunity to practice your changes.
- **Nightly review:** At the end of each day, you'll take a look back at the day to see what you did well and what you could do better.

This practice is going to transform your life in simple but profound ways, one day at a time. It will allow you to change, grow, and move steadily closer to the person you want to be—in your relationship and in your life. After all, that's really what these strategies and the whole A.R.T. Method are all about.

How to Be a Healthy Partner: Improving Your Relationship Skills

In the first step of the A.R.T. Method, you took a look at the things you do or fail to do that upset your partner. You also acknowledged what you consider to be your shortcomings as a partner—the areas in which you'd like to improve. In the second step of the A.R.T. Method, you reconsidered which of those behaviors and attitudes you could change and whether you were willing to do so. And you made decisions about how you might compromise in problem areas and which steps you could take toward attaining your own ideal as a partner.

Now it's time to start making those compromises and taking those steps.

Challenges and Changes. The first step is simple. Get yourself a piece of paper, and divide it in half by drawing a line down the middle, lengthwise. Across the top, write this title: "Healthy Partnership Challenges and Changes." On the left side, list all of your challenges: behaviors and attitudes that bother your partner and that you've decided you're willing to change—any behaviors and attitudes that you don't like in yourself as a partner and you want to improve. Then, on the right side, directly across from each item, write down the corresponding change, compromise, or improvement you'd like to make. And you're done!

If you like, you might also make a copy of the list to carry in your pocket, purse, or wallet, so you can remind yourself throughout the day what your goals are. Before you move on, look over your list of Healthy Partnership Challenges and Changes, and take a moment to feel proud about how much courage and willingness you've shown, and how much work you've done to arrive at this point.

Morning Affirmations. Each morning, before you get started with your day, set aside a few minutes to consider your list of Healthy Partnership Challenges and Changes. Don't worry; it won't take long. You can spend as little as three minutes, and with some practice, it'll make your whole day go better.

First, find a nice quiet place in your home where you can sit comfortably and undisturbed for a few minutes. Take your list of Healthy Partnership Challenges and Changes along with you. Sit down, and take a moment to close your eyes, take a few deep breaths, clear your mind, and get calm. Try not to be distracted by thoughts of the coming day and all the things that you have to do; you can dive into that in just a few minutes. Right now you're taking time for yourself. So try to just stay in the moment, and focus on this important work.

Next, take a look at your list. Review your old attitudes and actions and the new attitudes and actions that will replace them today. Take them in one at a time, paying special attention to any pair that seems to leap out at you or seems especially pertinent to whatever has been going on in your relationship.

Then, when you're ready, say quietly (or in your head, if you prefer) the following affirmation:

"I affirm my commitment to becoming a healthy partner and having healthy relationships. I am willing and able to make these changes and grow toward these goals. Just for today, I'll do my best to move in the direction of my ideal attitudes and actions and to treat myself and others with consideration and respect. I'm doing this for me, because I deserve better."

Finally, take a moment to let these positive thoughts resonate, to feel proud of yourself for showing up for these growth opportunities and taking such good care of yourself. Then get up, put your list away, and get ready to have a great day.

Daily Practice. Your goal each day is to be guided throughout the day by your affirmations to become a healthy partner. Of course, I don't mean that's all you'll be thinking of; far from it! You have a big, busy life and many things to do. Instead, you can think of these affirmations as a set of guidelines or suggestions that inform your decisions and actions. It's like being on a diet. When you're trying to lose a little weight or watching your cholesterol levels, you don't spend the whole day thinking of nothing but grams of fat and carbs and calories. But you do keep thoughts about the diet in the back of your mind; you'll stay away from snacks and make thoughtful choices about what to eat at mealtime.

Congratulate yourself for every single occasion on which you were able to make progress and every effort you made toward growth, because just the fact that you're trying is a real triumph.

This daily practice is just the same. You won't spend your whole day thinking about how to become a healthier partner. But you will keep your challenges and changes at the back of your mind. You'll strive to stay away from situations that trigger old behaviors. And during interactions with others, especially your partner, you'll be mindful of the challenges you face and the changes you've committed to making for yourself.

Nightly Review. At the end of the day, before you go to bed, return to the place where you did your morning affirmations. Again, take a moment to close your eyes, take a few deep breaths, clear your mind, and get calm.

With your list of Healthy Partnership Challenges and Changes in hand, review your day. Take a look at which challenges you faced. Note whether you were able to practice the new action or attitude you've committed to, or if you fell back into old patterns. (You may do this review in your head if you prefer, but I think you'll find it helpful to write down the review in a notebook, so you can track your progress.) As you do so, remember that this is hard work. The sorts of transformations you're working toward don't happen overnight. So try to show yourself as much compassion and patience as possible, and give yourself the kind of encouragement you'd give a best friend who's tackling an exciting project that he or she had always dreamed of doing.

When you've finished your nightly review (it doesn't have to take more than a couple of minutes), take a moment to congratulate yourself for every single occasion on which you were able to make progress and every effort you made toward growth, because just the fact that you're trying is a real triumph.

How to Live the Healthy Model: Taking Action Instead of Acting Out

In the first step of the A.R.T. Method, you acknowledged the mechanisms you employ to cope with the pain of a bullying relationship, and you identified any other behaviors that allow the relationship to continue as it is or make it worse. In the second step of the A.R.T. Method, you became ready to give up those behaviors and opened yourself and your relationship to positive changes.

Now it's time to do just that—to live the healthy model.

Challenges and Changes. The first step works just the way it did in the previous strategy. First get yourself a piece of paper, and divide it in half by drawing a line down the middle, lengthwise. This time, the title you'll write at the top is "Healthy Model Challenges and Changes." On the left side, list all of your challenges: the coping mechanisms and self-defeating or destructive behaviors you've decided you're willing to change. Then, on the right side, directly across from each item, write down the positive, self-loving, esteem-building behavior with which you're going to replace the negative one. And you're done! If you like, you might also make a copy of the list to carry in your pocket, purse, or wallet, so you can remind yourself throughout the day what your goals are.

Before you move on, look over your list of Healthy Model Challenges and Changes, and take a moment to feel proud about how much courage and willingness you've shown and how much work you've done to arrive at this point.

Morning Affirmations. You'll do this set of morning affirmations the same way you did in the first strategy (you can even do it at the same time). Each morning, before you get started with your day, set aside a few minutes to consider your list of Healthy Model Challenges and Changes. First, find a nice quiet place in your home where you can sit comfortably and undisturbed for a few minutes, and take your list of Healthy Model Challenges and Changes along with you. Sit down, and take a moment to close your eyes, take a few deep breaths, clear your mind, and get calm.

Next, take a look at your list. Review your old coping mechanisms and destructive behaviors and the actions and behaviors that will replace them today. Take them in one at a time, paying special attention to any pair that seems to leap out at you or seems especially pertinent to whatever has been going on in your relationship.

Take a moment to feel proud about how much courage and willingness you've shown and how much work you've done to arrive at this point.

Then, when you're ready, say quietly (or in your head, if you prefer) the following affirmation:

> "I affirm my commitment to living the healthy model, changing instead of coping, taking action instead of acting out. I am willing and able to make these changes and grow toward this positive, healthy model of living. Just for today, I'll do my best to move in the direction

of my goals and to treat myself and others with consideration and respect. I'm doing this for me, because I deserve better!"

Finally, take a moment to let these positive thoughts resonate, to feel proud of yourself for showing up for these growth opportunities and taking such good care of yourself.

Then get up, put your list away, and get ready to have a great day.

Daily Practice. Your goal each day is to be guided throughout the day by your affirmations to live the healthy model. To put the affirmations into action, you'll practice what I like to call "doing the opposite" or "taking contrary action," another form of acting as if.

To practice doing the opposite, look out for moments when you feel yourself falling back into old coping mechanisms and self-destructive behaviors. When you get that feeling, take contrary action—that is, act contrary to your impulses. Do the opposite of what you feel you want to do, because you don't really want to. Who would want to fall back into those old, self-destructive, self-defeating ways? No one—and certainly not you, after all your hard work. In spite of that work, you may feel compelled to act in old, familiar ways, because you've been acting that way for so long that it feels intuitive and even comfortable.

You can change your thinking by changing your actions. So the more contrary action you take, the easier this new way of behaving will be.

That's what I mean by "contrary action." When faced with one of those old impulses, you'll do the opposite of what your impulse is to do in the moment, because you know it's better for you in the long run.

As we've discussed, you can change your thinking by changing your actions. So the more contrary action you take, the easier this new way of behaving will be. Eventually, the action will change the way you think and feel, until it's not contrary any more. Instead, you'll be instinctively, intuitively living the healthy model.

Nightly Review. You'll do a nightly review just the way I described it for the previous strategy. (You can even do all your reviews at the same time.) At the end of the day, before you go to bed, return to the place where you did your morning affirmations. Take a moment to close your eyes, take a few deep breaths, clear your mind, and get calm.

With your list of Healthy Model Challenges and Changes in hand, review your day. Take a look at which challenges you faced and which coping mechanisms and destructive behaviors you were tempted to use. Note whether you were able to do the opposite and practice the healthy actions you've committed to. Or did you fall back into old patterns?

Again, as you review your day, remember that changing is hard work. The sorts of transformation you're working toward don't happen overnight. So try to show yourself as much compassion and patience as possible, and give yourself the kind of encouragement you'd give a best friend. And when you've finished your nightly review, take a moment to congratulate yourself for every single occasion on which you were able to make progress and every effort you made toward growth, because just the fact that you're trying is a real triumph.

How to Maintain a Healthy Attitude: Nurturing New Messages About Yourself

In the first step of the A.R.T. Method, you examined the destructive, esteem-destroying messages you get from your Inner Bully and the old unconscious ideas and fears that keep you from standing up for yourself, speaking up for what you deserve, and walking away from toxic situations.

In the second step of the A.R.T. Method, you became willing to let go of those ideas and attitudes. You affirmed that you deserve love and respect. And you committed to developing and embracing healthy, esteem-building ideas and attitudes about yourself and your life.

Now it's time to put those ideas and attitudes front and center—and live them, every day.

Challenges and Changes. Listing your challenges and changes works just the way it did for the previous two strategies. First get yourself a piece of paper, and divide it in half by drawing a line down the middle, lengthwise. Title this page "Healthy Attitude Challenges and Changes." On the left side, list all of your challenges: old ideas, Inner Bully messages, negative thought patterns, and self-defeating or esteem-eroding attitudes that you've decided you're willing to change. Then, on the right side, directly across from each item, write down the positive new idea, self-loving message, positive thought pattern, or esteem-building attitude with which you're going to replace the old one. If you like, you might also make a copy of the list to carry in your pocket, purse, or wallet, so you can remind yourself throughout the day what your goals are.

Show yourself as much compassion and patience as possible, and give yourself the kind of encouragement you'd give a best friend.

Before you move on, look over your list of Healthy Attitude Challenges and Changes, and take a moment to feel proud of how much courage and willingness you've shown and how much work you've done to arrive at this point.

Morning Affirmations. You'll do this set of morning affirmations the same way you did for the first two strategies (you can even do all three at the same time). Each morning, before you get started with your day, set aside a few minutes to consider your list of Healthy Attitude Challenges and

Changes. First, find a nice quiet place in your home where you can sit comfortably and undisturbed for a few minutes. Take your list of Healthy Attitude Challenges and Changes along with you. Sit down, and take a moment to close your eyes, take a few deep breaths, clear your mind, and get calm.

Next, take a look at your list. Review your old negative ideas and attitudes and the actions and behaviors that will replace them today. Take them in one at a time, paying special attention to any pair that seems to leap out at you or seems especially pertinent to whatever has been going on in your relationship.

Then, when you're ready, say quietly (or in your head, if you prefer) the following affirmation:

> "I affirm my commitment to maintaining a healthy attitude and replacing old negative ideas, attitudes, and messages with new positive ones. I am willing and able to make these changes and grow toward this positive, healthy attitude. Just for today, I'll do my best to move in the direction of my goals and to treat myself and others with consideration and respect. I'm doing this for me, because I deserve better!"

Finally, take a moment to let these positive thoughts resonate, to feel proud of yourself for showing up for these growth opportunities and taking such good care of yourself.

Then get up, put your list away, and get ready to have a great day.

Daily Practice. Your goal each day is to be guided throughout the day by your affirmations to keep a healthy attitude. Having done your morning affirmations, you'll find yourself increasingly attuned to the moments when old negative ideas, attitudes, and thought patterns creep back in. You'll learn to recognize immediately the awful, ugly, unmistakable voice of the Inner Bully. And when that happens, you'll do your best to replace the negative thought or attitude with the positive one.

You can do this just as we discussed in the section on talking back to your Inner Bully (for a refresher course, turn to Chapter 5). When you catch yourself thinking esteem-destroying thoughts or beginning to act on bad attitudes, stop and talk back. Tell the Inner Bully to shut up and go away! Then gently remind yourself that those negative ideas and attitudes are not true. Push them aside, and bring in the positive, self-loving messages to replace them.

Nightly Review. You'll do this nightly review the same way it was described for the previous strategies. (You can even review all three of your lists at the same time.) At the end of the day, before you go to bed, return to the place where you did your morning affirmations. Again, take a moment to close your eyes, take a few deep breaths, clear your mind, and get calm.

With your list of Healthy Attitude Challenges and Changes in hand, review your day. Take a look at which challenges you faced, which old ideas and negative messages you might have heard. Were you able to replace them with the healthy, positive attitudes you've committed to, or did you fall back into negative, defeatist thinking? Again, as you reflect on your day, remember that the sort of transformation you're working toward doesn't happen overnight. Be compassionate and patient with yourself. And when you've finished your nightly review, take a moment to congratulate yourself for every single occa-

You'll learn to recognize immediately the awful, ugly, unmistakable voice of the Inner Bully. And when that happens, you'll do your best to replace the negative thought or attitude with the positive one.

sion on which you were able to make progress and every effort you made toward growth, because just the fact that you're trying is a real triumph.

TAKE ACTION—ALL THE TIME!

I encourage you, if you possibly can, to work on all three strategies of the healthy model every day. You don't have to spend hours on them—just a few minutes each morning and evening for affirmations and review. And if you do that, you'll find that your daily practice becomes increasingly easy and intuitive every day. If working on all three lists every day feels overwhelming, do just one each day, in an ongoing three-day rotation. Or if you're really busy and just can't make the time to do more, choose three days each week, and work with one list of challenges and changes on each of those days, each week.

You're working on making big, deep changes— unlearning self-defeating thought patterns, negative attitudes, and destructive behaviors that have been ruling your life for years.

Remember that the more time, energy, and attention you can give to this work, the better. You're working on making big, deep changes—unlearning self-defeating thought patterns, negative attitudes, and destructive behaviors that have been ruling your life for years. It's not going to happen overnight. As with everything, the best way to make real progress is to practice as much and as consistently as possible.

And though it may seem to take up time in your busy schedule, what could be a more important use of your time than something that will make your life so much better? What could be more important than taking care of yourself? I hope by now you know the answer: nothing!

Moving Forward, Moving On 10

The New You—with or Without Your Partner

- Moving forward with your changing relationship
- Should you stay or go? How to tell, when to decide
- Rediscovering yourself: the adventure of a lifetime
- Twenty tips for great confidence

Parents can only give good advice or put them [children] on the right paths, but the final forming of a person's character lies in their own hands.

—ANNE FRANK

Congratulations! You're now an official practitioner of the A.R.T. Method. You're moving forward in your relationship and in your life, as a healthy partner and a healthy person, with healthy attitudes and healthy self-esteem. And in this chapter you're going learn how to continue moving forward—with or without your partner.

It may very well be that the changes you're making will galvanize and inspire your partner to start healing as well. Your partner may join you in this process of growth and change, working with you to transform your relationship. It won't be easy, and it won't happen overnight, but with hard work, patience, cooperation, and compromise, it absolutely can happen. Sometimes that's exactly what happens for my clients, and perhaps that will be what happens for you.

Unfortunately, not everyone is as strong and committed to personal growth as you are, so not everyone can break out of the bullying cycle as you've done. Therefore, the reality is that your partner might remain trapped in that cycle. He or she may be unwilling or unable to change those bullying behaviors and learn to treat you with the love and respect you deserve. If that's the case, then you'll need to treat yourself with love and respect by making the hard but self-loving decision to move on—*from* the relationship, and *with* your life.

The very thought of leaving your partner might seem unimaginable, even impossible, but it's not. It may be difficult and painful, but it can't be nearly as difficult and painful as remaining in a relationship where you're subjected to bullying and emotional abuse. You deserve so much better than that. And with the A.R.T. Method, you've learned so much and come so far that you now know you just can't settle for less than you deserve.

The A.R.T. Method will get you through anything with grace; you can use it every single day to help you keep moving forward in your relationship.

Instead, take action and take care of yourself, no matter how challenging it is to do so. Because that's what you need, and that's what you deserve. And in this chapter, I'll guide you through every step of this process.

THE A.R.T. METHOD—EVERY DAY

If you've done the work laid out in Chapters 7 through 9, you already know the A.R.T. Method helps you take on and transform major life issues. What you don't know yet is that the A.R.T. Method will get you through anything with grace; you can use it every single day to help you keep moving forward in your relationship. Don't worry—I don't mean you have to do all those exercises over again! Instead, you can use the tools, techniques, and principles you've acquired by doing the exercises to take on whatever challenges life brings you.

When conflict or tension arise in your relationship with your partner or any other aspect of your life, you can use the A.R.T. Method to face each experience with new courage and confidence—and grow from it. Whatever the situation, just acknowledge the problem, rethink your options, and take action. Here's how it works:

On any given day, when a challenge or conflict arises, the very first thing you should do is pause. Don't react! Don't let your old ideas and attitudes take charge and run the show. Instead, hit the pause button.

Then, if possible, take a couple of minutes alone. Suppose, for example, that your partner makes a critical comment, and you feel hurt or angry about the criticism. Instead of reacting, simply excuse yourself from the conversation for a moment, and go into another room. This will give you the time and space to practice your day-to-day version of the A.R.T. Method. And that will make it possible for you to *respond*, rather than *reacting*, to whatever happens.

But what if you aren't able to pause or take a moment for yourself? Instead, you get caught up in the conflict and fall back into old attitudes and actions. Try not to beat yourself up about it. Just end the interaction as soon as you're able, and then take those minutes alone. You need them to calm and center yourself, especially if you've been drawn into a conflict.

Acknowledge the Problem

You learned how to acknowledge the problem in Chapter 7, when you answered questions about the state of your relationship and got completely honest with yourself about it. You'll do the same thing with the current situation.

Take a moment to close your eyes, take a few deep breaths, clear your mind, and get calm. Then ask yourself the following three questions:

1. How is this person treating me, and how does it make me feel?
2. How am I enabling or exacerbating the conflict?
3. What old ideas and attitudes prevent me from living up to my ideal in this situation?

You can answer these questions in your mind or write them down if you have the time. Either way, the most important thing is to keep your answers as simple as possible, to be as honest as you can in this particular moment, and to fully acknowledge the reality of your situation.

Reassess Your Options

You learned how to reassess your options in Chapter 8, when you learned to take a new look at old issues and get a fresh, healthy perspective on how you deserve to be treated and how you want to treat others. That's what you need to do next. With your answers to the previous questions in mind, ask yourself the following three questions:

1. How do I want and deserve to be treated by this person?
2. What can I do to stop increasing the problem and instead increase the solution?
3. What new ideas and attitudes will I bring in to replace the old ones?

Take Action

You learned how to take action in Chapter 9, where you used the new awareness, options, and perspectives you gained in the previous two steps of the A.R.T. Method to speak out against being bullied, stand up for your feelings, and grow toward your own partnership ideals. You'll apply those lessons to your current situation. With your answers to the previous questions in mind, ask yourself the following three questions:

1. How can I most effectively let this person know that his or her bullying behavior isn't acceptable to me?
2. How can I bring my solutions to this situation and live the healthy model?
3. How will I act on my new ideas and attitudes, so I can grow toward my ideal in this situation?

When you've answered these questions, you'll have a strategy. That means you can go back to your partner with courage and confidence, and take action!

Small Steps, Big Changes

You've already experienced how the A.R.T. Method can work on the big stuff—letting go of the past, getting a new perspective on the present, moving toward the future with a brave, bold attitude. It can also work on the "small" stuff, the conflicts and challenges that make up our daily lives. The more you practice the A.R.T. Method on these small things, the more you'll see yourself and your life changing in big ways.

So when you feel overwhelmed by the need to make large-scale changes in your relationship and your life, remember that you don't have to—and shouldn't try to—tackle those changes all at once. Instead, just face one moment, one challenge at a time, using the A.R.T. Method. Take care of the small things, and the big things will take care of themselves!

YOU'RE THE ONLY ONE YOU CAN CHANGE (SO FOCUS ON YOURSELF)

I've mentioned that you may see your partner's actions and attitudes changing as you practice your new approach to the relationship. That's completely true, but don't make the mistake of thinking you changed your partner. You didn't and you can't. We can't change anyone else. The only person we can change is ourselves. So if you see your partner changing, remember that he or she is making those changes him- or herself.

Yes, the changes may be a reaction or response to the changes you've made. They may be influenced by you. But they're not controlled by you. Always remember that you don't have power over anyone's changes but your own. You're only in charge of yourself. You can't make your partner change, no matter how hard you try, and my experience shows that the harder you try, the worse you'll both feel.

When you think about it, isn't that a relief? It means you're not responsible for your partner changing. You're responsible only for your own attitudes and actions. How your partner reacts or responds to your new approach is out of your hands. So once you've taken the actions, your work is simply to pay attention, see what happens, and use that information to help you decide what further action you need to take.

Of course, accepting that you can't change your partner isn't always easy. Sometimes it may be incredibly upsetting, especially if you have clear ideas about what you want to happen, how you want your partner to change, or how you want your relationship to go. You may be tempted to ignore the fact that you're not in charge of the situation and try to make things go your way. As I said earlier, this will succeed only in making both you and your partner frustrated and angry. So instead, do everything you can to keep your focus on yourself—what you're doing, how you're changing, your own ideals, attitudes, and actions. The more you do that, the better you'll feel, and the better things will go for you.

Of course, when I say keep the focus on yourself, I mean you should concentrate on what you're doing to grow as a partner, such as using the strategies for living the healthy model discussed in Chapter 9 and using the A.R.T. Method every day. But I also mean you should start paying attention to your own wants and needs, and seeing that they get met. For all these years, you've been living out the lies of your childhood, acting on your low self-esteem, and neglecting your wants and needs. Now it's time to make up for that.

The more you practice the A.R.T. Method on these small things, the more you'll see yourself and your life changing in big ways.

Start treating yourself like someone you love and respect, and do the things for yourself that you would do for someone you love and respect. Spend more time with friends and family members who make you feel good about yourself. Tackle a project at home or work that you've been putting off; you won't believe how great you'll feel when it's finished. Take care of yourself physically by going to see the doctor and dentist or by getting a massage or facial. Volunteer for a cause you support. Take time for yourself, for doing the things you love to do, whether that's gardening or jogging, reading or cooking, spending time outdoors or at the movies.

These are all great ways to keep the focus on you and your growth. Because you gain self-esteem by doing estimable things such as these, they're also great ways to begin feeling better and better about yourself.

WORKING WITH YOUR PARTNER:
TIME, PRACTICE, AND PATIENCE

Now you know that you need to let your partner make whatever changes he or she is going to make without your interference, however well meant. You also need to give your partner—and yourself—plenty of time to transform your relationship. Remember that you've established your dynamic as a couple over many months or, more likely, years. A total transformation isn't going to happen in a day, a week, or a month.

Your partner may not (and probably won't) immediately respond to the changes you're making with positive feedback and changes of his or her own. That's OK! You two have been doing things the same way for a long time, and it may take a while for your partner to catch up with your changes. Be patient. Don't give up. Keep up your own efforts, and remember that you have a pretty big head start on your partner.

Start paying attention to your own wants and needs, and seeing that they get met.

If, after some time, your partner shows receptivity to your communication and willingness to work with you, even just a little, then keep up the good work. Keep using your new tools and techniques, and share them with your partner if it seems appropriate. Offer encouragement and support for your partner's efforts.

Maybe you'll find that your relationship has improved but is still rocky much of the time. Or things are going well, and then out of the blue you have one of your old, awful interactions. You somehow seem to forget all about your new approach and fall back into your former, self-defeating patterns. If this happens, try not to get discouraged. So you're not perfect. So what? You're making progress. As long as the two of you are able to keep growing and changing together, that's what counts.

SHOULD I STAY OR SHOULD I GO? HOW TO TELL, WHEN TO DECIDE

Should you stick it out, stay in your relationship, and keep working to improve it? Or should you leave your partner and start fresh on your own? That decision is not easy. In fact, making the decision may be one of the hardest things you ever do. But you have the tools and the strength to make the appropriate choice for yourself.

When considering your options, keep in mind that what you're asking for from your partner—to be treated with consideration and respect—is not just reasonable. It's a basic, fundamental component of any relationship, of any kind, between any two people. A partner who loves and respects you will be glad that you're asking for what you need, grateful that you're taking action to make change possible for both of you, and willing to modify his or her behavior or discuss compromises to make sure you're happy. Even bullying partners who suffer from the rage of generations can step up to the plate, start dealing with their issues, and improve their partnership skills. It may be a struggle for them. But you've done it, and so can they.

As I've explained, these changes aren't going to happen immediately, but they *must* happen if you're going to stay in the relationship. It has been said that one definition of insanity is doing the same thing over and over, expecting different results. If you've been practicing the healthy model in your relationship for a while, and day after day your partner continues to bully you in the same old way, it would be a little insane for you to stick around and subject yourself to more of the same.

Of course, you'll want to do your best and be patient with your partner, up to a point. But you also need to be completely honest with yourself about your partner's responses to and participation in your efforts to improve the relationship. If, after a few weeks or a few months, you see little or no change and it's still bullying business as usual with your partner, then it's time to take action and move on. After all, you wouldn't stay in a house full of toxic fumes that made you sick. You wouldn't live in a neighborhood where weekly earthquakes wrecked your home and your nerves. But that's exactly what it's like when you stay in a bullying relationship: you risk your physical and emotional health, your current and future happiness.

If it becomes clear that your partner is either unwilling or unable to change, I hope you'll be able to see that you need to evacuate this dangerous situation as soon as possible. Don't subject yourself to any more emotional abuse. Don't waste another day of your life. The time to take action is *now*.

Tools for Evaluation: The Three Guiding Principles of the A.R.T. Method

Making a decision to stay or leave won't be easy, but you can use the three guiding principles of the A.R.T. Method to help you evaluate the situation and make the appropriate choice. As you consider what's best for you, keep in mind the principles you've already learned and relied upon:

What other people think of us has only as much power over us as we let it have.

- When thinking about your relationship, trust your gut.
- Don't be embarrassed or ashamed about your situation.
- Know your self-worth.

We have nothing to lose that's more valuable than our self-respect, our self-esteem, and our sense of self-worth.

- You deserve to be treated with kindness, compassion, respect, and love—by yourself first and foremost!
- What you're afraid of losing may not be worth keeping.
- Almost anything that you put ahead of preserving and protecting your sense of self-worth you will lose.

Do it scared!

- Courage isn't about being fearless; it's about not letting your fear hold you back.
- Act as if.
- If nothing changes, nothing changes.

MOVING ON: A NEW BEGINNING

Few changes in life are as difficult as ending a relationship, even an unhealthy, emotionally abusive one. Especially if you and your partner have been together for a long time, the thought of leaving your partner will bring up all kinds of feelings. Even when you've become entirely convinced that ending the relationship is your best and only possible choice, actually preparing to act on your decision might stir up fear, grief, loneliness, anger, panic, and elation, to name just a few emotions.

How to handle these feelings? Don't get overwhelmed! Use the skills you acquired learning the A.R.T. Method: Do the right thing, do it for yourself, and do it scared. Get support; you don't need to go it alone. Most of all, remember that you're not just leaving a relationship; you're embarking on the adventure of a lifetime. You're going to rediscover yourself and build a brand-new life, based on healthy ideas and attitudes, self-esteem, and self-respect.

Do the Right Thing, Do It for Yourself, and Do It Scared

I've talked about this principle so much that you hardly need to hear it again. But since you might be applying it to a very big step, review it just a bit more. By now you know the basics of this principle very well: Don't react to your own feelings; respond to them. And don't worry about anyone else's opinion on the matter; do this for yourself.

Do the right thing, no matter how scared you are to do it. Of course you're going to be scared about leaving your partner. Who wouldn't be? Especially if you've been together for a long time, it may be difficult to even imagine life without your partner, no matter how difficult life *with* your partner has become.

If your partner is the primary earner in your household, you may be concerned about how you'll support yourself or reluctant to give up your lifestyle. You may worry about how separation will affect your children, or whether you'll lose your mutual friends. You may fear that no one will ever care for you again, that you won't find another partner, or that your friends and family will condemn you for "giving up." If you're feeling any of these things, I suggest you turn to Chapter 3 and reread the section on rationalization for a reality check about how truly, literally dangerous it is to let fear of an unknown future keep you trapped in a relationship you know is toxic.

There's no getting around it: you will experience changes in your life when you leave your partner—perhaps radical changes. But what these changes will bring you is priceless: confidence, courage, and self-esteem. And with assets like these, in time you'll be able to build a life filled with all the things you want, on a firm foundation of self-respect.

That's worth facing your fears for, isn't it? You bet it is. So act as if, take contrary action, and make your move. Do it scared; that's what heroes do.

Get Support: You Don't Need to Go It Alone

If you decide to leave your relationship, you shouldn't face the challenge alone. Even if you can do it by yourself, why would you want to? There are so many people and resources to help get you through it in so many ways. I encourage you to avail yourself of them as much as you can.

Too many people make the mistake of thinking that needing anything from other people is a sign of weakness. In my mind, only the strongest, smartest people understand when they need outside help and ask for it. Doing that takes real strength of character and confidence—the kind I know you have.

Rely on Friends and Family. The people who have been with you the longest, heard about your relationship with your bullying partner, and witnessed the effect it has had on you will probably be thrilled to hear that you're making a move to take care of yourself. Most of your friends, family members, and colleagues will probably be very supportive and will go out of their way to lend you a hand. So don't be shy about asking. It may feel uncomfortable at first, but remember that by asking for help, you're giving a significant compliment. You're letting people know that you trust them enough to open up to them in a very vulnerable moment, and I can't think of anyone who isn't flattered and honored by that kind of trust.

When you ask friends for help, you're also giving them an opportunity to be helpful, to have the experience of giving of themselves. I'm sure you've had that kind of experience at least once and perhaps many times, so you know how great it feels. Don't hesitate, then, to share it with others. Don't worry about imposing; you've learned to set your own boundaries, and you can trust others to do the same. Most people are pretty good at saying yes only when they mean it and saying no when they mean no. So take what your friends say at face value; when they say something's no problem, believe them!

Unfortunately, almost every family and circle of friends includes a few people who simply can't be supportive. Some people may judge you, discourage you, play on your doubts, focus on the negative aspects of the situation, and feed your fears. Usually, I've found that the people who can't just be loving, supportive, and glad that you've left an emotionally abusive relationship are the very same ones who have their own issues with their partners, with bullies, and with the rage of generations. Your courage and changes scare these people. They experience your transformation as a critique, even though of course it has nothing to do with them. As a result, they won't be able to offer you the support you need and deserve.

Accept their limitations, and when it comes to getting support for this life change, steer clear. Instead, stick with the people who can fully support you in your decision, whatever their own opinions about it are. Surround yourself with optimistic, upbeat friends who love their lives, inspire you in your own life, and make you feel great about yourself. You'll be amazed at how contagious a good attitude can be!

Make Use of Organizations and Institutions. From the American Psychological Association to career counseling to assertiveness training, there's no end to the help you can get as you begin your new life. In Appendix A, you'll find a list of references and organizations that can provide you with support through this transition. Don't hesitate to reach out and check in with any group that sounds like it might be useful to you. You might not end up needing it, but it might turn out to be exactly what you need. Why not investigate?

Legal Issues and Assistance. While you are in the later stages of deciding to leave your partner, you will be consulting an attorney in your community with experience in such matters. If you haven't already done that but you've decided to leave, then it's time to get a lawyer. Selecting the right person for you is important. You should speak with several candidates before choosing one who will help you pursue the options you want for yourself at this point. Your friends may know of likely choices, but a better way is to ask the local bar association for a list of lawyers specializing in marital or personal relationships.

In some states, when a couple is seeking divorce, joint counseling procedures are voluntary or mandatory. Sometimes the counseling leads to creation of an agreement between the two persons; it's similar to a prenuptial agreement but "postnuptial" in content, and it can make both partners feel more secure while working to preserve the relationship. If the agreement can actually come to pass, it works well for a renewal of a loving and respectful relationship.

Your attorney can help you if you decide you want to preserve the relationship. You should be sensitive to that in your initial interviews in selecting counsel. If reconciliation attempts fail and your decision to move on is final, your attorney will inform you how to proceed in the circumstances and in your best interest. Most likely the two of you will try to work out an amicable agreement with your partner and his or her attorney. If you are not married to your partner and the separation involves joint residence and property concerns or even custody matters, which are not quickly resolved, let the lawyers work it out.

Divorce, however, is an entirely separate matter. The law tries to be equitable to both partners. You need not fear that your partner will be able to strip you of your legal entitlement. Consultation with an attorney will likely assure you of that. Your attorney should advise you how to avoid a hostile environment by taking a responsible and amicable position, as well as what you can expect if proceedings do turn hostile.

The Adventure of a Lifetime: Rediscovering Yourself

As I said earlier, the most important point to remember in all this is that you're not just saying good-bye to something. You're setting yourself free to begin a whole new life. You're getting ready to rediscover who you are, what you want for yourself, and all that you can dream and accomplish! It may be scary, but it should also be thrilling.

Even in the healthiest of relationships, we can sometimes lose ourselves. In your relationship with a bullying partner, you may have given up so much of yourself that you don't even remember who you are. This is your chance to start fresh and get to know a bright, passionate, fascinating person with all sorts of skills and interests, dedicated to personal growth and change: you. So try to think of this as an opportunity, not a hardship. It's the kind of experience many people would love to have—beginning again with a clean slate and the whole world available to them.

You're getting ready to rediscover who you are, what you want for yourself, and all that you can dream and accomplish!

Here are just a few of the things you can do as you begin life on your own, rediscover who you are, and learn to nurture and care for yourself:

- Reconnect with friends and family.
- Go back to school or take classes of any kind.
- Take up a new hobby.
- Transform your home, in big ways or small, to really reflect your own tastes.
- Travel, near or far, to places you've been wanting to visit.
- Try dating. (You don't have to get serious—just have a good time.)

Twenty Tips to Build Confidence and Vitality for Your New Life

Paired with your everyday practice of the A.R.T. Method, the following simple, commonsense tips will help you build your self-esteem and gain confidence that will shine through in every area of your life, whether you're with friends or strangers, in private or public, on a date or in the office, at home or out taking on the world!

1. **Be physically active and eat healthy.** Research shows that people who take care of their bodies feel better about themselves overall. Just exercising (or playing a sport, or even taking a walk) a few times a week, getting enough sleep, and making healthful food choices can stabilize your moods, give you more energy and focus, and boost your self-esteem.

2. **Surround yourself with photos.** Buy a bunch of frames at a housewares store, and fill them with photos of the people you love. Or make a collage of pictures that represent the experiences you aspire to: traveling the world, going back to school, learning to play a musical instrument, or sailing. These images will remind you of the people who care for you and the experiences you can look forward to.

3. **Stop apologizing all the time!** Are you one of those people who's always saying you're sorry . . . for everything and anything? Stop apologizing! You don't have any reason to apologize (unless you stepped on someone's foot). You have a right to live your life and do your thing, whatever it is. From now on, each time you feel compelled to say you're sorry, pause and affirm that you're equal to everyone else and have nothing to be sorry about.

4. **Don't worry if someone doesn't like you.** Not everybody's going to like you. Who cares? It doesn't mean there's anything wrong with you. Remember, what other people think of you is none of your business. Instead of dwelling on it and getting upset about it, remind yourself that it's their loss. Then forget about it, and concentrate on the people who *do* like you.

5. **Commit random acts of kindness.** Do something that makes someone else feel good. Call someone you haven't talked with for a while, just to say hello. Let someone go ahead of you in line. Give a small gift to a friend who's feeling down. You'll feel better if you brighten someone else's day—guaranteed.

6. **Flirt with a good-looking stranger.** I'm not saying you should throw yourself into the arms of the next attractive person who passes by. But there's nothing wrong with a little flirting. It's harmless fun and a great way to remind yourself that you're attractive and desirable.

7. **Find time to do the things you like.** No matter how busy you are, be sure you make time each week for fun activities that recharge your batteries and allow you to enjoy your talents. Whether you make the world's best brownies or pitch a mean fastball, remind yourself of the things you're good at by doing them—often.

8. **Watch a tearjerker or a tragedy.** How can a sad movie make you feel better? It helps you cry if you need to, and that kind of emotional release is good for you. Plus, sad, sappy flicks can remind you that, compared with some people's, your problems really aren't all that bad!

9. **Go for a walk.** Feeling annoyed, angry, overwhelmed? Can't get any privacy at home? Step outside, and walk around the block. Or head for a local park and let yourself wander. The exercise will help clear your

head, calm you down, and give you some much-needed perspective.

10. **Like what you see.** Get an instant image boost: Look in the mirror, and instead of examining your so-called bad parts, focus on the things you like best. Be generous with yourself, take note of your good features, and admire them.

11. **Don't be a drama queen.** So what if you screwed something up? So what if something's not going your way? That doesn't mean you'll "never" be good at anything or that things "always" go wrong for you. Get over it, move on, and keep trying.

12. **Find a job.** If you're not currently working outside the home, consider getting a job, even part-time. You'll gain a sense of independence from making your own money and discovering skills you didn't know you had. You could also take on a position as a volunteer for an organization you admire. Or get an internship, and use it as an opportunity to gain new work experience.

13. **Quit a job.** Some people love to bully and boss others around—and you might be working for one of them. If you've really tried to be a good employee but your boss constantly criticizes you, maybe it's time to move on. Why put up with it when you can find a job where you'll be appreciated instead of picked on?

14. **Send a bunch of e-mails and letters.** If you're feeling disconnected, isolated, or lonely, get in touch by sending messages to people you haven't communicated with for a while. You'll be excited and feel popular and loved when they reply.

15. **Get rid of it.** Make a pile of clothes you don't wear anymore, books you never read, and furniture that's been gathering dust in the attic for who knows how long. Then find out what charity you can donate it to.

You'll feel great when there's extra space in your shelves and closets, and good about giving what you can't use to others less fortunate than you.

16. **Change your style a little—or a lot.** Even if you're happy with the way you look, it can be great for your self-confidence to change things up a little. Try a new hair style or color. Experiment with your makeup. Sample a new perfume. Add a few new pieces to your wardrobe, or a few new outfits. Even one really nice new item can make you feel attractive and pampered, and put you in a great mood.

17. **Treat yourself.** When you accomplish something you're proud of, whether it's spring cleaning, a big presentation at work, or a difficult conversation with your partner that you handled particularly well, reward yourself. It doesn't have to be extravagant, but treat yourself—perhaps to a new CD, a scented bubble bath, or a special meal.

18. **Say it with confidence.** Do you end every sentence on a high note, as if you're asking a question? It's hard to feel confident, and for people to take you seriously, if you sound like you're asking for approval whenever you speak. Instead, before you open your mouth, take a moment to feel sure of yourself and your right to share thoughts and ask questions. Then speak with confidence.

19. **Finish it.** Set aside an hour or two to finish that project you've been meaning to get done forever, whether it's a craft project you left halfway complete or a book you've been reading. You'll feel ten times better not to have it hanging over you anymore.

20. **Start it.** Is there something you've been wanting to do for ages, like learn to speak Japanese or make French pastries? Visit your best friend from high school or the town your ancestors came from? Take figure drawing

or kung fu classes? Stop smoking or start waking up earlier? Then do it! You already know how good it feels to take action. Think how good it'll feel to do something you've been dreaming of for so long.

PARTING THOUGHTS

Look at yourself and how far you've come. Isn't it amazing? You're on your way, moving forward with your new life. You've learned, changed, and grown so much since you began reading this book. And I hope that you continue to do so for the rest of your life!

Of all the lessons you've learned, the most important lesson to remember, the one I hope you'll always keep in your mind and heart and gut, is this: *You deserve to be treated with love and respect.* You deserve to be treated that way by your partner and in all your relationships. But it has to start with you. Begin by living the healthy model, and practice love and respect for yourself. When you decide that love and respect for yourself are going to be your first priority, I promise that everything you put second in your life will be first-rate.

Of all the lessons you've learned, the most important lesson to remember, the one I hope you'll always keep in your mind and heart and gut, is this: You deserve to be treated with love and respect.

appendix

Additional Resources

A

BOOKS

Encouragements for the Emotionally Abused Woman: Wisdom and Hope for Women at Any Stage of Emotional Abuse Recovery. Beverly Engel. New York: Ballantine Books, 1994. ISBN: 044 990878X.

Can be useful as a tool for healing, especially for those who cannot or will not seek outside assistance. Gives supportive quotes, stories, affirmations, and suggestions to help women through the process of recovery.

Adult Bullying. Peter Randall. London: Routledge, 1997. ISBN: 0415 126738.

A straightforward look at the roots of bullying behaviors and their effects in later life from the perspectives of both the bully and the victim. Focuses on workplace and community situations more than personal relationships.

Bullying in Adulthood: Assessing the Bullies and Their Victims. Peter Randall. East Sussex, England: Routledge, 2001. ISBN: 0415 236932.

Similar to Randall's *Adult Bullying* but more academic with less focus on how to overcome the problem and more discussion of its origin.

Bullies, Tyrants, and Impossible People: How to Beat Them Without Joining Them. Ronald M. Shapiro, Mark A. Jankowski, and James Dale. New York: Crown Business, 2005. ISBN: 140 0050111.

Takes a look at most interactions as negotiations and breaks down "difficult people" into three categories. Provides steps and tools to overcome challenges with each type, supported by lots of anecdotal evidence and situational examples. Has information for workplace and personal relationships.

Take the Bully by the Horns: Stop Unethical, Uncooperative, or Unpleasant People from Running and Ruining Your Life. Sam Horn. New York: St. Martin's Griffin, 2003. ISBN: 0312 320221.

Short, easy-to-read chapters with lots of aphorisms, quizzes, and role-playing scenarios to help readers learn, practice, and integrate the skills discussed. Focused primarily on personal and family relationships, rather than the workplace.

Emotional Blackmail: When the People in Your Life Use Fear, Obligation, and Guilt to Manipulate You. Susan Forward and Donna Frazier. New York: Harper Paperbacks, 1998. ISBN: 006 0928972.

Deals primarily with personal and family relationships that involve more subtle forms of bullying in the guise of manipulation and coercion. Provides tools to break ingrained patterns that can lead to the blackmailing of oneself.

Aggression and Destructiveness: Psychoanalytic Perspectives. Celia Harding. East Sussex, England: Routledge, 2006. ISBN: 1583918841.

A collection of essays written by psychoanalytic professionals and dealing with various types of aggression in relationships. While the first two sections are useful in general, the third section, "Destructiveness in Disguise and as Disguise," has essays that provide insight into bullying behaviors and their effects.

New Perspectives on Bullying. Ken Rigby. Philadelphia: Jessica Kingsley Publishers, 2002. ISBN: 185302872X.

With sections focusing on young people, a pervasive look at bullying throughout the life cycle. Provides chapters on understanding motivations and personalities of victims and bullies, the effects of bullying, and attitudes surrounding the topic.

WEBSITES

APA Help Center
http://locator.apahelpcenter.org/index.cfm

A referral service of the American Psychological Association to help patients find a psychologist. Also available by phone (see telephone listings). The APA can only give provider contact information and cannot check on insurance coverage or give testimonials as to the quality of care from individual providers.

Bully OnLine's Bullying in the Family
http://www.bullyonline.org/related/family.htm
    The main site is run by the United Kingdom's National Workplace Bullying Advice Line, but a section is dedicated to issues outside of the workplace. Includes an explanation and discussion of the "serial bully" and provides additional information on abuse, personality disorders, and behaviors concerning bullying of all types.

Life After Adult Bullying
http://www.lifeafteradultbullying.com
    The site was constructed by a bullying victim in the United Kingdom and has bullying information for personal relationships and the workplace, including the creator's personal struggle and recovery methods. Includes worldwide links to additional resources.

Selfhelp Magazine
http://www.selfhelpmagazine.com/resources/dv/dvresour4.html #How_to_Get_Help
    An extensive list of useful resources, both national and local, covering a variety of topics, including domestic violence and emotional abuse.

TELEPHONE

APA Help Center
1-800-964-2000
    A referral service of the American Psychological Association to help patients find a psychologist. Also available online (see website listings). The APA can only give provider contact information and cannot check on insurance coverage or give testimonials as to the quality of care from individual providers.

National Domestic Violence Hotline
1-800-799-SAFE (7233)

Available nationally twenty-four hours a day in a variety of languages. Staffed by professionals trained to listen, provide support, and give referrals and additional information on all types of abuse, including emotional abuse and bullying.

appendix B

Emotional- and Domestic-Abuse Agencies, State by State

Alabama Coalition Against Domestic Violence
P.O. Box 4762
Montgomery, AL 36101
Phone: 334-832-4842
Fax: 334-832-4803
24-hour hotline: 800-650-6522
Website: www.acadv.org
E-mail: info@acadv.org
  Nonprofit organization that provides a help line, shelters, legal information, education, and public policy information.

Alaska Network on Domestic Violence and Sexual Assault
Phone: 907-586-3650
Website: www.andvsa.org
  A network of nonprofit organizations that provides help and information for victims of domestic violence and sexual assault. Does not have crisis services but instead acts as a clearinghouse for the member organizations.

Arizona Coalition Against Dometic Violence
301 E Bethany Home Road, Suite C 194
Phoenix, AZ 85012
Phone: 602-279-2900 or 800-782-6400
Fax: 602-279-2980
Legal advocacy hotline: 800-782-6400 or 602-279-2900
Website: www.azcadv.org
E-mail: acadv@azcadv.org
  Advocacy and educational organization that provides information and resources to victims of domestic violence and abuse.

Services include the legal advocacy hotline, a list of shelters, and easy-to-understand fact sheets.

Arkansas Coalition Against Domestic Violence
1401 W Capitol, Suite 170
Little Rock, AR 72201
Phone: 800-269-4668
Website: www.domesticpeace.com
Nonprofit organization that provides direct assistance to victims in the form of shelter lists, a toll-free hotline, and general information on abuse. Also performs instructional sessions for advocates, legal organizations, and educators.

California Partnership to End Domestic Violence
P.O. Box 1798
Sacramento, CA 95812
Phone: 916-444-7163 or 800-524-4756
Fax: 916-444-7165
Website: www.cpedv.org
E-mail: info@cpedv.org
Organization primarily focused on education, advocacy, and community outreach. Also provides a list of local hotline numbers and referrals for victim resources and services.

Colorado Coalition Against Domestic Violence
P.O. Box 18902
Denver, CO 80218
Phone: 303-831-9632 or 888-788-7091
Fax: 303-832-7067
Website: www.ccadv.org
Advocates that provide training, outreach, access to technology, empowerment sessions for victims, and statewide program funding. Website has a list of local crisis numbers and a fact sheet on how to stay safe.

Connecticut Coalition Against Domestic Violence
90 Pitkin Street
East Hartford, CT 06108
Phone: 860-282-7899 or 800-281-1481
Fax: 860-282-7892

24-hour in-state hotline: 888-774-2900
Website: www.ctcadv.org
E-mail: info@ctcadv.org
Statewide networks of advocacy and community programs that provide help and information for domestic-abuse victims in the form of education, a resource library, and the hotline, which routes calls to appropriate services.

Delaware Coalition Against Domestic Violence
100 W 10th Street, #703
Wilmington, DE 19801
Phone: 302-658-2958 or 800-701-0456
Fax: 302-658-5049
Website: www.dcadv.org
E-mail: dcadv@dcadv.org
Nonprofit organization that serves as educator and advocate in the realm of domestic abuse. Does not provide direct crisis services but has extensive information for victims on counseling, legal assistance, shelters, and advocacy services.

DC Coalition Against Domestic Violence
5 Thomas Circle, NW
Washington, DC 20005
Phone: 202-299-1181
Fax: 202-299-1193
Website: www.dccadv.org
E-mail: help@dccadv.org
Organization that provides services to both victims and organizations. Services for victims include an extensive resource manual of information with listings of local hotlines, shelters, medical facilities, food banks, religious organizations, and counseling services.

Florida Coalition Against Domestic Violence
425 Office Plaza
Tallahassee, FL 32301
Phone: 850-425-2749 or 800-500-1119; 850-621-4202 TDD
Fax: 850-425-3091
Website: www.fcadv.org
Statewide organization that supports education, outreach, training, advocacy, and local domestic-abuse services. Publishes

a *Domestic Violence Service Directory* that lists Florida Certified Domestic Violence Centers by city and by county. Referrals to local services available by calling the 800 number.

Georgia Coalition Against Domestic Violence
3420 Norman Berry Drive, #280
Atlanta, GA 30354
Phone: 404-209-0280
Fax: 404-766-3800
Website: www.gcadv.org
Umbrella organization of certified shelters and member programs that work on projects in economic justice, public policy, legal advocacy, and victim assistance. Provides information for both the abused and the abuser to seek help.

Hawaii State Coalition Against Domestic Violence
716 Umi Street, Suite 210
Honolulu, HI 96819-2337
Phone: 808-832-9316
Fax: 808-841-6028
Website: www.hscadv.org
Private statewide coalition of domestic-abuse programs coordinated to provide education and training to communities and service providers, offer technical assistance to victims and families, and act as a clearinghouse for information resources. Has a list of local phone numbers for direct victim services in emergency situations.

Idaho Coalition Against Sexual and Domestic Violence
815 Park Boulevard, #140
Boise, ID 83712
Phone: 208-384-0419 or 888-293-6118
Fax: 208-331-0687
24-hour hotline: 800-669-3176
Website: www.idvsa.org
E-mail: domvio@mindspring.com
Nonprofit group that offers education, technical support, and general assistance to shelters, support groups, counselors, and other organizations. Provides contact information for additional resources, including the Idaho CareLine, which offers informa-

tion on a wide range of programs and services even beyond domestic abuse.

Illinois Coalition Against Domestic Violence

801 S 11th Street
Springfield, IL 62703
Phone: 217-789-2830
Fax: 217-789-1939
Website: www.ilcadv.org
E-mail: ilcadv@ilcadv.org

Membership organization of domestic-abuse groups that provide training, technical assistance, and public education materials and implement public policy. A lending library of information and a statewide map of services are available for victims and community members.

Indiana Coalition Against Domestic Violence

1915 W 18th Street
Indianapolis, IN 46202
Phone: 317-917-3685
Fax: 317-917-3695
24-hour hotline: 800-332-7385
Website: www.violenceresource.org
E-mail: icadv@violenceresource.org

Organization that provides education and advocacy through community programs and a resource center. The twenty-four-hour hotline offers help in crisis situations, including emotional support, practical advice, counseling, legal information, and referral services.

Iowa Coalition Against Domestic Violence

515 28th Street, #104
Des Moines, IA 50312
Phone: 515-244-8028
Fax: 515-244-7417
In-state hotline: 800-942-0333
Website: www.icadv.org

Coalition of domestic-abuse programs statewide that encourages collaboration and provides assistance and education to the programs. Publishes listings of national, state, and local domestic-abuse projects that offer help to victims.

Kansas Coalition Against Sexual and Domestic Violence
634 SW Harrison Street
Topeka, KS 66603
Phone: 785-232-9784
Fax: 785-266-1874
24-hour hotline: 888-363-2287
Website: www.kcsdv.org
E-mail: coalition@kcsdv.org

Statewide network of domestic-abuse programs that provide support and safety to victims. Publishes a listing of organizations by county and operates a hotline that offers crisis intervention, referral to community programs, general information, and emotional support.

Kentucky Domestic Violence Association
P.O. Box 356
Frankfort, KY 40602
Phone: 502-695-2444
Fax: 502-695-2488
Website: www.kdva.org

Organization that offers networking, support, and advocacy for domestic-abuse programs throughout the state. Offers contact information for programs that cover legal advocacy, case management, safety planning, support groups, and individual counseling, among other services for victims.

Louisiana Coalition Against Domestic Violence
P.O. Box 77308
Baton Rouge, LA 70879
Phone: 225-752-1296 or 888-411-1333
Fax: 225-751-8927
Website: www.lcadv.org

Statewide network of individuals and organizations involved in direct services to victims and community education and advocacy. Provides a list of local victim service organizations and information on safety planning and intervention programs.

Maine Coalition to End Domestic Violence
170 Park Street
Bangor, ME 04401

Phone: 207-941-1194
Fax: 207-941-2327
24-hour hotline: 866-834-4357
Website: www.mcedv.org
E-mail: info@mcedv.org

Coalition working with local programs to coordinate community action, education, and advocacy. Member projects include the twenty-four-hour hotline, referral and information services, support groups, legal information, outreach, and advice for friends of victims.

Maryland Network Against Domestic Violence

6911 Laurel-Bowie Road, #309
Bowie, MD 20715
Phone: 301-352-4574 or 800-634-3577
Fax: 301-809-0422
Website: www.mnadv.org
E-mail: mnadv@aol.com

Organization focused mainly on advocacy, training, and education. Provides information and lists of local domestic-abuse service agencies, including some directed at specialized communities, such as immigrants, military members, persons with disabilities, and religious groups.

Jane Doe, Inc.
Massachusetts Coalition Against Sexual Assault and Domestic Violence

14 Beacon Street, #507
Boston, MA 02108
Phone: 617-248-0922; 617-263-2200 TTY/TTD
Fax: 617-248-0902
24-hour hotline: 877-785-2020
Website: www.janedoe.org
E-mail: info@janedoe.org

Network of direct-service providers, business partners, health care professionals, government agencies, law enforcement officials, and others that educate and inform victims and communities to provide help and prevent abuse. Provides referral services for crisis intervention and further information and programs for non-emergency situations.

Michigan Coalition Against Domestic and Sexual Violence
3893 Okemos Road, #B-2
Okemos, MI 48864
Phone: 517-347-7000; 517-381-8470 TTY
Fax: 517-347-1377
Website: www.mcadsv.org
E-mail: general@mcadsv.org
Statewide group that networks over seventy domestic- and sexual-abuse programs and over two hundred allied organizations and individuals. Operates a resource center, which provides information for victims, community members, and survivors. Publishes a referral list of service providers by city.

Minnesota Coalition for Battered Women
1821 University Avenue W, #S-112
St. Paul, MN 55104
Phone: 651-646-6177
Fax: 651-646-1527
Crisis line: 651-646-0994 or 800-289-6177
Website: www.mcbw.org
E-mail: mcbw@mcbw.org
Statewide organization of local, regional, and state programs that offer resources and referrals for individuals, training programs for service providers, and information for community outreach and education.

Mississippi Coalition Against Domestic Violence
P.O. Box 4703
Jackson, MS 39296
Phone: 601-981-9196 or 800-898-3234
Fax: 601-981-2501
Website: www.mcadv.org
Organization that offers technical assistance, community outreach, and professional education to individuals and groups. Maintains a clearinghouse and resource library of service providers, statistics, and general resources for victims and community members. Also provides victim referral services.

Missouri Coalition Against Domestic Violence
718 E Capitol Avenue
Jefferson City, MO 65101

Phone: 573-634-4161
Fax: 573-636-3728
Website: www.mocadv.org
E-mail: mcadv@sockets.net

Statewide grassroots organization comprising community-based domestic-abuse programs. Victim services contact information available by local area.

Montana Coalition Against Domestic and Sexual Violence

P.O. Box 818
Helena, MT 59624
Phone: 406-443-7794 or 888-404-7794
Fax: 406-443-7818
Website: www.mcadsv.com
E-mail: mcadsv@mt.net

Organization that represents over fifty programs statewide that provide victim services, advocate for public-policy changes, and provide public education and project development. A regional list of direct-service providers and fact sheets on surviving abuse are available for victims and friends of victims.

Nebraska Domestic Violence and Sexual Assault Coalition

825 M Street, #404
Lincoln, NE 68508
Phone: 402-476-6256 or 800-876-6238
Fax: 402-476-6806
Website: www.ndvsac.org
E-mail: info@ndvsac.org

Statewide advocacy organization that serves as a clearinghouse for information including program listings with contact information, the resource library for those in-state wishing to learn more about domestic abuse, relevant website links, and legal information.

Nevada Network Against Domestic Violence

100 W Grove Street, #315
Reno, NV 89509
Phone: 775-828-1115 or 800-230-1955
Fax: 775-828-9911
Hotline: 800-500-1556
Website: www.nnadv.org

Statewide organization that provides resources, training, and technical assistance to domestic-abuse programs. Primarily lists member programs for victim assistance. Also offers a few additional programs for those not served by member programs.

New Hampshire Coalition Against Domestic and Sexual Violence
P.O. Box 353
Concord, NH 03302
Phone: 603-224-8893 or 866-644-3574
Fax: 603-228-6096
Website: www.nhcadsv.org

Statewide umbrella organization for fourteen member programs that provide services to victims, work on prevention initiatives, and educate communities. Offers specific information for health care providers and employers and a complete listing of crisis centers in the state.

New Jersey Coalition for Battered Women
1670 Whitehorse Hamilton Square
Trenton, NJ 08690
Phone: 609-584-8107 or 800-572-7233
Fax: 609-584-9750
Website: www.njcbw.org
E-mail: info@njcbw.org

Organization that provides information, training, conferences, advocacy, and statistics to prevent abuse and help victims. Publishes a *Guide to Services* containing information for victims by county and links to other state coalitions.

New Mexico State Coalition Against Domestic Violence
200 Oak NE, #4
Albuquerque, NM 87106
Phone: 505-246-9240 or 800-773-3645
Fax: 505-246-9434
Website: www.nmcadv.org

Organization that acts as a clearinghouse for information, resources, and referrals for victims, community members, and other organizations. Operates a lending library and provides contact information for direct-service providers by location.

New York State Coalition Against Domestic Violence
350 New Scotland Avenue
Albany, NY 12054
Phone: 518-482-5464 or 800-942-6906;
800-942-6908 Spanish
Fax: 518-482-3807
Website: www.nyscadv.org
E-mail: nyscadv@nyscadv.org
   Nonprofit organization comprising member programs that provide community outreach, education, training, and policy development. A directory of services based on location is available by calling the toll-free numbers or visiting the Resources page of the website.

North Carolina Coalition Against Domestic Violence
115 Market Street, #400
Durham, NC 27701
Phone: 919-956-9124 or 888-232-9124
Fax: 919-682-1449
Website: www.nccadv.org
   Coalition of agencies and individuals serving victims and communities through outreach, public-policy initiatives, training institutes, and abuser intervention programs. Provides contact information for service providers by county, by type, and by special population.

North Dakota Council on Abused Women's Services
418 E Rosser Avenue, #320
Bismark, ND 58501
Phone: 701-255-6240 or 888-255-6240
Fax: 701-255-1904
Website: www.ndcaws.org
E-mail: ndcaws@ndcaws.org
   A network of twenty-one member programs targeting prevention, education, and intervention through services that include awareness projects, outreach programs, scholarship funds, and victim resources. The *ND Resource Directory* provides a searchable listing of service providers by type or region.

Action Ohio Coalition for Battered Women
P.O. Box 15673
Columbus, OH 43215
Phone: 614-221-1255
Fax: 614-221-6357
Website: www.actionohio.org
E-mail: actionoh@ee.net

Advocate organization that provides resources and referrals for domestic-abuse victims, professional education, community outreach, technical assistance, and public-awareness training. Features information for some special populations, such as the elderly and the rural population.

Oklahoma Coalition Against Domestic Violence and Sexual Assault
3815 N Santa Fe Ave., Suite 124
Oklahoma City, OK 73118
Phone: 405-524-0700
Fax: 405-524-0711
Safeline: 800-522-7233
Website: www.ocadvsa.org

Coalition that encourages collaboration among local, state, and national agencies and programs by maintaining a resource library, publishing a newsletter, helping with education and training, and working directly with service providers. The website includes an extensive list of member organizations and local hotlines.

Oregon Coalition Against Domestic and Sexual Violence
380 SE Spokane Street, #100
Portland, OR 97202
Phone: 503-230-1951
Fax: 503-230-1973
Website: www.ocadsv.com

Coalition of programs that provides information and referrals, consulting, education, training, and public-policy advocacy. Offers contact information for local service providers based on county.

Pennsylvania Coalition Against Domestic Violence
6400 Flank Drive, #1300
Harrisburg, PA 17112
Phone: 717-545-6400 or 800-932-4632
Fax: 717-545-9456
Website: www.pcadv.org
Private nonprofit organization that functions as a statewide network of domestic-abuse services. Provides referrals but does not offer emergency services.

Rhode Island Coalition Against Domestic Violence
422 Post Road, #202
Warwick, RI 02888
Phone: 401-467-9940 or 800-494-8100
Fax: 401-467-9943
Website: www.ricadv.org
E-mail: ricadv@ricadv.org
Statewide organization of six member programs that provides victim resources, community outreach, public education, and advocacy. Lists types of services, such as crisis intervention, emotional support, and legal assistance, available through member programs.

South Carolina Coalition Against Domestic Violence and Sexual Assault
P.O. Box 7776
Columbia, SC 29202
Phone: 803-256-2900 or 800-260-9293
Fax: 803-256-1030
Website: www.sccadvasa.org
Statewide coalition of all domestic-abuse programs and rape crisis centers. Offers contact information for member organizations that provide victim services, and works on community outreach and education.

South Dakota Coalition Against Domestic Violence and Sexual Assault
P.O. Box 141
Pierre, SD 57501
Phone: 605-945-0869 or 800-572-9196

Fax: 605-945-0870
Website: www.southdakotacoalition.org
E-mail: sdcadvsa@rapidnet.com

Coalition of member groups that educate, advocate, and raise awareness regarding domestic abuse. Provides a list of local crisis contacts for victims.

Tennessee Coalition Against Domestic and Sexual Violence

P.O. Box 120972
Nashville, TN 37212
Phone: 615-386-9406 or 800-289-9018
Fax: 615-383-2967
Website: www.tcadsv.org
E-mail: tcadsv@tcadsv.org

Private nonprofit organization that supports over thirty-five programs statewide that provide support groups, counseling, transportation, advocacy, legal and medical assistance, emergency shelter, outreach, and community education.

Texas Council on Family Violence

P.O. Box 161810
Austin, TX 78716
Phone: 512-794-1133 or 800-525-1978
Fax: 512-794-1199
Website: www.tcfv.org

Organization that supports service providers, advocate groups, counseling professionals, and prevention programs. A service directory provides information on shelters and support services throughout the state.

Utah Domestic Violence Council

320 W 200 S, #270-B
Salt Lake City, UT 84101
Phone: 801-521-5544
Fax: 801-521-5548
Website: www.udvac.org

Nonprofit group that functions as an umbrella organization for twenty-three statewide domestic-abuse programs. Coordinates events with these programs and provides victims with information referrals.

Vermont Network Against Domestic Violence and Sexual Assault

P.O. Box 405
Montpelier, VT 05601
Phone: 802-223-1302
Fax: 802-223-6943
24-hour domestic-violence hotline: 800-228-7395
24-hour sexual-assault hotline: 800-489-7273
Website: www.vtnetwork.org
E-mail: vtnetwork@vtnetwork.org

Feminist organization that creates a network of localized programs that focus on prevention, education, advocacy, and victim services.

Virginians Against Domestic Violence

2850 Sandy Bay Road, #101
Williamsburg, VA 23185
Phone: 757-221-0990 or 800-838-8238
Fax: 757-229-1553
Website: www.vadv.org
E-mail: vadv@tni.net

Organization of individuals and agencies that inform and educate community and government leaders. Besides giving referral services to victims, provides information and assistance for friends of victims, crisis workers, and the general public via their 800 number.

Women's Coalition of St. Croix (Virgin Islands)

Box 2734
Christiansted
St. Croix, VI 00822
Phone: 340-773-9272
Fax: 340-773-9062
Website: www.wcstx.com
E-mail: wcsc@pennswoods.net

Organization that sponsors support groups, shelters, training, education, legal and medical advocate programs, and a resource library for victims and community members.

Washington State Coalition Against Domestic Violence
711 Capitol Way, #702
Olympia, WA 98501
Phone: 360-586-1022
Fax: 360-586-1024

1402 3rd Avenue, #406
Seattle, WA 98101
Phone: 206-389-2515 or 800-886-2880
Fax: 206-389-2520
Website: www.wscadv.org
E-mail: wscadv@wscadv.org

Statewide nonprofit organization that works primarily through education, training, advocacy, and support actions. Provides referral services for victims of domestic abuse and features six support networks for individual communities: Jewish Network, Immigrant and Refugee Network, Lesbian/Bisexual/Transgender/Gay Network, Native Network, Survivors in Service Caucus, and Women of Color Caucus.

West Virginia Coalition Against Domestic Violence
4710 Chimney Drive, #A
Charleston, WV 25302
Phone: 304-965-3552
Fax: 304-965-3572
Website: www.wvcadv.org

Coalition of organizations that provide counseling, education, and information for victims of domestic abuse. Publishes a detailed map of locations for help and targeted information for individual populations such as the elderly, faith communities, people with disabilities, people of color, and those in lesbian and gay relationships.

Wisconsin Coalition Against Domestic Violence
307 S Paterson Street, #1
Madison, WI 53703
Phone: 608-255-0539
Fax: 608-255-3560
Website: www.wcadv.org
E-mail: wcadv@wcadv.org

Nonprofit organization that links individuals, community groups, and domestic-abuse programs to run a variety of initiatives that focus on different communities such as the elderly, people of color, children and youth, immigrants, and those in rural areas. Also operates a prevention program linked with a Coordinated Community Response service.

Wyoming Coalition Against Domestic Violence and Sexual Assault
P.O. Box 236
409 S Fourth Street
Laramie, WY 82073
Phone: 307-755-5481 or 800-990-3877
Fax: 307-755-5482
Website: www.wyomingdvsa.org
E-mail: Info@mail.wyomingdvsa.org

Organization that acts as a network to connect local programs with governmental and private agencies to further education and advocacy regarding domestic abuse. Offers information on a variety of topics, including how to help friends who may be in abusive relationships.

bibliography

Crawford, Trish. "Why Do Bullies Get Away With It?" *Life*, September 18, 2006, p. B01.

Magazine article showing the prevalence of bullying in society in schools, sports, and daily life.

Follingstad, Diane, and D. DeHart. "Defining Psychological Abuse of Husbands Towards Wives: Contexts, Behaviors, and Typologies." *Journal of Interpersonal Violence* 15(9), September 2000, pp. 891–920.

Professional-journal article presenting the results of a study performed to help define behaviors considered to be psychological abuse. Many of the psychologists who participated rated behaviors consistent with bullying to be psychologically abusive at least on some level.

Goulston, Mark. "My Dinner with a Bully." Resource Centers: Leading Edge section of *Fast Company* website, www.fastcompany.com/resources/leadership/goulston/083004.html.

Anecdotal article written by a UCLA professor about his initial sessions with a man who bullied in both the family and the workplace and the change that he decided to make in his life.

Lee, Raymond T., and C. Brotheridge. "When Prey Turns Predatory: Workplace Bullying as a Predictor of Counteraggression/Bullying, Coping, and Well-Being." *European Journal of Work and Organizational Psychology* 15(3), September 2006, pp. 352–377.

Study of workplace bullying in Canada that provides information about how victims' coping methods affect their physical and mental health.

Minton, Stephen James, and P. Minton. "The Application of Certain Phenomenological/Existential Perspectives in Understanding the Bully-Victim Cycle." *Existential Analysis* 15(2), July 2004, pp. 230–242.

   A professional and somewhat academic look at the bully-victim cycle, focusing on the origins and features of workplace and personal-relationship bullying.

Retzinger, Suzanne. "Shame, Anger, and Conflict: Case Study of Emotional Violence." *Journal of Family Violence* 6(1), March 1991, pp. 37–59.

   Academic article that looks at an actual verbal argument between a couple to discern patterns of conflict and examples of emotional violence that included shaming, disrespect, and alienation.

Schwartz, Amy, S. Andersen, and T. Strasser. "Psychological Maltreatment of Partners." In *Case Studies in Family Violence*, 2nd edition, edited by Robert Ammerman and Michel Hersen, pp. 349–373. New York: Kluwer Academic Publishers, 2000.

   A chapter using two case studies to look at various aspects of psychological maltreatment, such as methods of abuse, medical problems, social concerns, and treatment.

Shaw, Jennifer. "Lacanian Demand and the Tactics of Emotional Abuse." *Journal for the Psychoanalysis of Culture and Society* 10(2), August 2005, pp. 186–196.

   Academic article that looks at emotional abuse through the lens of psychoanalytic theory. The "Nature of Abuse" section includes a list categorizing tactics of emotional abusers. The "Immobilization and Abuse" section examines those tactics in order to see how the abuse manifests itself.

Smullens, SaraKay. "The 5 Cycles of Emotional Abuse: Investigating a Malignant Victimization." *Annals of the American Psychotherapy Association* 5(5), September–October 2002, pp. 16–18.

   Article presenting a clear, concise description of forms and impacts of emotional abuse, reasoning behind the lack of study of the subject, and the five-cycle process of abuse. The ideas presented are framed primarily in terms of parent or caretaker relationships but refer to intimate relationships as well.

index